TRIBAL SQL

By

Dave Ballantyne, John Barnett, Diana Dee,

Kevin Feasel, Tara Kizer, Chuck Lathrope,

Stephanie Locke, Colleen Morrow,

Dev Nambi, Bob Pusateri,

Mark S. Rasmussen, Wil Sisney,

Shaun J. Stuart, David Tate, Matt Velic

First published by Simple Talk Publishing, 2013

Technical Review and Edit: Kat Hicks
Editor: Tony Davis
Cover Image: Rain Cao
Typeset: Peter Woodhouse and Gower Associates

Table of Contents

Using Database Mail to Email Enable Your SQL Server   261
John Barnett

Nine Habits to Secure a Stellar Performance Review   435
Wil Sisney

About This Book

The Tribal Authors

Dave Ballantyne
Dave is a freelance SQLServer database developer/designer and has been working in the IT field for over 20 years, during the past 15 of which he has been specializing within the SQL Server environment.
Dave is a regular speaker at UK events such as SQL Bits and user groups and is founder of the SQLLunch User Group.

John Barnett
John has been working in IT now for over 15 years. Over this time he's had a variety of roles in the public and private sectors. Responsibilities have included database administration, system administration and applications support and development. Most recently this has been in the UK Higher Education sector, supporting and developing with a variety of vendor-supported and in-house applications.

Diana Dee
Diana is a Microsoft Certified Trainer who has taught Microsoft courses to IT professionals and college students since 1996. She has been a course developer throughout her computer teaching career. She has revised and developed database design, administration, and querying courses for an online University and for a major training company.
Diana has presented at five SQL Saturdays (so far).

Kevin Feasel
Kevin Feasel is a database administrator at American Health Holding, a subsidiary of Aetna, where he specializes in SSIS development, performance tuning, and pulling rabbits out of hats on demand. A resident of Durham, North Carolina, he can be found cycling the trails along the triangle whenever the weather's nice enough.

Tara Kizer

Tara Kizer is a Database Administrator and has been using SQL Server since 1996. She has worked at Qualcomm Incorporated since 2002 and supports several 24x7 mission-critical systems with very high performance and availability requirements. She obtained her Bachelor of Science in Mathematics with emphasis on Computer Science from San Diego State University in 1999. She has been a Microsoft MVP since July of 2007 and is an active member at SQLTeam.com where she posts under the name tkizer. Tara lives in San Diego, California with her husband and kids. You can reach her via her blog, *Ramblings of a DBA* (HTTP://WEBLOGS.SQLTEAM.COM/TARAD).

Chuck Lathrope

Chuck Lathrope is a Seattle-based SQL Server administrator with over twenty years of IT experience. He was a Top-5 nominee in the Red Gate Exceptional DBA Award in 2009. Currently, he manages a team of DBAs who support a very large SQL Server replication environment across many datacenters in the USA. Chuck often speaks at SQL Saturday events on replication. He blogs at WWW.SQLWEBPEDIA.COM, and tweets via his account @SQLGuyChuck.

Stephanie Locke

Stephanie Locke (@SteffLocke) is an experienced analyst and BI developer within the Finance and Insurance industries. Steph runs her local SQL Server User Group, is one of the organizers of SQLRelay (HTTP://SQLRELAY.CO.UK/) and contributes to the community at large via blogging at HTTP://STEFF.ITSALOCKE.COM/, presenting, and forums.

Colleen Morrow

Colleen Morrow began her career in databases providing technical support for Informix Software. After a brief foray into programming, she decided to try her hand in database administration. She's been at it ever since. Colleen spent 12 years at her previous position as a DBA for a large law firm, focusing primarily on SQL Server for the last 9 years. In October of 2012 she moved to her current position as a Database Engineer at a software company where she provides consulting services on database administration and performance tuning. But a little bit of the programmer inside lives on; you'll often find her writing PowerShell or T-SQL scripts to make life a little easier.

Dev Nambi

Dev is a data geek, developer, and aspiring polymath. He works with databases, statistics, and curiosity to solve problems using data. He is currently working in the University of Washington's Decision Support group.

Bob Pusateri

Bob is a Microsoft Certified Master and has been working with SQL Server since 2006. He is currently a Database Administrator at Northwestern University where he uses data compression to manage databases over 25 TB in size for their Medical Enterprise Data Warehouse.
He lives near Chicago, Illinois with his wife, Michelle and their big orange kitty, Oliver. You can reach Bob on Twitter at @SQLBob, or through his blog, "The Outer Join" at HTTP://WWW.BOBPUSATERI.COM.

Mark S Rasmussen

Mark, a SQL Server MVP, has worked extensively with SQL Server through his years as a consultant as well as in his current position as the CTO of iPaper A/S. He has primarily been working on performance tuning as well as diving into the internals of SQL Server. Besides SQL Server, Mark is also proficient in the .NET development stack, with a decade of experience. Fueled by his interest in development and the nitty-gritty details, Mark has created OrcaMDF, an open source parser for SQL Server data files, written in C#. He enjoys presenting, and frequently speaks at local user groups as well as international events. Mark keeps a blog at HTTP://IMPROVE.DK and tweets at @improvedk.

Wil Sisney

Wil is a database administrator specializing in performance, core administration and SQL Server Integration Services. He also spends a lot of time training on SQL Server and blogs about new training opportunities. He teaches others about SQL Server through corporate training, user groups and events like SQL Saturday.

Shaun J Stuart

Shaun J. Stuart is the Senior SQL Server DBA at the largest credit union in Arizona. He has a Bachelor's degree in electrical engineering, but has been working with databases for over 15 years. He started his database career as a database developer before moving into the database administrator role. He became a Microsoft Certified Professional on SQL Server 7.0 and is a Microsoft Certified Technology Specialist (MCTS) on SQL Server 2005 and 2008 and a Microsoft Certified IT Professional (MCITP) on SQL Server 2008. Shaun blogs about SQL Server at WWW.SHAUNJSTUART.COM and can occasionally be found on Twitter as @shaunjstu.

Shaun would like to thank Jen McCown for her work in creating and shepherding this Tribal SQL Project and Thomas LaRock, whose article about sampling on Simple-Talk.com inspired him to implement this process.

David Tate

David Tate is a full-stack software consultant but his family thinks that he fixes wireless computer printers. David uses his work energy to create things that do not compare to the simple elegance of the tree outside his window. He is consistently bad at choosing reheating times for the microwave and his channel-changing algorithm is despised by all that have lived with him.

In his spare time he likes to ride bicycles. He once saw a bird that looked like Madonna. He blogs at HTTP://DAVIDTATE.ORG and tweets @mixteenth.

Matt Velic

Matt Velic is a Database Developer for Sanametrix in Washington, DC. He enjoys helping others succeed by ensuring that they've got the proper resources and support. Towards that goal, Matt is a co-leader of the official PASSDC User Group, helps to organize DC SQL Saturday events, finds new speakers for PASS's "Oracle and SQL Server" Virtual Chapter, blogs, presents, and loves hanging out on Twitter.

Computers 4 Africa

All the Tribal SQL authors have agreed to donate their royalties to Computers 4 Africa (HTTP://WWW.COMPUTERS4AFRICA.ORG.UK/INDEX.PHP).

Computers 4 Africa is a registered charity operating as a social enterprise. We collect redundant IT, which is refurbished and data-wiped before being sent out to African schools, colleges, and selected community projects.

Our mission is to help lift the continent of Africa out of the poverty trap by equipping the next generation to work in a global environment. This is the 21st Century version of "....teach a man to fish.....". We do this by supplying the best value computers in the areas where we operate.

At our central processing unit in Kent we receive working redundant computers through collections and local donations from around the UK. The donated equipment is then treated and sent out to beneficiaries in Africa.

Beneficiaries pay a contribution towards the cost of preparing and shipping the equipment – but at the best price available in their locality – that is our ambition. In this way we make modern IT available to those that would otherwise never get to use a computer in their years at school. Computers 4 Africa targets the poorest causes by donating 10% of the computers we send out.

The Tribal Reviewers and Editors

Numerous people in the SQL community gave up their time to review and edit the efforts of the Tribal authors, at various stages in the evolution of this project. Let's start at the beginning…

Jen McCown @MidnightDBA

Jen and Sean McCown, the MidnightDBAs, conceived the idea for Tribal SQL late in 2011, keen to find a way to let people hear the knowledge and passion of some of the some lesser-known voices in the SQL Server community. Jen encouraged abstracts, peer reviewed the submissions and coordinated the whole process to the point where a complete initial draft of Tribal SQL was born.

Jen McCown is a SQL Server consultant, and DBA with over 15 years' experience. She is Senior Editor at MidnightDBA.com, where she creates training videos, the "DBAs at Midnight" web show, blogs, reviews, and podcasts. Jen is a member, volunteer, and speaker in PASS, and the PASS Women in Technology virtual chapter. She lives in Dallas, Texas in the vicinity of approximately 6.5 million other humanoids.

Volunteer Reviewers

Many people gave their time freely, technically reviewing chapters during the writing of the initial chapter drafts. We'd like to say thank you to:

Joseph D. Antoni @jdanton	**Nicholas Cain** @SirSQL	**Justin Dearing** @zippy1981
Neil Hambly @Neil_Hambly	**Stephan Lawson** @SQLArcher	**Shannon Lowder**
Jen McCown @MidnightDBA	**Sean McCown** @KenpoDBA	**Frank Moore**
John Morehouse @SQLRUs	**Scott Murray**	**Brent Ozar** @BrentO
Craig Purnell @CraigPurnell	**Thomas Rushton** @ThomasRushton	**Meredith Ryan** @coffegrl
Ben Seaman @thetornpage	**Steve Stedman** @SQLEmt	**Thomas Stringer** @SQLLife
Jason Thomas @de_unparagoned	**Robert Volk** @sql_r	**Ed Watson** @SQLGator
Jason Yousef @Huslayer	**Melody Zacharias** @SQLMelody	**James Zimmerman**

Tony Davis @Red Gate

Tony grabbed a coffee (or was it a beer?) with Jen at the PASS Community Summit 2013. Enthused and impressed by the project, he persuaded Red Gate to support it, and applied his editorial expertise to helping shape the content into the book you hold in your hands now.

Tony Davis is an Editor with more than 14 years' experience, specializing in SQL Server, and currently working for Red Gate Software, based in Cambridge (UK). He edits and writes for both Simple-talk.com and SQLServerCentral.com, sites with a combined audience of over 1.5 million subscribers. He is the editor behind most of the SQL Server-related books (see HTTP://WWW.SIMPLE-TALK.COM/BOOKS/) published by Red Gate, and spends much of his time helping others write about SQL, but is also the lead author of the book, *SQL Server Transaction Log Management*.

Kat Hicks

During the second round of reviews, Kat technically reviewed and edited the completed drafts of Chapters 6–10 and 15.

Kat Hicks, DBA extraordinaire, works at Rackspace in beautiful San Antonio, TX, and she's been databasing for over 12 years. MS SQL has been her primary focus, from 6.5 all the way through 2012. She has a slew of letters after her name too – but she's still more certifiable than certified. Her favorites (apart from her wonderful family) include horror movies, superheroes, great fiction, cramming as many words and commas as possible into a single sentence and, last but not least, writing random T-SQL scripts to make her life easier.

The Tribal Sponsors

The MidnightDBAs, Jen and Sean McCown

We are SQL Server consultants, DBAs, and Microsoft MVPs with over 30 years of database experience between us. We write articles and blogs, provide training, and volunteer for the Professional Association for SQL Server, and that's just in our spare time. We are happiest when we're making data systems run better, or showing someone else how.

For years now, we've been putting out free technology tutorial videos on the **MidnightDBA** website (WWW.MIDNIGHTDBA.COM). Our favorite subject matter is SQL Server and PowerShell, but we'll present on whatever strikes our fancy. You can also find recordings of the classes we teach at user groups and international conferences, and of our live weekly IT web show, **DBAs@Midnight**. All of these videos are designed to help data professionals do their jobs more effectively, and to serve as a reference for our own use from time to time!

Tribal SQL was a wonderful project, and we're thrilled that so many people were brave enough to take part. The authors worked hard on this, because they had something to say. The editors worked hard to help them say it. Red Gate worked very hard to make sure we were all correct and presentable. To everyone involved: thanks for making Tribal SQL a reality!

Red Gate Software

Red Gate (WWW.REDGATE.COM) makes ingeniously simple tools for SQL and .NET professionals around the world. Our purpose is to make life easier for developers and DBAs, which is why we have a small but dedicated publishing team focused on providing great educational content for our audience. With our publishing content on WWW.SIMPLE-TALK.COM and WWW.SQLSERVERCENTRAL.COM, we want to help people be more confident, and more adept, at their jobs. Whether that's by reading an article about a specific topic, or seeing an announcement for a local user group, or downloading some free scripts that'll make your job easier, we try to help and support people learning to become better SQL or .NET professionals.

We're very happy that we've been able to play a part in this community project, to produce a book filled with tribal knowledge – things all SQL DBAs and developers should know. We're also delighted to be able to support and bring into the limelight so many new authors. This project is about the authors, the SQL Tribe, and we hope you enjoy reading what they have to say.

Introduction

A while back, I invited the unpublished masses to submit abstracts for a new-author-written SQL book – called Tribal SQL – and the people spoke. The chosen ones are now feverishly writing their first drafts! – Jen McCown, March 2012

In late 2011, Sean and Jen McCown finished their weekly web show, and relaxed with the chat room audience. Talk ranged to the recently published *SQL Server MVP Deep Dives, Volume 2*, in which 64 SQL Server MVPs, Jen included, contributed a chapter each, with proceeds going to charity.

Everyone loved the model, but lamented that only MVPs could take part. Wouldn't it be nice if new voices in the SQL Community could contribute? Jen asked if anyone would be interested in such a project, and four people immediately volunteered. Tribal SQL was born.

When prospective authors asked, "What kind of book will this be? What should I write about?" Jen's response was simple: ***This is a book for DBAs, for things you think they really ought to know... so what do you think belongs in it?***

Fifteen experienced SQL people, all previously unpublished authors, have contributed a chapter each to share their hard-won knowledge. The result? We have insights into how to reduce data size and optimize performance with compression, verify backups, tune SQL Server with traces and extended events, audit SQL Server activity, implement replication, and more. Side by side with these, we have chapters on the importance to DBAs of communicating clearly with their co-workers and business leaders, presenting data as useful information that the business can use to make decisions, adopting a more Agile approach to their work, and learning sound project management skills.

Tribal SQL is a reflection of a DBA's core and long-standing responsibilities for database security, availability and performance. Tribal SQL is a discussion of new ideas about how the DBA role is evolving, and what it means to be a DBA in today's businesses.

Code Examples

We provide a code download bundle containing every script in this book, and a few more that were too large to present in the text. You can find it on the Tribal SQL website (HTTP://TRIBALSQL.COM) or download it directly from the following URL: HTTP://WWW.SIMPLE-TALK.COM/RedGateBooks/TribalSQL/Tribal_Code.zip

Most of the examples use versions of the readily available AdventureWorks database. For SQL Server 2008 and later, you can download it from Microsoft's codeplex site: HTTP://MSFTDBPRODSAMPLES.CODEPLEX.COM/RELEASES/

Feedback and Errata

We've tried our very best to ensure that this book is useful, technically accurate, and written in plain, simple language. If we've erred on any of these elements, or you just want to let us know what you think of the book, we want to hear from you.

Please post your feedback and errata to the Tribal SQL book page, here: HTTP://TRIBALSQL.COM/FEEDBACK.

SQL Server Storage Internals 101

Mark S. Rasmussen

In this chapter, I offer a concise introduction to the physical storage internals behind SQL Server databases. I won't be diving into every detail because my goal is to provide a simple, clear picture of how SQL Server stores data.

Why is this useful? After all, the day-to-day routine of most SQL Server developers and DBAs doesn't necessarily require detailed knowledge of SQL Server's inner workings and storage mechanisms. However, armed with it, we will be in a much better position to make optimal design decisions for our systems, and to troubleshoot them effectively when things go wrong and system performance is suffering.

There are so many optimization techniques in a modern RDBMS that we're unlikely to learn them all. What if, instead of striving to master every technique, we strive to understand the underlying structures that these techniques try to optimize? Suddenly, we have the power of deductive reasoning. While we might not know about every specific feature, we can deduce *why* they exist as well as *how* they work. It will also help us to devise effective optimization techniques of our own.

In essence, this is a simple manifestation of the ancient Chinese proverb:

> *Give a man a fish and you feed him for a day; teach a man to fish and you feed him for a lifetime.*

It's the reason I believe every SQL Server DBA and developer should have a sound basic understanding, not just of what storage objects exist in SQL Server (heaps and indexes), but of the underlying data structures (pages and records) that make up these objects, what they look like at the byte level and how they work. Once we have this, we can make much better decisions about our storage requirements, in terms of capacity, as well as the storage structures we need for optimal query performance.

The Power of Deductive Reasoning

I want to start with a story that explains how I came to appreciate fully the value of knowing what SQL Server actually stores on disk and how. It is also a cautionary tale of how ignorance of the basic underlying structures of the database means that you don't have the right set of tools to evaluate and design an effective SQL Server solution.

When I first started out with SQL Server, and before I developed any deep knowledge of it, a print magazine retailer asked me to create a system for presenting their magazines online and tracking visitor patterns and statistics. They wanted to know how many views a given magazine page attracted, on an hourly level.

Quick to fetch my calculator, I started crunching the numbers. Assuming each magazine had an average of 50 pages, each page being viewed at least once an hour, this would result in roughly half a million rows (*50 pages * 365 days * 24 hours*) of data in our statistics table in the database, per year, per magazine. If we were to end up with, say, 1,000 magazines then, well, this was approaching more data than I could think about comfortably and, without any knowledge of how a SQL Server database stored data, I leapt to the conclusion that it would not be able to handle it either.

In a flash of brilliance, an idea struck me. I would split out the data into separate databases! Each magazine would get its own statistics database, enabling me to filter the data just by selecting from the appropriate statistics database, for any given magazine (all of these databases were stored on the same disk; I had no real grasp of the concept of I/O performance at this stage).

I learned my lesson the hard way. Once we reached that magic point of having thousands of magazines, our database backup operations were suffering. Our backup window, originally 15 minutes, expanded to fill 6 hours, simply due to the need to back up thousands of separate databases. The DDL involved in creating databases on the fly as well as creating cross-database queries for comparing statistics...well, let's just say it wasn't optimal.

Around this time, I participated in my first SQL Server-oriented conference and attended a Level 200 session on data file internals. It was a revelation and I immediately realized my wrongdoing. Suddenly, I understood why, due to the way data was stored and traversed, SQL Server would *easily* have been able to handle all of my data. It struck me, in fact, that I'd been trying to replicate the very idea behind a clustered index, just in a horribly inefficient way.

Of course, I already knew about indexes, or so I thought. I knew you created them on some columns to make queries work faster. What I started to understand thanks to this session and subsequent investigations, was how and why a certain index might help and, conversely, why it might not. Most importantly, I learned how b-tree structures allowed SQL Server to efficiently store and query enormous amounts of data.

Records

A **record**, also known as a row, is the smallest storage structure in a SQL Server data file. Each row in a table is stored as an individual record on disk. Not only table data is stored as records, but also indexes, metadata, database boot structures and so forth. However, we'll concentrate on only the most common and important record type, namely the **data record**, which shares the same format as the index record.

Data records are stored in a **fixedvar** format. The name derives from the fact that there are two basic kinds of data types, *fixed length* and *variable length*. As the name implies, fixed-length data types have a static length from which they never deviate. Examples are 4-byte integers, 8-byte datetimes, and 10-byte characters (char(10)).

Variable-length data types, such as varchar(x) and varbinary(x), have a length that varies on a record-by-record basis. While a varchar(10) might take up 10 bytes in one record, it might only take up 3 bytes in another, depending on the stored value.

Figure 1 shows the basic underlying fixedvar structure of every data record.

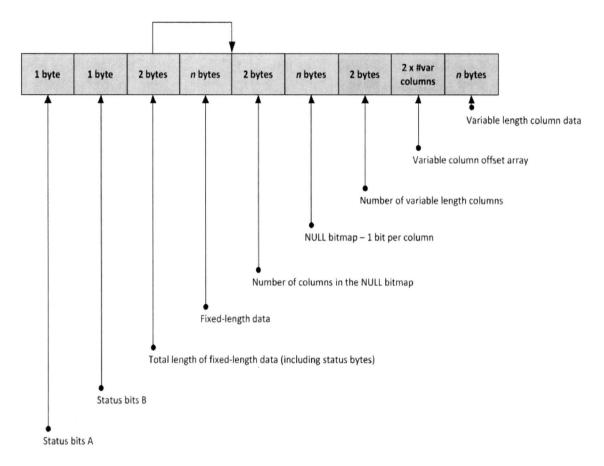

Figure 1:   Structure of a data record at the byte level.

Every data record starts with two status bytes, which define, among other things:

- the record type – of which the data and index types are, by far, the most common and important

- whether the record has a null bitmap – one or more bytes used to track whether columns have null values

- whether the record has any variable-length columns.

The next two bytes store the total length of the fixed-length portion of the record. This is the length of the actual fixed-length data, plus the 2 bytes used to store the status, and the 2 bytes used to store the total fixed length. We sometimes refer to the fixed-length length field as the **null bitmap pointer**, as it points to the end of the fixed-length data, which is where the null bitmap starts.

The **fixed-length data** portion of the record stores all of the column data for the fixed-length data types in the table schema. The columns are stored in physical order and so can always be located at a specific byte index in the data record, by calculating the size of all the previous fixed-length columns in the schema.

The next two areas of storage make up the **null bitmap**, an array of bits that keep track of which columns contain null values for that record, and which columns have non-null values in the record. As fixed-length data columns always take up their allotted space, we need the null bitmap to know whether a value is null. For variable-length columns, the null bitmap is the means by which we can distinguish between an empty value and a null value. The 2 bytes preceding the actual bitmap simply store the number of columns tracked by the bitmap. As each column in the bitmap requires a bit, the required bytes for the null bitmap can be calculated by dividing the total number of columns by 8 and then rounding up to the nearest integer: `CEIL(#Cols / 8)`.

Finally, we have the variable-length portion of the record, consisting of 2 bytes to store the number of variable-length columns, followed by a **variable-length offset array**, followed by the actual variable-length data.

Figure 2 shows an expanded example of the sections of the data record relating to variable-length data.

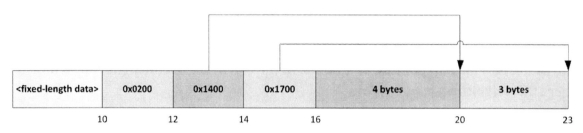

Figure 2: Variable-length data portion of a data record.

We start with two bytes that indicate the number of variable-length columns stored in the record. In this case, the value, 0x0200, indicates two columns. Next up is a series of two-byte values that form the variable-length offset array, one for each column, pointing to the byte index in the record where the related column data ends. Finally, we have the actual variable-length columns.

Since SQL Server knows the data starts after the last entry in the offset array, and knows where the data ends for each column, it can calculate the length of each column, as well as query the data.

Pages

Theoretically, SQL Server could just store a billion records side by side in a huge data file, but that would be a mess to manage. Instead, it organizes and stores records in smaller units of data, known as pages. Pages are also the smallest units of data that SQL Server will cache in memory (handled by the buffer manager).

There are different types of pages; some store data records, some store index records and others store metadata of various sorts. All of them have one thing in common, which is their structure. A page is always exactly 8 KB (8192 bytes) in size and contains two major sections, the header and the body. The header has a fixed size of 96 bytes and has the same contents and format, regardless of the page type. It contains information such as how much space is free in the body, how many records are stored in the body, the object to which the page belongs and, in an index, the pages that precede and succeed it.

The body takes up the remaining 8096 bytes, as depicted in Figure 3.

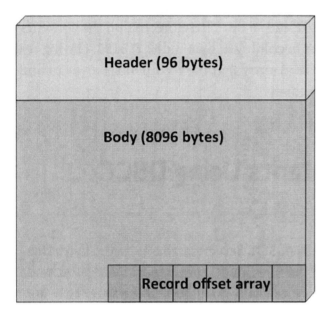

Figure 3:   The structure of a page.

At the very end of the body is a section known as the **record offset array**, which is an array of two-byte values that SQL Server reads in reverse from the very end of the page. The header contains a field that defines the number of **slots** that are present in the record offset array, and thus how many two-byte values SQL Server can read. Each slot in the record offset array points to a byte index in the page where a record begins. The record offset array dictates the **physical order** of the records. As such, the very last record on the page, logically, may very well be the first record, physically. Typically, you'll find that the first slot of the record offset array, stored in the very last two bytes of the page, points to the first record stored at byte index 96, which is at the very beginning of the body, right after the header.

If you've ever used any of the DBCC commands, you will have seen record pointers in the format (X:Y:Z), pointing to data file X, page Y and slot Z. To find a record on page Y, SQL Server first needs to find the path for the data file with id X. The file is just one big array of pages, with the very first page starting at byte index 0, the next one at byte index 8192, the third one at byte index 16384, and so on. The page number correlates directly with the byte index, in that page 0 is stored at byte index 0*8192, page 1 is stored at byte index 1*8192, page 2 is stored at byte index 2*8192 and so on. Therefore, to find the contents of page Y, SQL Server needs to read 8192 bytes beginning at byte index Y*8192. Having read the bytes of the page, SQL Server can then read entry Z in the record offset array to find out where the record bytes are stored in the body.

Investigating Page Contents Using DBCC Commands

It's surprisingly easy to peek into the innards of SQL Server databases, at the bytes that make up your database. We can use one of the three DBCC commands: DBCC TRACEON, DBCC PAGE, and DBCC IND. Microsoft has not officially documented the latter two, but people use them so widely that you can assume that they're here to stay.

DBCC IND provides the relevant page IDs for any object in the database, and then DBCC PAGE allows us to investigate what's stored on disk on those specific pages. Note that DBCC PAGE and IND are both ready-only operations, so they're completely safe to use.

DBCC PAGE

By default, SQL Server sends the output from DBCC PAGE to the trace log and not as a query result. To execute DBCC PAGE commands from SSMS and see the results directly in the query results window, we first need to enable Trace Flag 3604, as shown in Listing 1.

```
--Enable
DBCC TRACEON (3604);

--Disable
DBCC TRACEOFF (3604);
```

Listing 1:   Enabling and disabling Trace Flag 3604.

The trace flag activates at the connection level, so enabling it in one connection will not affect any other connections to the server. Likewise, as soon as the connection closes, the trace flag will no longer have any effect. Having enabled the trace flag, we can issue the DBCC PAGE command using the following syntax:

DBCC PAGE (<Database>, <FileID>, <PageID>, <Style>)

Database is the name of the database whose page we want to examine. Next, the FileID of the file we want to examine; for most databases this will be 1, as there will only be a single data file. Execute Listing 2 within a specific database to reveal a list of all data files for that database, including their FileIDs.

```
SELECT * FROM sys.database_files WHERE type = 0;
```

Listing 2:   Interrogating sys.database_files.

Next, the PageID of the page we wish to examine. This can be any valid PageID in the database. For example, the special file header page is page 0, page 9 is the equally special boot page, which is only stored in the primary file with file_id 1, or any other data page that exists in the file. Typically, you won't see user data pages before page 17+.

Finally, we have the Style value:

- 0 – outputs only the parsed header values. That is, there are no raw bytes, only the header contents.

- 1 – outputs the parsed header as well as the raw bytes of each record on the page.

- 2 – outputs the parsed header as well as the complete raw byte contents of the page, including both the header and body.

- 3 – outputs the parsed header and the parsed record column values for each record on the page. The raw bytes for each record are output as well. This is usually the most useful style as it allows access to the header as well as the ability to correlate the raw record bytes with the column data.

Listing 3 shows how you'd examine the rows on page 16 in the primary data file of the AdventureWorks2008R2 database.

```
DBCC PAGE (AdventureWorks2008R2, 1, 16, 3);
```

Listing 3:   Using DBCC PAGE on AdventureWorks.

```
PAGE: (1:16)

PAGE HEADER:
m_pageId = (1:16)                   m_headerVersion = 1              m_type = 1
m_typeFlagBits = 0x4                m_level = 0                     m_flagBits = 0x200
m_objId (AllocUnitId.idObj) = 7     m_indexId (AllocUnitId.idInd) = 0   Metadata: AllocUnitId = 458752
Metadata: PartitionId = 458752      Metadata: IndexId = 1          Metadata: ObjectId = 7
m_prevPage = (0:0)                  m_nextPage = (1:130)           pminlen = 73
m_slotCnt = 51                      m_freeCnt = 4067               m_freeData = 8027
m_reservedCnt = 0                   m_lsn = (45:460:24)            m_xactReserved = 0
m_xdesId = (0:0)                    m_ghostRecCnt = 0              m_tornBits = 2036781508

Allocation Status
GAM (1:2) = ALLOCATED               SGAM (1:3) = NOT ALLOCATED
PFS (1:1) = 0x60 MIXED_EXT ALLOCATED   0_PCT_FULL                  DIFF (1:6) = CHANGED
ML (1:7) = NOT MIN_LOGGED

Slot 0 offset 0x60 Length 77
Record Type = PRIMARY_RECORD        Record Attributes =  NULL_BITMAP    Record Size = 77

Memory Dump @0x000000002709A060
0000000000000000:   10004900 00000300 00000000 01000003 †..I............
0000000000000010:   00000000 00000000 0001001f 00000001 †...............
0000000000000020:   00570000 00010056 00000001 00140000 †.W.....V........
0000000000000030:   00000000 00120000 00000000 00190000 †...............
0000000000000040:   00000000 00010000 000c0000 00†††††††††...........

Slot 0 Column 1 offset 0x4 Length 8 Length (physical) 8
auid = 196608

Slot 0 Column 2 offset 0xc Length 1 Length (physical) 1
type = 1

...
```

Looking at the output, you'll be able to see the page ID stored in the header (m_pageId), the number of records stored on the page (m_slotCnt), the object ID to which this page belongs (m_objId) and much more.

After the header, we see each record listed, one by one. The output of each record consists of the raw bytes (Memory Dump), followed by each of the column values (Slot 0 Column 1..., and so on). Note that the column values also detail how many (physical) bytes they take up on disk, making it easier for you to correlate the value with the raw byte output.

DBCC IND

Now that you know how to gain access to the contents of a page, you'll probably want to do so for tables in your existing databases. What we need, then, is to know on which pages a given table's records are stored. Luckily, that's just what DBCC IND provides and we call it like this:

```
DBCC IND (<Database>, <Object>, <IndexID>)
```

We specify the name of the database and the name of the object for which we wish to view the pages. Finally, we can filter the output to just a certain index; 0 indicates a heap, while 1 is the clustered index. If we want to see the pages for a specific non-clustered index, we enter that index's ID. If we use -1 for the IndexID, we get a list of all pages belonging to any index related to the specified object.

Listing 4 examines the Person.Person table in the SQL Server 2008 R2 Adventure-Works database, and is followed by the first five rows of the results (your output may differ, depending on the release).

```
DBCC IND (AdventureWorks2008R2, 'Person.Person, 1);
```

Listing 4:   Using DBCC IND on AdventureWorks.

	PageFID	PagePID	IAMFID	IAMPID	ObjectID	IndexID	PartitionNumber	PartitionID	iam_chain_type	Page Type
1	1	734	NULL	NULL	341576255	1	1	72057594043695104	In-row data	10
2	1	747	1	734	341576255	1	1	72057594043695104	In-row data	2
3	1	19904	1	734	341576255	1	1	72057594043695104	In-row data	1
4	1	19905	1	734	341576255	1	1	72057594043695104	In-row data	1
5	1	19906	1	734	341576255	1	1	72057594043695104	In-row data	1

There are a couple of interesting columns here. The **PageType** column details the type of page. For example, **PageType** 10 is an allocation structure page known as an IAM page, which I'll describe in the next section. **PageType** 2 is an index page and **PageType** 1 is a data page.

The first two columns show the file ID as well as the page ID of each of those pages. Using those two values, we can invoke **DBCC PAGE** for the first data page, as shown in Listing 5.

```
DBCC PAGE (AdventureWorks2008R2, 1, 19904, 3);
```

Listing 5:   Using DBCC PAGE to view the contents of a data page belonging to the Person.Person table.

Heaps and Indexes

We've examined the structure of records and the pages in which SQL Server stores them. Now it's time for us to go a level higher, and look at how SQL Server structures pages in *heaps* and *indexes*. If a table contains a clustered index, then that table is stored in the same way as an index. A table without a clustered index is a "heap."

Heaps

Heaps are the simplest data structures, in that they're just "a big bunch of pages," all owned by the same object. A special type of page called an **index allocation map** (IAM) tracks which pages belong to which object. SQL Server uses IAM pages for heaps and indexes, but they're especially important for heaps as they're the only mechanism for finding the pages containing the heap data. My primary goal in this chapter is to discuss index structure and design, so I'll only cover heaps briefly.

Each IAM page contains one huge bitmap, tracking 511,232 pages, or about 4 GB of data. For the sake of efficiency, the IAM page doesn't track the individual pages, but rather groups of eight, known as **extents**. If the heap takes up more than 4 GB of data, SQL Server allocates another IAM page to enable tracking the pages in the next 4 GB of data, leaving in the first IAM page's header a pointer to the next IAM page. In order to scan a heap, SQL Server will simply find the first IAM page and then scan each page in each extent to which it points.

One important fact to remember is that a heap guarantees no order for the records within each page. SQL Server inserts a new record wherever it wants, usually on an existing page with plenty of space, or on a newly allocated page.

Compared to indexes, heaps are rather simple in terms of maintenance, as there is no physical order to maintain. We don't have to consider factors such as the use of an ever-increasing key for maintaining order as we insert rows; SQL Server will just append a record anywhere it fits, on its chosen page, regardless of the key.

However, just because heap maintenance is limited, it doesn't mean that heaps have no maintenance issues. In order to understand why, we need to discuss **forwarded records**.

Unlike in an index, a heap has no key that uniquely identifies a given record. If a non-clustered index or a foreign key needs to point to a specific record, it does so using a pointer to its physical location, represented as (`FileID:PageID:SlotID`), also known as a **RID** or a **row identifier**. For example (1:16:2) points to the third slot in the 17th page (both starting at index 0) in the first file (which starts at index 1).

Imagine that the pointer to record (1:16:2) exists in 20 different places but that, due perhaps to an update to a column value, SQL Server has to move the record from page 16 as there is no longer space for it. This presents an interesting performance problem.

If SQL Server simply moves the record to a new physical location, it will have to update that physical pointer in 20 different locations, which is a lot of work. Instead, it copies the record to a new page and converts the original record into a **forwarding stub**, a small record taking up just 9 bytes storing a physical pointer to the new record. The existing 20 physical pointers will read the forwarding stub, allowing SQL Server to find the wanted data.

This technique makes updates simpler and faster, at the considerable cost of an extra lookup for reads. As data modifications lead to more and more forwarded records, disk I/O increases tremendously, as SQL Server tries to read records from all over the disk.

Listing 6 shows how to query the `sys.dm_db_index_physical_stats` DMV to find all heaps with forwarded records in the `AdventureWorks` database. If you do have any heaps (hopefully not), then monitor these values to decide when it's time to issue an `ALTER TABLE REBUILD` command to remove the forwarded records.

```
SELECT   o.name ,
         ps.forwarded_record_count
FROM     sys.dm_db_index_physical_stats(DB_ID('AdventureWorks2008R2'), NULL, NULL,
                             NULL, 'DETAILED') ps
         INNER JOIN sys.objects o ON o.object_id = ps.object_id
WHERE    forwarded_record_count > 0
```

Listing 6:   Using `sys.dm_db_index_physical_stats` to monitor the number of forwarded records in any heaps in a database.

Indexes

SQL Server also tracks which pages belong to which indexes through the IAM pages. However, indexes are fundamentally different from heaps in terms of their organization and structure. Indexes, clustered as well as non-clustered, store data pages in a guaranteed logical order, according to the defined index key (physically, SQL Server may store the pages out of order).

Structurally, non-clustered and clustered indexes are the same. Both store index pages in a structure known as a **b-tree**. However, while a non-clustered index stores only the b-tree structure with the index key values and pointers to the data rows, a clustered index stores both the b-tree, with the keys, and the actual row data at the leaf level of the b-tree. As such, each table can have only one clustered index, since the data can only be stored in one location, but many non-clustered indexes that point to the base data. With non-clustered indexes, we can include copies of the data for certain columns, for example so that we can read frequently accessed columns without touching the base data, while either ignoring the remaining columns or following the index pointer to where the rest of the data is stored.

For non-clustered indexes, the pointer to the actual data may take two forms. If we create the non-clustered index on a heap, the only way to locate a record is by its physical location. This means the non-clustered index will store the pointer in the form of an 8-byte row identifier. On the other hand, if we create the non-clustered index on a clustered index, the pointer is actually a copy of the clustered key, allowing us to look up the actual data in the clustered index. If the clustered key contains columns already part of the non-clustered index key, those are not duplicated, as they're already stored as part of the non-clustered index key.

Let's explore b-trees in more detail.

b-tree structure

The b-tree structure is a tree of pages, usually visualized as an upside-down tree, starting at the top, from the **root**, branching out into **intermediate** levels, and finally ending up at the bottom level, the **leaf level**. If all the records of an index fit on one page, the tree only has one level and so the root and leaf level can technically be the same level. As soon as the index needs two pages, the tree will split up into a root page pointing to two child pages at the leaf level. For clustered indexes, the leaf level is where SQL Server stores all the data; all the intermediate (that is, non-leaf) levels of the tree contain just the data from the key columns. The smaller the key, the more records can fit on those branch pages, thus resulting in a shallower tree depth and quicker leaf lookup speed.

The b-tree for an index with an integer as the index key might look something like the one shown in Figure 4.

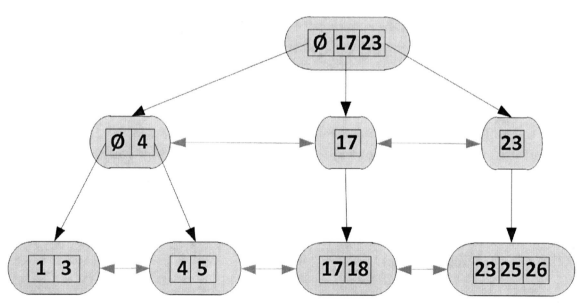

Figure 4:   A b-tree structure for an index with an integer key.

The bottom level is the leaf level, and the two levels above it are branches, with the top level containing the root page of the index (of which there can be only one). In this example, I'm only showing the key values, and not the actual data itself, which would otherwise be in the bottom leaf level, for a clustered index. Note that the leftmost intermediate level pages will always have an Ø entry. It represents any value lower than the key next to it. In this case, the root page Ø covers values 1–16 while the intermediate page Ø covers the values 1–3.

The main point to note here is that the pages connect in multiple ways. On each level, each page points to the previous and the next pages, provided these exist, and so acts as a doubly-linked list. Each parent page contains pointers to the child pages on the level below, all the way down to the leaf level, where there are no longer any child page pointers, but actual data, or pointers to the actual data, in the case of a non-clustered index.

If SQL Server wants to scan a b-tree, it just needs a pointer to the root page. SQL Server stores this pointer in the internal `sys.sysallocunits` base table, which also contains a pointer to the first IAM page tracking the pages belonging to a given object. From the root page, it can follow the child pointers all the way until the first leaf-level page, and then just scan the linked list of pages.

The power of b-trees: binary searches, a.k.a. seeking

You've probably heard the age-old adage that scans are bad and seeks are good, and with good reason because, in general, these are wise words.

As discussed previously, in a heap there is no order to the data, so if SQL Server wants to find a specific value, it can only do so by scanning *all* of the data in the heap. Even if we run a "`SELECT TOP 1`" query, SQL Server may still need to scan the entire table to return just that single row, if the first row of the result set happens to be the very the last record in the heap. Of course, if we happen to have a non-clustered index on the heap that includes the required columns, SQL Server may perform a seek operation.

Conversely, finding a specific value in a b-tree is extremely efficient. By exploiting the fact that the b-tree logically sorts all of the values by index key, we can use an algorithm called **binary search** to find the desired value in very few operations.

Imagine a game where Player A thinks of a number between 1 and 10 that Player B has to guess. On each guess from Player B, Player A must only offer one of three replies: "correct," "lower" or "higher."

Player A thinks of a number. Player B, a wise opponent, asks if the number is "5." Player B responds "higher," so B now knows that the number is 6, 7, 8, 9, or 10. Aiming for the middle of the set again, B guesses "8." A responds "higher" so now B knows it's either 9 or 10. B guesses "9" and A responds with "correct." By always going for the median value, Player B cut the number of values in half on each guess, narrowing down the possible values very quickly.

SQL Server uses similar logic to traverse the b-tree to find a specific value. Let's say SQL Server, in response to a query, needs to find the record corresponding to Key 5, in Figure 4. First, it looks at the middle key on the root page, 17, indicating that the page to which it points contains values of 17 and higher. Five is smaller than 17 so it inspects the middle key of all the keys lower than 17. In this simple example, there is only the Ø key so it follows this link to the page in the next level and inspects the value of the middle key. As there are only two keys, it will round up, look at the rightmost key, holding the value 4, and follow the chain to the leaf-level page containing Keys 4 and 5, at which point it has found the desired key.

If, instead, the search is for the Key 22, SQL Server starts in the same way but this time, after 17, inspects the middle key of all the keys higher than 17. Finding only Key 23, which is too high, it concludes that the page to which Key 17 points in the second level contains the values 17–22. From here, it follows the only available key to the leaf level, is unable to find the value 22 and concludes that no rows match the search criteria.

The downside to b-trees: maintenance

Though they enable efficient seeking, b-trees come with a price. SQL Server has to ensure that the records remain sorted in the correct key order at all times. In Figure 5, on the left we have a very small tree, with just an integer as the key. It contains two levels, consisting of a root page with two child pages. We'll assume that each of the leaf-level pages contains a lot of data besides just the keys, so can't hold more than two records. If we want to insert the value 15, SQL Server has to introduce a third leaf page. It can't just add the new row on a third page at the end, as it must insert the value 15 between 10 and 20. The result is a **page split**. SQL Server simply takes the existing page, containing the values 10 and 20, and splits it into two pages, storing half the rows on the new page, and half of them on the original page. There is now enough space for SQL Server to insert the value 15 on the half-empty original page, containing the value 10.

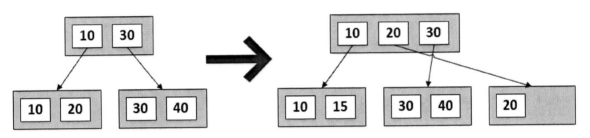

Figure 5:   A page split.

After splitting the page, we now have three pages in the leaf level and three keys in the root page. The page split is a costly operation for SQL Server in its own right, compared to simply inserting a record on an existing page, but the real cost is paid in terms of the fragmentation that arises from splitting pages. We no longer have a physically contiguous list of pages; SQL Server might store the newly allocated page in an entirely different area of disk. As a result, when we scan the tree, we'll have to read the first page, potentially skip to a completely different part of the disk, and then back again to continue reading the pages in order.

As time progresses and fragmentation gets worse, you'll see performance slowly degrading. Insertions will most likely run at a linear pace, but scanning and seeking will get progressively slower.

An easy way to avoid this problem is to avoid inserting new rows between existing ones. If we use an ever-increasing identity value as the key, we always add rows to the end, and SQL Server will never have to split existing pages. If we delete existing rows we will still end up with half-full pages, but we will avoid having the pages stored non-contiguously on disk.

Crunching the Numbers

Based on this understanding of the underlying structure of data records and pages and indexes, how might I have made better design and capacity planning choices for the magazine statistics database? Listing 7 shows a basic schema for the new design.

```
CREATE TABLE MagazineStatistics
    (
        MagazineID INT NOT NULL ,
        ViewDate SMALLDATETIME NOT NULL ,
        ViewHour TINYINT NOT NULL ,
        PageNumber SMALLINT NOT NULL ,
        ViewCount INT NOT NULL
    );

CREATE CLUSTERED INDEX CX_MagazineStatistics
  ON MagazineStatistics (MagazineID, ViewDate, ViewHour, PageNumber);
```

Listing 7:   New schema design for the `MagazineStatistics` table.

It is surprisingly simple. Part of the beauty here was in designing a schema that doesn't need any secondary indexes, just the clustered index. In essence, I'd designed a single clustered index that served the same purpose as my thousands of separate databases, but did so infinitely more efficiently.

Index design

There's one extremely high-impact choice we have to make up front, namely, how to design the clustered index, with particular regard to the `ViewDate` column, an ever-increasing value that tracks the date and hour of the page view. If that's the first column of the clustered index, we'll vastly reduce the number of page splits, since SQL Server will simply add each new record to the end of the b-tree. However, in doing so, we'll reduce our ability to filter results quickly, according `MagazineID`. To do so, we'd have to scan all of the data.

I took into consideration that the most typical query pattern would be something like *"Give me the total number of page views for magazine X in the period Y."* With such a read pattern, the schema in Listing 7 is optimal since it sorts the data by `MagazineID` and `ViewDate`.

While the schema is optimal for reading, it's suboptimal for writing, since SQL Server cannot write data contiguously if the index sorts by `MagazineID` first, rather than by `ViewDate` column. However, within each `MagazineID`, SQL Server will store the records in sorted order thanks to the `ViewDate` and `ViewHour` columns being part of the clustered key.

This design will still incur a page split cost as we add new records but, as long as we perform regular maintenance, old values will remain unaffected. By including the `PageNumber` column as the fourth and last column of the index key, it is also relatively cheap to satisfy queries like *"Give me the number of page views for page X in magazine Y in period Z."*

While you would generally want to keep your clustered key as narrow as possible, it's not necessary in this case. The four columns in the key only add up to 9 bytes in total, so it's still a relatively narrow key compared, for example, to a 16-byte `uniqueidentifier` (GUID).

The presence of non-clustered indexes or foreign keys in related tables exacerbates the issue of a wide clustering key, due to the need to duplicate the complete clustered key. Given our schema and query requirements, we had no need for non-clustered indexes, nor did we have any foreign keys pointing to our statistics data.

Storage requirements

The `MagazineStatistics` table has two 4-byte integers, a 2-byte `smallint`, a 4-byte `smalldatetime` and a 1-byte `tinyint`. In total, that's 11 bytes of fixed-length data. To calculate the total record size, we need to add the **two** status bytes, the **two** fixed-length length bytes, the **two** bytes for the null bitmap length indicator, as well as a **single** byte for the null bitmap itself. As there are no variable-length columns, the variable-length section of the record won't be present. Finally, we also need to take into account the **two** bytes in the record offset array at the end of the page body (see Figure 3). In total, this gives us a record size of 20 bytes per record. With a body size of 8096 bytes, that enables us to store 8096 / 20 = 404 records per page (known as the *fan-out*).

Assuming each magazine had visitors 24/7, and an average of 50 pages, that gives us 365 * 24 * 50 = 438,000 records per magazine, per year. With a fan-out of 404, that would require 438,000 / 404 = 1,085 data pages per magazine, weighing in at 1,085 * 8 KB = 8.5 MB in total. As we can't keep the data perfectly defragmented (as the latest added data will suffer from page splits), let's add 20% on top of that number just to be safe, giving a total of 8.5 + 20% = 10.2 MB of data per magazine per year. If we expect a thousand magazines per year, all with 24/7 traffic on all pages, that comes in at just about 1,000 * 10.2 MB = 9.96 GB of data per year.

In reality, the magazines don't receive traffic 24/7, especially not on all pages. As such, the actual data usage is lower, but these were my "worst-case scenario" calculations.

Summary

I started out having no idea how to calculate the required storage with any degree of accuracy, no idea how to create a suitable schema and index key, and no idea of how SQL Server would manage to navigate my data. That one session on SQL Server Internals piqued my interest in understanding more and, from that day on, I realized the value in knowing what happens internally and how I could use that knowledge to my advantage.

If this chapter has piqued your interest too, I strongly suggest you pick up *Microsoft SQL Server 2008 Internals* by Kalen Delaney et al., and drill further into the details.

SQL Server Data Compression

Bob Pusateri

Data compression, one of the many features introduced in SQL Server 2008, can help decrease the size of a database on disk, by reducing wasted space and eliminating duplicate data. Additionally, data compression can increase the speed of queries that perform high amounts of I/O, to and from disk, since each I/O operation can read or write more data.

Numbers will always vary from one environment to the next but, at my organization, the strategic deployment of data compression cut our overall database size on disk by nearly 50% and the execution time for key queries and processes by an average of 30%.

Nevertheless, DBAs must not take lightly the decision of when and where to deploy data compression; while its syntax is rather simple, the operations performed behind the scenes are not. This chapter aims to give you a good understanding of how data compression works so you can make an informed decision when deploying it.

Compression Basics

Data file compression technology has existed for many years and provides a simple way to reduce the size of data, save storage space, and minimize transfer time when sending data between locations.

However, database compression is far more challenging than standard file compression because with a database it is critical that the compression does not compromise data access speed, for both queries and modifications.

Simply compressing a SQL Server data file (typically files with **.mdf** or **.ndf** extensions) with a compression technology such as ZIP would yield a good compression ratio in many cases, but would degrade the performance of both reads and writes. In order to read a file compressed in this manner, SQL Server would have to decompress the entire file. If we also make changes, then it would subsequently have to recompress the entire file. These operations take considerable time and CPU cycles, even if we only need to change a few bytes of the file. Most of the work that SQL Server does involves making small changes to large files, so compressing the entire file, as described, would be rather inefficient.

Overview of SQL Server compression

Given that SQL Server divides data files into 8 KB pages and that it takes less time to compress or decompress a smaller amount of data, there is a clear advantage in compressing data pages individually instead of entire files. In fact, that is exactly how SQL Server data compression works.

Benefits

Compressing data does not reduce a page's 8 KB size. Instead, SQL Server compresses records stored on the page, which allows more records per page. SQL Server reads data as pages, *i.e.* one read will retrieve one 8 KB page from disk or memory. Therefore, with compression enabled, SQL Server requires fewer reads to return the same amount of data.

SQL Server is an in-memory database and the data format in memory exactly matches that used on disk. In other words, with data compression enabled, we have compressed data, and so more data per page, both in the buffer cache and on disk. This makes both logical I/O (reads and writes to memory) and physical I/O (reads and write to disk) quicker and more efficient.

By fitting more data in memory, we can reduce the necessity for disk reads, since it becomes more likely that the required data will already be in memory. Since logical I/O is orders of magnitude faster than physical I/O, this can also boost query performance relative to non-compressed data.

Typically, reads from disk account for a considerable portion of query execution time, so fewer disk reads generally means much faster queries. This is particularly evident for queries that involve large scans but is also advantageous for some seek operations.

Costs

Data compression and decompression takes place in an area of the SQL Server Storage Engine known as the "Access Methods." When a user issues a query, the Access Methods code requests the required rows from the buffer manager, which will return the compressed data pages from its cache, after loading them from disk if necessary and will decompress these data rows before passing them off to the relational engine. Conversely, when writing data, during an INSERT or UPDATE statement, the Access Methods code will compress the rows it receives from the relational engine and write the compressed pages to the buffer cache.

In other words, every time a query reads or writes a record, the Access Methods code must decompress or recompress the record, on the fly. This requires additional CPU resources and is the primary "cost" of using data compression.

For this reason, systems with high CPU usage may not be good candidates for data compression. Nothing in computing is free and if you want the benefits of compression then you will pay for them in terms of CPU utilization. Fortunately, the reduced disk usage and performance increase that accompany compression, more than compensate typically for this expense.

Types and granularity

SQL Server offers two compression settings or levels: **row compression** and **page compression**. The former converts fixed width data types to variable width in order to remove unused space from columns, and the latter (the more CPU-intensive of the two) removes duplicate values across multiple rows and columns on a page.

We configure SQL Server data compression, not on tables or their indexes, but on the **partitions** that comprise these tables and indexes. Of course, this doesn't mean we must partition our tables or indexes in order to use compression, because a non-partitioned object is simply one with a single partition. What it does mean is that we can, if desired, have a different compression setting for each object partition, rather than having to share a single setting for all. For example, a partition containing infrequently accessed data can have a high level of compression (*i.e.* page), whereas a partition containing frequently accessed records can have a lower setting (*i.e.* row), or be uncompressed. We'll discuss this in more detail a little later in the chapter.

Since compression occurs on a per-partition basis, we can view compression settings in the `data_compression` and `data_compression_desc` columns of the `sys.partitions` catalog view. Each partition will have a value of NONE, ROW, or PAGE.

Just because you have a hammer

By now, you might be wondering why we don't just deploy data compression everywhere. As my first DBA team leader used to say, "Just because you have a hammer doesn't mean every problem is a nail." Data compression is an excellent tool, but it is not always the most appropriate solution. As stated earlier, you will pay with higher CPU utilization for data compression's advantages, in order to compress and decompress the data on the fly. Generally, we DBAs view higher CPU usage as a bad thing but in this case it can be worth it, as many types of query will complete faster as a result. Along with many other aspects of SQL Server, there are no hard and fast rules for deploying compression, but we'll discuss some general guidelines later in this chapter.

Version and edition requirements

In its current form, data compression was first available in SQL Server 2008 Enterprise Edition. It remains an Enterprise Edition-only feature in SQL Server 2008 R2 and SQL Server 2012. Data compression is also available in SQL Server Evaluation Edition and SQL Server Developer Edition, since they support all the features of Enterprise Edition, but of course, Microsoft does not license these editions for use in a production environment.

As an Enterprise-only feature, data compression will probably cost you some cash in addition to CPU resources. SQL Server 2012's increased pricing and core-based licensing model for Enterprise Edition means that, unfortunately, you'll be paying more than for previous versions.

There is also the "gotcha" of not being able to restore a database utilizing Enterprise-only features onto any lesser edition of SQL Server. The restore will fail and, worse yet, this failure will occur at the very end of the restore process, meaning you might waste significant time before arriving at that result.

Row Compression

The first of the two available data compression settings is **row compression**. As its name suggests, row compression compresses data within individual rows on a page. Row compression can offer excellent compression ratios in many situations, and is less resource intensive than page compression.

The primary purpose of row compression is to squeeze unused space from columns in each row, whenever possible. Variable width types such as `VARCHAR` only consume the space necessary to store a value, but fixed-width types such as `CHAR` and `INT` are, by definition, the same size regardless of the stored value.

Row compression is able to save more space by utilizing a different record structure and storing fixed width data types as if they were variable width. The data types presented to users and applications outside of the database remain unchanged, but the storage engine treats them differently behind the scenes. The best way to demonstrate this is with a few examples.

Imagine a table that contains just one column, an integer. Being a fixed-width data type, an integer column for an uncompressed row takes up 4 bytes of space no matter what value it stores. With row compression enabled, SQL Server adjusts column sizes such that they only consume the space necessary to store the value in a particular row. As shown in Figure 1, the values NULL and 0 will consume no space at all with compression enabled (more on how this works later). The value 1 requires only one byte, saving three unused bytes. The value 40,000 requires three bytes, yielding a saving of one byte.

Integer Value Stored	Bytes (uncompressed)	Bytes (compressed)
NULL	4	0
0	4	0
1	4	1
40,000	4	3

Figure 1:   Integer column compression savings.

Character types can also benefit from row compression. Let's envision an uncompressed table with two columns, an ID column of type SMALLINT, and a Name column of type CHAR(8). Since a SMALLINT requires two bytes and CHAR(8) requires eight, each row requires ten bytes for data, as shown in Figure 2.

92		S	A	M					
4346		N	I	C	K				
120		M	I	C	H	E	L	L	E

Figure 2:   Two-column table, uncompressed.

With row compression enabled, our table looks very different, as shown in Figure 3. The ID values for Sam and Michelle are less than 128, meaning they would fit into a single byte instead of two. Nick's ID is large enough that it requires both bytes. As for the Name columns, Michelle requires all eight bytes, while Sam and Nick have unused bytes that can be removed from the end.

92	S	A	M					
4346	N	I	C	K				
120	M	I	C	H	E	L	L	E

Figure 3:   Two-column table with row compression.

Where all three rows previously required ten bytes each, with row compression enabled the first row now consumes only four, the second row uses six, and the third uses nine, a net space saving of over 36%, for the three rows combined.

As a side effect, the columns no longer begin at specific offsets. In the uncompressed example, the first two bytes of each row are part of the ID column and the third byte is the beginning of the name. In the compressed version, the name column might start at the second byte if the ID value is small enough, or even the first byte if the ID value is 0 or NULL. Since fixed-width columns are now essentially variable width, no longer can SQL Server use offsets to find these columns. Instead, the compressed record structure contains **column descriptors** that store the exact size of each variable width column, so that SQL Server knows where each column starts. For this service, column descriptors consume 4 bits per column per row. The special cases of NULL and 0 values are also stored in the column descriptor, which explains why those values can consume zero bytes.

As demonstrated in the previous examples, compression ratios will vary, based on both the value of the data stored and the data type of the column that is storing it. Storing five characters in a column of type CHAR(10) will see 50% compression, while storing those same five characters in a CHAR(100) column will achieve 95% compression. Chances are good with row compression that choosing an appropriate data type, when designing a table, will lead to lower compression ratios. Conversely, some values will consume all the space allocated to their column and thus compression will have no effect on them at all.

Another feature of row compression is **Unicode compression**, made available in SQL Server 2008 R2. Unicode compression utilizes the Standard Compression Scheme for Unicode (SCSU) to reduce the number of bytes required to store Unicode text. It supports the NCHAR and NVARCHAR data types, with specified lengths, but not NVARCHAR(MAX). For most Western languages, it results in a 50% saving, so each character will require only one byte instead of two. In the event that Unicode compression does not provide any advantage, SQL Server will not apply it.

The majority of SQL Server data types can benefit from row compression when the values stored in them allow for it. Notable exceptions are LOB (Large Object) types such as TEXT/NTEXT, IMAGE, NVARCHAR(MAX), XML, or FILESTREAM. A more complete list of data types affected by row compression is available in Books Online at HTTP://MSDN.MICROSOFT.COM/EN-US/LIBRARY/CC280576.ASPX.

Page Compression

While row compression squeezes unused space out of each column on a row-by-row basis, page compression takes a more drastic approach and removes duplicate values across multiple rows and columns on a page. This method can yield higher compression ratios than row compression but, because of its relative complexity, it also utilizes more CPU.

Page compression comprises three operations. First, SQL Server performs row compression as described in the previous section. Second is **column prefix compression**, and finally **page dictionary compression**.

Figure 4 shows a data page, containing three rows and three columns, which has already been row compressed.

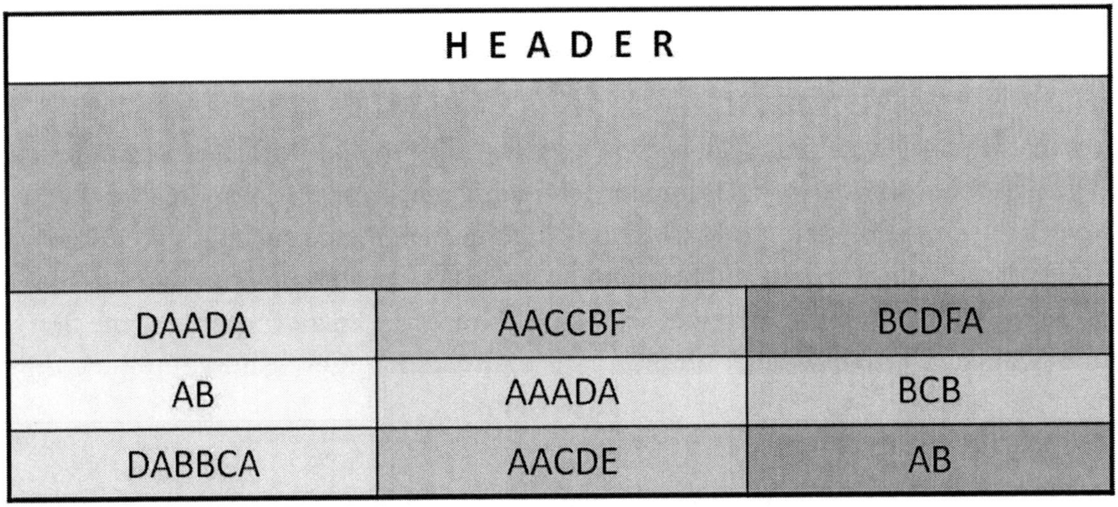

HEADER		
DAADA	AACCBF	BCDFA
AB	AAADA	BCB
DABBCA	AACDE	AB

Figure 4:   Data page before column prefix compression has been applied.

Let's see how the two page-compression operations affect the structure of this data page.

Stage 1: Column prefix compression

After row compression completes, SQL Server applies the first page compression operation (column prefix compression), which examines the values in a column and tries to find the prefix shared by the greatest number of values. This operation looks at the byte patterns stored, so it doesn't matter what data type each column contains. The term "prefix compression" refers to the fact that SQL Server considers pattern matches only when reading the bytes in order starting at the beginning. For example, consider the following two values in hexadecimal notation:

- 0xAABC1234

- 0xAABCC234

The common prefix is "0xAABC". Even though both values share the fourth byte "34", it is not part of the prefix because the third bytes "12" and "C2" differ.

If SQL Server finds a common prefix for the data in the column, the largest value containing that prefix is stored in a special record known as the **anchor record**, located right after the page header in a region known as the **Compression Information structure**, or **CI structure** for short. The anchor record is no different from any other record on the page, with the exception that it is marked as being the anchor, and so SQL Server does not return it with query results. If the column data has no common prefix value, then a NULL value is stored in the anchor record. Figure 5 shows the anchor record for the first column populated with the value "DABBCA", since this is the largest value containing the prefix, "DA", found in two of the values in this column.

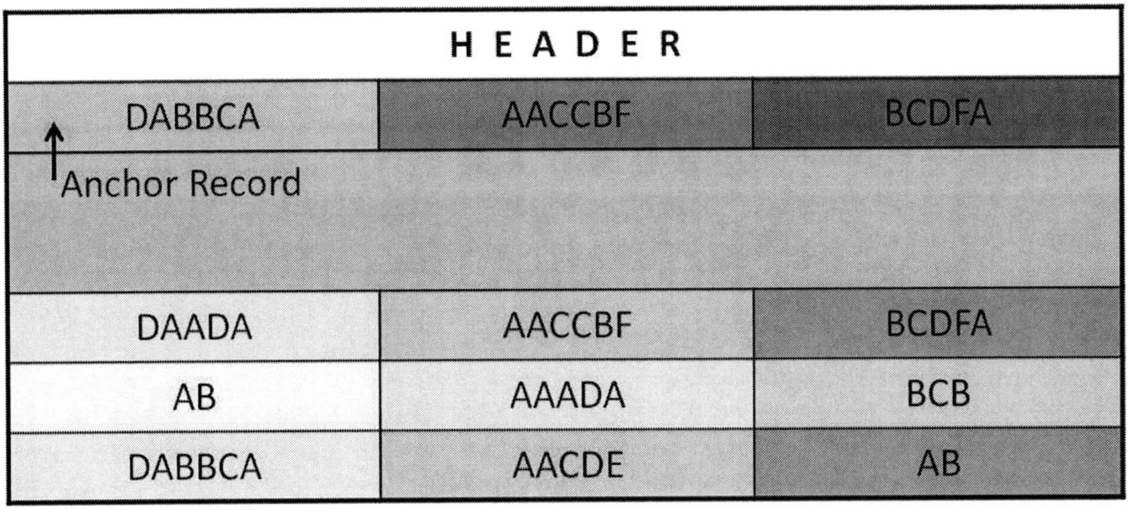

HEADER		
DABBCA	AACBF	BCDFA
Anchor Record		
DAADA	AACBF	BCDFA
AB	AAADA	BCB
DABBCA	AACDE	AB

Figure 5: Data page after the anchor record has been determined.

Having determined the anchor record, SQL Server adjusts the values stored in the data rows so they are relative to the anchor record. For any data rows that share a common prefix with the anchor row, it replaces the shared bytes with a number indicating how many prefix bytes should come from the anchor. For example, in Figure 5, the compressed form of the first record, DAADA, is 2ADA.

If a row value does not match the prefix of the anchor value, SQL Server adds a "0" to the stored value, indicating that the actual value is composed of the first 0 bytes of the anchor record followed by the row value. Therefore, in the second row of the first column, the value AB becomes 0AB.

For any rows that match the anchor record exactly, such as the third row in the first column, SQL Server replaces the row value with a special "pseudo-null" value, which is different from a standard NULL. SQL Server knows that this pseudo-null simply means that it should copy the anchor value in its entirety.

Figure 6 shows the result of applying column prefix compression to all of the columns in the table.

HEADER		
DABBCA	AACCBF	BCDFA
2ADA	NULL	NULL
0AB	2ADA	2B
NULL	3DE	0AB

Figure 6:   Data page after column prefix compression has completed.

After column prefix compression is completed, **page dictionary compression**, the second and final stage of page compression begins.

Stage 2: Page dictionary compression

While column prefix compression de-duplicates values within a column, page dictionary compression de-duplicates values across all rows and columns on a page. It does this by building a dictionary of repeated values and utilizing that dictionary instead of storing the values more than once in a page. Values from any column can reference a dictionary entry because, like column prefix compression, page dictionary compression operates on stored byte patterns, which are data type agnostic.

The dictionary is stored in the CI structure immediately following the anchor record and takes the form of an array with a zero-based index. To populate the dictionary, SQL Server searches the page for repeating values in any column or row. If a value is present in more than one column, it adds it to the dictionary and changes the data to reference the dictionary entry. It does not add NULL values to the dictionary, as they consume no space.

In our ongoing example, the value 2ADA is present in the first and second columns, and 0AB is in both the first and the third, so both become dictionary entries and the actual row values become the index values of their positions in the dictionary, [0] and [1]. Figure 7 shows the final compressed state of the page.

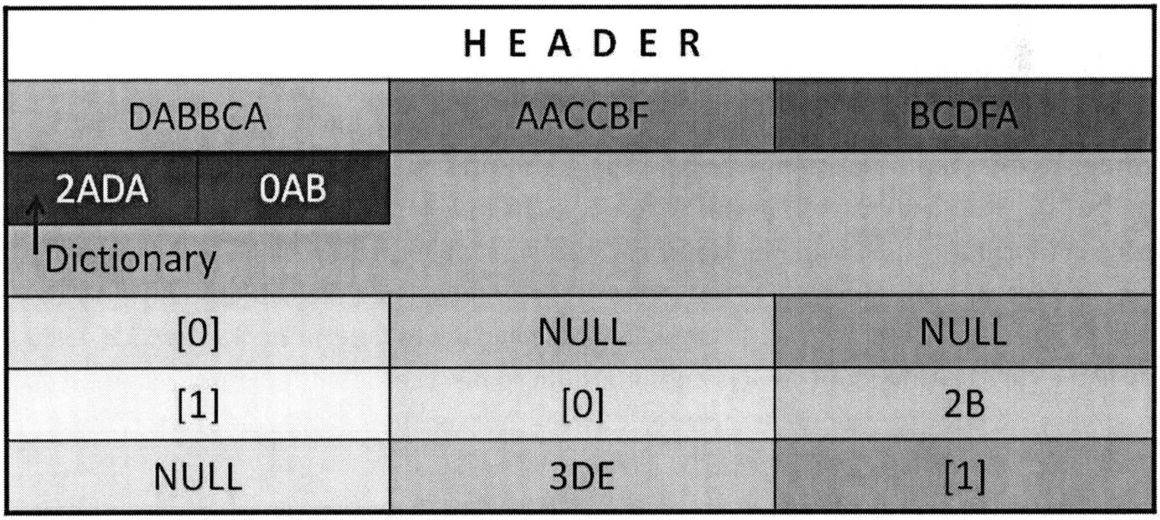

HEADER		
DABBCA	AACCBF	BCDFA
2ADA 0AB		
Dictionary		
[0]	NULL	NULL
[1]	[0]	2B
NULL	3DE	[1]

Figure 7: Data page with page dictionary compression completed.

Additional overhead of page compression

As demonstrated by the previous example, page compression is more complex and resource intensive than row compression. In order to select a record that is page compressed, SQL Server may have to look up a specific value in the dictionary, based on the index value stored in the row, and then construct the actual value based on the dictionary and anchor values. After that is complete, it will have to add back in any unused space removed by row compression, and then return the result to the client.

An added complication of page compression is that SQL Server does not maintain optimal page compression on the fly, in response to inserting, updating, or deleting rows on the page. It does not change the anchor or dictionary values. Instead, SQL Server keeps track of the number of modification operations on each page via a field in the CI structure. If SQL Server finds a page is full, and a predetermined number of modifications have occurred, it will attempt to re-apply compression to the entire page, just as when it was initially compressed. If this results in a significant space saving, the newly compressed page will replace the old one.

Finally, note that SQL Server only applies page compression to index pages at the leaf level of the tree structure. For pages at other levels of the index, it uses only row compression, even if we attempt to apply page compression. This is a tradeoff related to speed; it would take much longer to traverse the index if SQL Server had to reverse page compression at each level. Additionally, it is possible that not all leaf-level pages will be page compressed. As SQL Server creates and fills pages, they are initially only row compressed. Once the page is full, it evaluates each page to determine if the space saved by using page compression creates enough room to insert at least one more record. If so, it applies page compression. Otherwise, it leaves the page in its row-compressed state.

Where and When to Deploy Compression

The decision to deploy compression is not always straightforward, and neither is the choice between row and page compression; there is no single best practice for deploying compression. Hardware resource constraints, datasets, and workloads can profoundly affect the outcome and performance of both row and page compression, even if all the basic litmus tests indicate it should work.

Ultimately, the safest method for rolling out compression involves rigorous testing in a development environment followed by a careful, heavily monitored deployment to production. It is not unheard of to compress tables individually, first with row compression and then escalate to page compression, if warranted.

When considering either type of compression, the three most important considerations are as follows:

- **Compression ratio vs. CPU overhead** – if the data doesn't compress well, then you'll waste extra CPU cycles on compressing and decompressing the data, only to receive little or no space-saving benefit in return.

- **Overall performance impact of compression** – you'll want to confirm the impact of the CPU overhead, via monitoring, and see some positive benefits in terms of reduced disk reads and writes. Query response times should be equal or better than their pre-compression values. If compression reduces performance, it is not worth the cost.

- **Data usage patterns** – the read-write ratio of a partition may dictate the best type of compression.

Data compression ratio vs. CPU overhead

Microsoft provides the `sp_estimate_data_compression_savings` stored procedure, which returns an estimate of the space savings achieved for the target table, with either row or page compression. It does this by sampling 5% of the specified data and performing the compression operation in `tempdb`. While a tremendous help, this procedure comes with a few caveats. First, it will only return estimates for row *or* page compression, not both at the same time. In order to gauge the additional benefit of using page compression over row compression, you will need to run this procedure twice. Second, this procedure, like the compression feature in general, is only available in SQL Server Enterprise Edition and Developer Edition.

If you were hoping to use this procedure on your Standard Edition system to see if it is worth upgrading to Enterprise Edition, you will need to do your testing on either the Developer or Enterprise Evaluation Editions.

Assuming a dataset has an acceptable compression ratio, the next requirement for deploying compression is available CPU. If your server is unable to handle the additional CPU load, you may find that the performance degradation is too high a price to pay for the space savings.

The Microsoft SQL Server Customer Advisory Team (SQLCAT) produced a white paper on data compression best practices (see HTTP://TINYURL.COM/OABY8U4) where they state that, in their experience, row compression results in a CPU overhead of 10%, or less, and suggest:

> *"...if row compression results in space savings and the system can accommodate a 10 percent increase in CPU usage, all data should be row compressed."*

While my findings for CPU overhead align broadly with SQLCAT's, I wouldn't go out and blindly row-compress all my data; the space savings for some tables is so small that it is not worth the trouble. However, if your testing suggests a table's size will shrink by 20% or more, and the CPU capacity is available, I see no problem in applying row compression, combined with *careful monitoring* to ensure the database continues to perform as expected.

Page compression can result in greater space savings than row compression, but higher CPU overheads. I don't even consider page compression unless it can result in at least a 15 to 20% advantage over row compression. Even if this is the case, page compression might still not be appropriate.

Due to the associated CPU overhead, SQLCAT's advice for page compression is more cautious. They recommend first applying page compression to tables and indexes that are utilized less frequently, in order to confirm system behavior, before moving to more frequently accessed ones. They advise page-compressing all objects across the board only for large-scale data warehouse systems with sufficient CPU resources. I still prefer to estimate the benefits of compression and apply it where warranted rather than enabling it everywhere. Even if your system has a tremendous amount of CPU power to spare, the fastest operations are the ones you never perform.

Performance monitoring

There's a lot of great third-party software available for keeping an eye on CPU and other performance-related aspects of your servers. Many of these tools keep statistics over time, which is great for benchmarking and finding changes in performance trends. If you don't have a tool like that, Perfmon is a good alternative that's included with Windows and won't cost you anything. Brent Ozar has an excellent tutorial on his website, explaining how to use Perfmon to collect SQL Server performance data over time (see: HTTP://BRENTOZAR.COM/GO/PERFMON.

When monitoring the effects of data compression, I would pay particular attention to the following counters:

- **% processor time** – since CPU is the resource with which we're most concerned, you'll want to watch out for anything more than a modest increase in processor utilization.

- **Disk Reads / sec** and **Disk Writes / sec** – ideally, you'll see a decrease in disk activity since SQL Server should be reading and writing fewer pages to and from disk.

I hope that you will already have a benchmark of your database and application performance with which to compare your post-compression results. If not, you can use Brent's method to record performance metrics for a few days before starting to compress objects and then compare these values to metrics recorded after compressing, to see what changed.

Data usage patterns

Data usage patterns play an important role in determining whether to deploy row or page compression. The best candidates for page compression are object partitions containing records that are:

- **accessed infrequently** – archive data will reap the benefits of space savings while rarely having to pay the CPU cost for decompression.

- **updated infrequently** – modification operations are more likely to incur the added expense of periodic re-compression, as discussed earlier.

- **scanned frequently** – maximum I/O savings will occur when SQL Server can read as many records as possible from the same page. Making multiple requests to the same page leads to reduced physical I/O.

Partitions subject to a high level of writes, or few scans, might benefit more from row compression, since it does not require re-compression over time and is a simpler process overall.

If you have partitioned tables, you can consider deploying each type of compression as appropriate for the usage patterns of each partition. For example, partitions containing historical data, which is generally static and queried less frequently, are good candidates for page compression. Actively updated partitions might be better off with row compression or perhaps no compression at all.

Basic usage statistics for indexes can be obtained from the `sys.dm_db_index_usage_stats` DMV. Listing 1 shows how it can be used to determine the percentage of update and scan operations for each index in the current database.

```
SELECT   sc.name AS SchemaName ,
         o.name AS ObjectName ,
         i.name AS IndexName ,
         s.user_updates * 100.0 / ( s.user_seeks + s.user_scans
                                 + s.user_lookups + s.user_updates )
                                                     AS Update_Pct ,
         s.user_scans * 100.0 / ( s.user_seeks + s.user_scans + s.user_lookups
                             + s.user_updates ) AS Scan_Pct
FROM     sys.dm_db_index_usage_stats s
         INNER JOIN sys.objects o ON s.object_id = o.object_id
         INNER JOIN sys.schemas sc ON o.schema_id = sc.schema_id
         INNER JOIN sys.indexes i ON s.object_id = i.object_id
                                 AND s.index_id = i.index_id
WHERE    s.database_id = DB_ID()
         AND o.is_ms_shipped = 0
         AND ( s.user_seeks + s.user_scans
                             + s.user_lookups + s.user_updates ) > 0;
```

Listing 1:   Calculating index update and scan ratios.

The values displayed by `sys.dm_db_index_usage_stats` are initialized to empty any time the SQL Server service is started. If no operation has used an index since the last server restart, this view will not return it, so results may not be completely accurate if the server hasn't been up for a sufficiently long period to reflect the full workload.

A Brief Review of Data Compression Syntax

We specify compression settings at the time of object creation, using the clause:

```
WITH (DATA_COMPRESSION = {NONE | ROW | PAGE})
```

For example, Listing 2 creates a `dbo.Sales` table with row compression.

```
CREATE TABLE dbo.Sales
    (
      SaleID INT NOT NULL ,
      SaleDate DATETIME2(0) NOT NULL ,
      Price DECIMAL(9, 2) NOT NULL
    )
    WITH (
        DATA_COMPRESSION= ROW);
 GO
```

Listing 2: Applying row compression when creating a new table.

SQL Server uses a different record format for compressed data, so the only way to change compression settings on an existing table or index is to perform a rebuild. Listing 3 rebuilds dbo.Sales to use page compression.

```
 ALTER TABLE dbo.Sales REBUILD WITH (DATA_COMPRESSION=PAGE);
```

Listing 3: Changing the compression type for a table.

Changing the compression setting for a table affects only its clustered index or heap. Other objects such as non-clustered indexes never inherit compression settings. If we create a non-clustered index on a compressed table, that index will be uncompressed, unless we explicitly apply data compression.

```
SELECT   OBJECT_NAME(i.object_id) AS TableName ,
         i.name AS IndexName ,
         partition_number ,
         data_compression_desc
FROM     sys.partitions AS p
         INNER JOIN sys.indexes AS i ON i.object_id = p.object_id
                                    AND i.index_id = p.index_id
WHERE    i.object_id = OBJECT_ID('dbo.Sales');
GO
CREATE INDEX IDX_Sales_Price ON dbo.Sales (Price);
GO
```

```
SELECT   OBJECT_NAME(i.object_id) AS TableName ,
         i.name AS IndexName ,
         partition_number ,
         data_compression_desc
FROM     sys.partitions AS p
         INNER JOIN sys.indexes AS i ON i.object_id = p.object_id
                                     AND i.index_id = p.index_id
WHERE    i.object_id = OBJECT_ID('dbo.Sales');
GO
```

	TableName	IndexName	partition_number	data_compression_desc
1	Sales	NULL	1	PAGE
2	Sales	IDX_Sales_Price	1	NONE

Listing 4: Non-clustered indexes do not inherit compression settings from the table.

We must specify the compression setting explicitly on creation, or rebuild the index.

```
-- DROP_EXISTING added as this index was already created in Listing 4
CREATE INDEX IDX_Sales_Price ON dbo.Sales (Price)
WITH (DATA_COMPRESSION=ROW, DROP_EXISTING=ON);

ALTER INDEX IDX_Sales_Price ON dbo.Sales
REBUILD WITH (DATA_COMPRESSION=NONE);
```

Listing 5: Defining or changing the compression type for a non-clustered index.

Inheritance only occurs when creating or dropping a clustered index, as demonstrated in Listing 6. The first operation creates a clustered index, which will retain the page compression setting of the heap created in Listing 2. The second operation changes the clustered index to row compression, and the third drops the clustered index, effectively creating a heap. The resulting heap retains the row compression setting of the clustered index. It is more efficient to keep the records in their compressed or uncompressed state than to have to create a new index or heap and change the compression at the same time.

```
CREATE CLUSTERED INDEX IDX_Sales_SaleID ON dbo.Sales (SaleID);
GO

/* re-run sys.partitions query from Listing 4
TableName       IndexName           partition_number   data_compression_desc
-----------------------------------------------------------------------------
Sales           IDX_Sales_SaleID    1                  PAGE
Sales           IDX_Sales_Price     1                  NONE
*/

ALTER INDEX IDX_Sales_SaleID ON dbo.Sales
REBUILD WITH (DATA_COMPRESSION=ROW);
GO

/* re-run sys.partitions query from Listing 4
TableName       IndexName           partition_number   data_compression_desc
-----------------------------------------------------------------------------
Sales           IDX_Sales_SaleID    1                  ROW
Sales           IDX_Sales_Price     1                  NONE
*/

DROP INDEX IDX_Sales_SaleID ON dbo.Sales;

/* re-run sys.partitions query from Listing 4
TableName       IndexName           partition_number   data_compression_desc
-----------------------------------------------------------------------------
Sales           NULL                1                  ROW
Sales           IDX_Sales_Price     1                  NONE
*/
```

Listing 6:   Compression inheritance with clustered indexes.

We can also apply compression to individual partitions of a table or index, using slightly different syntax. In order to demonstrate this, let's create a partitioned version of our Sales table.

70

```
CREATE PARTITION FUNCTION PF_Sales (DATETIME2(0))
AS RANGE RIGHT
FOR VALUES ('20110101','20120101','20130101');
GO

CREATE PARTITION SCHEME PS_Sales
AS PARTITION PF_Sales
ALL TO ([PRIMARY]);
GO

CREATE TABLE dbo.Sales_Partitioned
    (
        SaleID INT NOT NULL ,
        SaleDate DATETIME2(0) NOT NULL ,
        Price DECIMAL(9, 2) NOT NULL ,
        CONSTRAINT PK_Sales_Partitioned PRIMARY KEY CLUSTERED
          ( SaleDate, SaleID )
    )
ON  PS_Sales(SaleDate);
```

Listing 7:   Creating dbo.Sales_Partitioned.

This divides dbo.Sales_Partitioned into four partitions, based on the SaleDate column:

- P1 – SaleDate < 20110101

- P2 – SaleDate >= 20110101 and SaleDate < 20120101

- P3 – SaleDate >= 20120101 and SaleDate < 20130101

- P4 – SaleDate >= 20130101

Listing 8 shows how to apply row compression to Partition 4 and page compression to Partitions 1–3.

```
ALTER INDEX PK_Sales_Partitioned ON dbo.Sales_Partitioned
REBUILD PARTITION=ALL
WITH (DATA_COMPRESSION=ROW ON PARTITIONS(4),
DATA_COMPRESSION=PAGE ON PARTITIONS (1 TO 3));
```

Listing 8:   Applying compression to individual partitions.

Our data is now partitioned so that older, less frequently accessed data is page compressed for maximum space savings, while the current data is row compressed, to strike a balance between space savings and performance. We can confirm this by re-running our **sys.partitions** query from Listing 4 on **dbo.Sales_Partitioned**.

```
SELECT   OBJECT_NAME(i.object_id) AS TableName ,
         i.name AS IndexName ,
         partition_number ,
         data_compression_desc
FROM     sys.partitions AS p
         INNER JOIN sys.indexes AS i ON i.object_id = p.object_id
                                    AND i.index_id = p.index_id
WHERE    i.object_id = OBJECT_ID('dbo.Sales_Partitioned');
```

	TableName	IndexName	partition_number	data_compression_desc
1	Sales_Partitioned	PK_Sales_Partitioned	1	PAGE
2	Sales_Partitioned	PK_Sales_Partitioned	2	PAGE
3	Sales_Partitioned	PK_Sales_Partitioned	3	PAGE
4	Sales_Partitioned	PK_Sales_Partitioned	4	ROW

Listing 9:   View partition compression information for **dbo.Sales_Partitioned**.

Combining Data Compression with Backup Compression and Transparent Data Encryption

Whenever the topic of data compression arises, not far behind are questions about its use in conjunction with backup compression and transparent data encryption features, also introduced in SQL Server 2008.

Backup compression uses a block-based compression algorithm to compress the backup stream, which reduces the size of the backup file and increases the speed of the backup, since SQL Server needs to write less data to disk. Much like data compression, the price of backup compression is increased CPU utilization, but the performance improvement in the backup operation is usually substantial.

A database backup contains a copy of each page in the database. With data compression, SQL Server can store more records per page, thereby reducing the number of pages in the database. Therefore, uncompressed backups will decrease in size on databases with data compression enabled.

Enabling backup compression will shrink this backup size even further. I frequently use both data compression and backup compression together and see great benefits. Backup compression was limited to the Enterprise Edition in SQL Server 2008, but is included in the Standard Edition in SQL Server 2008 R2 and SQL Server 2012.

Compression algorithms generally work by identifying repeating patterns in data and removing duplicates, while encryption algorithms exist to eliminate repeating patterns and make data appear as random as possible. Therefore, on the surface, it would seem that **transparent data encryption** (TDE) is incompatible with data compression. However, the order in which we apply the compression and encryption operations is very important. Compressing encrypted data is not the same as encrypting compressed data.

Encrypting the data first would eliminate repetitive patterns, meaning data compression would have little left to work with. Conversely, compressing the data before encryption means that data compression would be able to take advantage of duplicates and repeating patterns before encryption eliminates them. SQL Server uses the latter method so that data compression and TDE can coexist. SQL Server TDE encrypts data only when writing it to disk, and decrypts it when reading from disk into memory. Data compression, on the other hand, keeps data in a compressed state both on disk and in memory, decompressing it only in the Access Methods as discussed earlier. This design means that TDE is transparent to data compression.

The fact that data compression and TDE can coexist doesn't mean that combining them is a simple decision. Doing so requires careful testing and monitoring to ensure there are no negative impacts to end-users. CPU resources should be substantive in servers requiring both data compression and encryption, as the load of performing both operations will fall on the processor. In my opinion, we should only enable TDE when strictly necessitated by business requirements and/or legislation. Transparent Data Encryption is only available in the Enterprise Edition.

Summary

The data compression options available in SQL Server 2008 and later are a powerful tool for reducing the size of a database and improving query performance in certain situations. Data compression comes at the cost of increased CPU utilization. However, if the appropriate form of compression is enabled on objects that can benefit from it, the performance gains observed will greatly outweigh their cost.

Verifying Backups Using Statistical Sampling

Shaun J. Stuart

Your database backups are only valid when you've proved you can restore the database

This little nugget of wisdom should be foremost in the mind of every DBA. Yes, you created the backup using the `WITH CHECKSUM` option and, once the backup was complete, you ran a `RESTORE VERIFYONLY` to validate that the backup was good. The problem is that this confirms only that no corruption occurred between the time the SQL Server wrote the data to disk and reading it for your backup. It will not detect any corruption that happened to the data in memory after data was updated, but before SQL Server hardened the data to the database file. In addition, many mishaps can befall your backup files, *after* you've taken and verified them. For example:

- A subsequent problem with the I/O subsystem corrupts the backup file.

- A developer makes a backup of a production database, to restore to a test system, and forgets to use the `COPY_ONLY` option, thus breaking your backup chain.

- Even worse, a developer creates the backup on an existing backup set and uses the `WITH INIT` option, wiping out all previous backups in that set.

- A mistake made when setting up the automated file deletion routine means it is deleting full backups that you might still need to restore later differential backups.

If a backup file is missing, won't restore because it is corrupt, or will restore but contains corrupted data, then the DBA needs to find out about this *before* he or she might need it for disaster recovery. The only way to do this, and simultaneously to offer reasonable levels of confidence in the validity of the backups, is to restore the database backups to a test server on a regular basis, and perform `DBCC CHECKDB` tests on the restored copy.

Performing manual test restores might be manageable with five servers, but it doesn't scale to tens or hundreds of servers. In this chapter, I offer a technique that, using the power of **statistical sampling**, allows you to restore a small subset of your backups and report to your boss that *"with 95% confidence, our backups are valid."* If that percentage isn't good enough for your boss, you simply need to nudge that percentage higher, by performing more test restores, and I'll show you how to determine how many backups you need to test to obtain the desired confidence level.

Why Backup Validation?

Many DBAs tend to believe that the chances of database or backup corruption are remote. Sixty-five billion neutrinos from the sun pass through Earth every second, but most never touch a thing. The chances seem slim that one will hit a small magnetic particle in your storage array, changing it from a one to a zero, and corrupting your file. The chances, though, are somewhat higher that the deliveryman accidentally knocks his hand truck into the SAN rack, while delivering your new blade server, causing a read/write head to bounce across the surface of a couple of platters, wiping out several sectors of bits.

Corruption is not a rare event. Consider Paul Randal's response to a reader who, having never personally encountered the problem in ten years, questioned how often corruption occurs in the real world:

> *"Hundreds to thousands of times every week across the world, in the tens of millions of SQL Server databases...Every single week I receive multiple emails asking for some advice about corruption recovery...I expect every DBA to see database corruption at some point during their career.*
> – *Paul Randal* (HTTP://WWW.SQLSERVERCENTRAL.COM/ARTICLES/CORRUPTION/96117/)

You do not want to find out about a corruption problem with your backups at the time you actually need to restore a database to a production system. Usually, this is a high-pressure situation. Something bad has happened and you need to fix it. The clock is ticking, you'll likely have at least one manager looking over your shoulder, and you need to get the database back online *now*. If you can't, you may find yourself smack in the middle of an R.G.E. (Résumé Generating Event).

To protect against this, you need to perform regular test restores of your backups.

Why Automate Backup Validation?

If you are at a company with a relatively small number of SQL Servers and databases, you can validate backups manually, as a background task, in amongst your regular daily tasks. However, firstly, you run the risk of letting this duty fall by the wayside when swept off your feet by other demands. Secondly, this method won't scale.

If you manage dozens of SQL Server instances with thousands of databases, you need *automation*. The typical DBA loves automation. It's not that DBAs are inherently lazy. It's just that automating repetitive tasks provides two main benefits: it ensures consistency across the SQL Server environment, and it frees up the DBA's time to address other, more pressing issues.

Having an automated backup testing procedure is vitally important when you move into larger environments. However, even if you've built a tool, or bought a third-party backup tool that helps automate the task of copying backups to a test server, restoring them and performing DBCC checks on the restored databases, it's still very difficult to schedule in the time to perform regular test restores on *every* database.

With my **statistical sampling procedure**, which you can use with native backups or third-party backup tools, you simply decide on the necessary "statistical" confidence level in the validity of your backups, and it will calculate how many databases you need to restore, randomly, in order to attain that confidence level in the validity of all backups on that server.

Armed with this magic number, there are many ways to implement an automated restore routine, depending on the tools at your disposal. In my case, I simply run a linked server T-SQL script to retrieve a list of all the databases and backup files from my servers, and assign a number to each file to establish the correct restore sequence. My automated restore routine then uses the T-SQL RAND function to select, randomly, the required "magic number" of databases, restores them to the test server, runs DBCC CHECKDB and then drops the restored databases.

Let's drill into the details.

Planning Considerations

In this section, I'll review the planning considerations such as necessary hardware, impact of compression and encryption technologies and so on.

You'll need a test server, with adequate drive space, onto which to restore your databases. I've found virtual machines make good candidates for this. You don't need a powerful machine with tons of RAM or fast processors, but you will likely need lots of disk space, at least enough to hold your biggest database. If you run an environment with multiple versions of SQL Server, your test server should have the latest version, since you can restore backups from older versions of SQL Server to a newer version, but not the other way around.

Ideally, your backup file repository will be available on a network share, or some other shared device that all your SQL Servers and your test server can access. If not, you'll need some way to move those backup files to a location that the test server can access.

If you are using any third-party backup tools that provide compression or other features, you'll need to make sure the test server has that software installed as well. If some servers use third-party backup and others use native SQL Server backups, you'll also need to devise some way to differentiate between the two (*e.g.* based on file name, though there are other ways).

If you are using Transparent Data Encryption, then in order to restore a TDE-protected database to a test server, you will need to restore the service master key to the test server.

Automating Restores with Statistical Sampling: the Parts

Our goal, ultimately, is to create a **backup verification** stored procedure that will perform the following steps:

- Connect to each required server.

- Retrieve a list of databases and their most recent backup files.

- Select, randomly, the required "magic number" of databases to restore – this number comes from the **statistical sampling** stored procedure.

- For each selected database, perform the test restore, run DBCC checks and drop the restored database.

It sounds simple enough, but there are many different parts to consider. The code download for this chapter includes an example backup verification stored procedure, called up_Backup_Verification_Process, which performs all the above steps, for verifying full backups only. I won't present all of the code in this chapter, but I will explain all the major parts, and describe the considerations for extending it to include testing of differential backups, as well as point-in-time restores. Included in the same code file are the required supporting tables to store the server list, store databases we don't wish to test, store configuration details such as the restore paths, and store the results of the tests, including errors.

Retrieving a list of databases and backup files from each server

We need a list of the servers whose backups we want to test, and a way to extract, for each database, a list of the relevant backup files to restore.

If you maintain a small number of servers, or only care about testing certain high-importance databases, it's not too onerous to populate manually a table containing both server names and their databases. However, in a larger, livelier environment, where new databases are added to servers at any time, manual maintenance becomes more of a burden.

A better method, and one that I use, is to store in a table (`Backup_Verification_ServerList` in the code download file) a list of servers on the test restore system; my server build procedure includes a step to add new servers to this list.

For each server in the list, the next task is to load onto the test server the list of databases and files for test restore, and the first step in that task is to decide what types of backups you want to test. In the simplest case, you may just need to restore the latest full backup for each database. It is also relatively simple to test both our full backup files, created once a week, say, as well as our differential backup files, created daily. We simply need to retrieve the latest full backup and the latest differential and restore them in order. However, if we wish to verify point-in-time restores, the logic gets a little more complex as we need to determine the last full backup followed by the chain of differential and transaction log files, and the correct restore order.

If all your backups are stored in a centralized location, it's possible to select the required files directly from that location, but this method is a bit tricky, as it will require reading file attributes or names from the operating system to determine the proper restore order. Obtaining any information from the file system is a weak point of T-SQL and so this type of information gathering typically involves VB scripting or PowerShell.

CMS and MOM

If you use a Centralized Management Server or Microsoft Operations Manager, you can pull database information from multiple servers from its tables.

Currently, I use a T-SQL approach. I have a linked server query (SSIS is an alternative, if you prefer to avoid linked servers) that cycles through the server list, grabs the backup history of all the databases from each server, and writes it into a table.

The T-SQL script in Listing 1 demonstrates this approach, querying the `backupset` table to retrieve the last full and incremental backups for each database. It provides the name of the databases that have been backed up on that server (`database_name` column), the type of backup (`type` column), and start and end times of the backup (`backup_start_ date` and `backup_finish_date` columns). I leave the code to return the last several transaction logs as an exercise for the reader. As discussed, it adds a little complexity, as we can't simply select the oldest one. We need to select all log backups dated later than the last full or differential backup. This is easy enough to do by searching the `backupset` table, ordering by the `backup_finished_date` column and looking for entries with an "I" (for differential backup) or "L" (for log backup) in the `type` column that were taken after the most recent entry with a "D" (for full backup).

Note that this code specifically excludes the `master` database (you may also want to exclude `msdb`). If you want to include these, be sure to rename the databases during your restore process to avoid overwriting the system databases on your test platform! However, later I'll explain why creating a copy of `master` during a test restore will thwart any `DBCC` checks you'd like to run on the restored database.

```
SELECT  a.server_name ,
        a.database_name ,
        b.physical_device_name ,
        a.[type] ,
        a.backup_finish_date ,
        LogicalFile = d.logical_name ,
        d.File_number
```

```
FROM      msdb.dbo.backupset a
          JOIN msdb.dbo.backupmediafamily b ON a.media_set_id = b.media_set_id
          JOIN ( SELECT    backup_finish_date = MAX(c1.backup_finish_date) ,
                           c1.database_name ,
                           c1.server_name
                 FROM      msdb.dbo.backupset c1
                           JOIN msdb.dbo.backupmediafamily c2
                                ON ( c1.media_set_id = c2.media_set_id )
                 WHERE     c1.type IN ( 'D' )
                 GROUP BY c1.database_name ,
                          c1.server_name
               ) c ON a.backup_finish_date = c.backup_finish_date
                   AND a.database_name = c.database_name
          JOIN msdb.dbo.[backupfile] d ON a.backup_set_id = d.backup_set_id
                                     AND d.file_type = 'D'
WHERE     a.type IN ( 'D' )
          AND a.database_name NOT IN ( 'master' )
          AND a.is_copy_only = 0

-- get differential backup entries
UNION
SELECT    a.server_name ,
          a.database_name ,
          b.physical_device_name ,
          a.[type] ,
          a.backup_finish_date ,
          LogicalFile = d.logical_name ,
          d.File_number
FROM      msdb.dbo.backupset a
          JOIN msdb.dbo.backupmediafamily b ON a.media_set_id = b.media_set_id
          JOIN ( SELECT    backup_finish_date = MAX(c1.backup_finish_date) ,
                           c1.database_name ,
                           c1.server_name
                 FROM      msdb.dbo.backupset c1
                           JOIN msdb.dbo.backupmediafamily c2
                                ON ( c1.media_set_id = c2.media_set_id )
                 WHERE     c1.type IN ( 'I' )
                 GROUP BY c1.database_name ,
                          c1.server_name
               ) c ON a.backup_finish_date = c.backup_finish_date
                   AND a.database_name = c.database_name
          JOIN msdb.dbo.[backupfile] d ON a.backup_set_id = d.backup_set_id
                                     AND d.file_type = 'D'
```

```
WHERE    a.type IN ( 'I' )
         AND a.database_name NOT IN ( 'master' )
         AND a.is_copy_only = 0
ORDER BY database_name ,
         a.backup_finish_date ;
GO
```

Listing 1:   Retrieving full and differential database backups for a test restore.

One other peculiarity to note is that SQL Server writes to the `backupset` table when we restore a database. This can lead to problems when we move a database from one server to another using a backup/restore process. The restore process on the destination server will result in an entry in the `backupset` table with a `server_name` value of the source server. Therefore, you may want to modify Listing 1 to verify that the `server_name` field matches the actual server to which you're connected.

A query such as this appears in the example `up_Backup_Verification_Process` stored procedure, adapted to write the results into a temporary table, called `##Backup_Verification_Restore`, from which we later choose random restores. For each server, we create a linked server if one doesn't already exist. You may need to create some logins on the various servers to allow your test server to connect and grab the backup history from the system tables. Typically, I store the linked server login details, along with other important details, such as the path to which to restore the database and log file, in a dedicated table (see the table `Backup_Verification_Configuration` in the code download).We then retrieve the database and file details, as shown Listing 1, and drop the linked servers. If any errors occur in retrieving the data and file details, I write the error into the `Backup_Verification_Log` table.

Finally, there may be databases that you wish to exclude from test restores, for some reason. For example, a database might be too big to make a test restore viable with the current disk space, so you want to exclude it until more space becomes available.

For such cases, I maintain an exclusion list in a table called `Backup_Verification_Exception_List`. Having retrieved into `##Backup_Verification_Restore` the full list of databases for each server, I simply have code that deletes from this table any that appear in the current exclusion list.

Performing test restores

Armed with a list of servers, and having retrieved the backup history for each database on each server, our `up_Backup_Verification_Process` stored procedure needs a way to pick random databases and associated backup files from this list, restore the files in the right order, run `DBCC CHECKDB` and then drop the restored database.

One way to pick, at random, the right number of databases to test, is to include a column in the backup file list table that assigns a number to each file using the `NEWID()` function. You can then sort by that number, which functionally gives you a randomized list, and just select the number of files you need by using the `TOP` clause in a `SELECT` statement (alternatively, we can generate random numbers between one and the maximum number of entries, using the T-SQL `RAND` function, and select the matching rows).

How do you determine how many to test? That's where the magic statistical formula comes into play, and I'll get to that in the next section.

Your routine will then need to restore the correct backup files for the selected database and restore them in the correct order. For example, if you want to perform a test restore for the last differential backup, the routine must retrieve the last full backup prior to that differential, and restore that full backup, with the `NORECOVERY` option, before restoring the differential. Testing transaction log backups will require similar logic, according to the following pseudo-code, in order to identify the prior full backup, most recent differential backup, and subsequent transaction log backups up to the one you want to test.

```
If…restoring last transaction log backup
   Identify all transaction log backups created since last differential backup
   Identify last differential backup
   Identify last full backup made prior to last differential backup
   Restore last full backup made prior to last differential backup
   Restore last differential backup
   Restore all transaction log backups in order from oldest to most recent
Endif
```

An important consideration during the test restore is handling failures. You have two options:

- On failure, let the whole procedure fail and send out an alert.

- Trap the failure and continue to the next backup file.

The first method is easiest, but has a rather obvious problem. If you need to test 30 backups to reach your desired confidence level and the first one fails, it means that your routine will not test the next 29 backups.

The second option is the more robust solution. You'll need to trap for any errors encountered during the process. The **TRY-CATCH** block, introduced in SQL Server 2005, helps here. You can log any errors to a table, then move on to restoring the next backup file.

```
Get backup to restore
Repeat
   Begin try block
      Restore database backup
   End try block
   Begin catch block
       Log failure of restore command to reporting table
   End catch block
   Get next backup to restore
Until no more backups to restore
```

Having tested the required number of backups, you can then report off your logging table.

The next step, optional but highly recommended, is to run a DBCC CHECKDB test against the restored database. SQL Server modifies data in memory and memory is flushed to disk only periodically (during checkpoints), so it is possible that the data can become corrupted in memory before it is written to the disk. In this case, the database would have no corruption that a backup checksum could detect, but it would have logical corruption, which the DBCC CHECKDB process would detect.

Having already restored the database, running an additional DBCC CHECKDB test is relatively easy; it adds minimal steps to the process, and adds another level of robustness to your verification process. This method is especially helpful when dealing with very large production databases whose maintenance window might not be wide enough to allow time for a full DBCC CHECKDB to complete.

If you do decide to incorporate a DBCC check, you'll need to exclude the master database from the check. Earlier, I advised either excluding the master database from the list of databases to test, or restoring the backup of the master database as a user database with a name other than master (otherwise you will overwrite the master database on your test server and really mess things up).

If you go down the latter route, and then run DBCC against your newly restored and renamed copy of master, it will report all kinds of errors. The master database has a special page that contains configuration information specific to the SQL Server instance from which it originated. This special page can only exist in the master database on a server and DBCC will report errors if it finds it in any user databases.

In short, if you include the master database in your backup plans and your backup/ restore testing, then **exclude** it from the DBCC checks on your test server. For the master database, you'll always need to run DBCC on the live copy.

Finally, your routine should drop the restored databases from your test server.

The magic happens here

The missing piece of this puzzle is the "magic formula" that determines how many backups you need to test (the **sample size**) in order to achieve your desired **confidence level** in the validity of *all* your backups. Allow me to draw back the curtain and show you how to do it.

First, we need to establish the meaning of the key terms that we use in the magic formula. Some of them will be familiar if you've ever read news stories about opinion polls. Others are a bit more technical. It may be tempting to change the values in the formula to arrive at the answer you want, but you need to understand the implications of such changes in order to ensure the formula is giving you meaningful results.

Sample size

The sample size is the required number of people in the survey. In our case, the sample size is the number of backups we need to test restore, in order to obtain a certain confidence level, given a certain **margin of error**, **response distribution**, and **population size** (all terms we'll discuss shortly).

Confidence level

This number represents how closely our sampling results represent the entire population. When we say we are 95% confident that the majority of people prefer vanilla ice cream to chocolate, our confidence level is 95%. This means we are confident that the results of our sampling will mirror those of the entire population 95% of the time.

In other words, if we asked a sample size of 100 people if they preferred vanilla ice cream or chocolate, and 70% said vanilla and we have a 95% confidence level, then if we repeatedly ask another random 100 people the same question, 95% of the time the respondents would favor vanilla 70% to 30%, over chocolate.

Margin of error

We are not sampling every person in the world, so we need to understand the margin of error (or confidence interval) on our confidence level, due to sampling. In other words, because our sampling is picking random people, there is the possibility that we will pick randomly a group of people whose tastes do not mirror the tastes of the entire population. The margin of error is a reflection of this possibility.

For example, if we say we have a margin of error of 1%, what we mean is that if we ask many groups of people which ice cream flavor they prefer, 1% of the time we will get a group whose response does not match the population as a whole. Using our ice cream example and a margin of error of 1%, if we asked 500 groups of 100 people which ice cream flavor they prefer, 5 of those groups might have 100% of the people preferring vanilla over chocolate, instead of the average 70% of the other groups.

I use an error margin of 1% for my backup testing purposes, but you can adjust that to suit your needs.

Response distribution

This one can be confusing. This number indicates how your results would vary if you repeated the entire sampling process many, many times. Suppose your first poll of 100 people resulted in 10% of the people favoring vanilla over chocolate ice cream, but in each of the next 9 polls, each with 100 different people, 70% preferred vanilla. If you based your predictions only on the first poll, you would reach a much different conclusion than if you looked at all 10 polls. You can look at response distribution as a measure of the "spread" between your various poll results. If each poll returned exactly the same results, your response distribution would be zero, but some polls might return a 69% vanilla over chocolate ratio, some might return 72% vanilla over chocolate, and so on. If, as in the example above, there are variations in results between polls, response distribution is a measure of that variation. As you might expect, this value, confidence level, and margin of error are closely related.

When it comes to sampling for quality checking, we can regard response distribution as the failure rate (this isn't strictly true but, for our purposes, we can think of it this way). The higher the response distribution, the larger the sampling size must be in order to attain the required confidence level.

The most conservative setting for response distribution is 50% because that results in the largest sample size (technically, 100% would give the largest, but if every one of your samples is failing, you have larger problems than statistical sampling can fix).

Again, though, if our backup failure rate really were 50%, we would surely know about it because backups would be failing left and right. If you're creating the backups using the WITH CHECKSUM option, performing a RESTORE VERIFYONLY for basic backup verification, and you have alerts configured for backup job failures, out of disk space events, and other common causes of backup problems, then your true failure rate is going to be much lower.

In my tests, I use a value of 0.1% (that's 0.001, or one failure in one thousand).

Population

This one is straightforward. Population is the total group size from which we are pulling our random samples. If we are trying to figure out what percentage of a city's residents prefer vanilla ice cream to chocolate, our population number is the city's population.

In our backup testing case, the population is the total number of backups from which we are pulling our random samples.

The magic formula: determining the required sample size

Now we just need some way to relate all these numbers and determine the required sample size. If you look in statistics books or on statistics websites, you will find equations for calculating the normal distribution (as well as for related terms such as *variance, mode* and *standard deviation*) that can be downright daunting:

$$f(x) = \frac{1}{\sqrt{2\pi\sigma^2}} e^{\frac{-(x-\mu)^2}{2\sigma^2}}$$

I don't know about you, but I wouldn't want to translate that into T-SQL. Luckily, we can avoid almost all of that stuff. Shanti Rao and Potluri Rao have created a website (HTTP://WWW.RAOSOFT.COM/SAMPLESIZE.HTML) that lets us experiment with all of our four variables (confidence level, margin of error, response distribution, and population) to see how they affect our sample size.

Their page uses Java and, if we examine the web-page source code, we can see they are performing their calculations using a numerical approximation. If you remember your early calculus classes, this is similar to approximating integrals using Riemann sums or trapezoidal approximations. I'm not going to go into an explanation of how the approximation was derived because that is outside our scope and, really, it's not knowledge that is needed by the typical DBA (also, I don't want to put anyone to sleep).

In Listing 2, I've translated their Java source into a T-SQL stored procedure. Java supports arrays whereas T-SQL doesn't, and that makes things a bit uglier.

```
CREATE PROCEDURE [dbo].[up_GetSampleSize]
    @ResponseDistribution FLOAT ,
    @Population FLOAT ,
    @ConfidenceLevel FLOAT ,
    @MarginOfError FLOAT ,
    @SampleSize FLOAT OUTPUT
AS /*  This procedure is used to determine the sample size you need to test
       out of a given population for a given set of response distribution,
       confidence level, and margin of error.
       The math is taken from http://www.raosoft.com/samplesize.html and has
       been translated from Java to T-SQL.

       For database verification purposes, reasonable values are:
           @ResponseDistribution = .1%
           @ConfidenceLevel = 95%
           @MarginOfError = 1%

       Example usage:
               DECLARE    @SampleSize FLOAT
               EXEC up_GetSampleSize    @ResponseDistribution = .1,
                         @Population = 3000,
                         @ConfidenceLevel = 95,
                         @MarginOfError=1,
                         @SampleSize=@SampleSize OUTPUT
    --   SJS
       Shaunjstuart.com
       9/7/11
*/
    SET NOCOUNT ON
    DECLARE @Y FLOAT
    DECLARE @Pr FLOAT
    DECLARE @Real1 FLOAT
    DECLARE @Real2 FLOAT
    DECLARE @P1 FLOAT
    DECLARE @P2 FLOAT
    DECLARE @P3 FLOAT
    DECLARE @P4 FLOAT
    DECLARE @P5 FLOAT
    DECLARE @Q1 FLOAT
    DECLARE @Q2 FLOAT
    DECLARE @Q5 FLOAT
    DECLARE @ProbCriticalNormal FLOAT
```

```
DECLARE @d1 FLOAT
DECLARE @d2 FLOAT

SET @P1 = -0.322232431088
SET @P2 = -1.0
SET @P3 = -0.342242088547
SET @P4 = -0.0204231210245
SET @P5 = -0.453642210148E-4
SET @Q1 = 0.0993484626060
SET @Q2 = 0.588581570495
SET @Q3 = 0.531103462366
SET @Q4 = 0.103537752850
SET @Q5 = 0.38560700634E-2


SET @ConfidenceLevel = @ConfidenceLevel / 100.0
SET @Pr = 0.5 - ( @ConfidenceLevel / 2.0 )
IF @Pr < 1.0E-8
    BEGIN
        SET @ProbCriticalNormal = 6.0
    END
ELSE
    BEGIN
        IF @Pr = 0.5
            BEGIN
                SET @ProbCriticalNormal = 0.0
            END
        ELSE
            BEGIN
                SET @Y = SQRT(LOG(1.0 / ( @Pr * @Pr )))
                SET @Real1 = @P5
                SET @Real2 = @Q5
                SET @Real1 = @Real1 * @Y + @P4
                SET @Real2 = @Real2 * @Y + @Q4
                SET @Real1 = @Real1 * @Y + @P3
                SET @Real2 = @Real2 * @Y + @Q3
                SET @Real1 = @Real1 * @Y + @P2
                SET @Real2 = @Real2 * @Y + @Q2
                SET @Real1 = @Real1 * @Y + @P1
                SET @Real2 = @Real2 * @Y + @Q1
                SET @ProbCriticalNormal = @Y + ( @Real1 / @Real2 )
            END
    END
```

```
    SET @d1 = @ProbCriticalNormal * @ProbCriticalNormal
        * @ResponseDistribution * ( 100.0 - @ResponseDistribution )
    SET @d2 = ( @Population - 1.0 ) * ( @MarginOfError * @MarginOfError )
        + @d1
    IF @d2 > 0.0
        BEGIN
            SET @SampleSize = CEILING(@Population * @d1 / @d2)
        END
    SELECT  @SampleSize;
```

Listing 2: The up_GetSampleSize stored procedure to determine the sample size.

The procedure takes our first four variables as inputs and returns the resulting sample size as an output parameter.

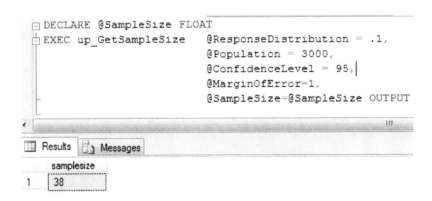

Of course, if you have a reasonably small population size (i.e. a small number of databases), then a single failure will have a greater impact on your confidence level, and so attaining a higher confidence level will mean testing a higher percentage of your population. In other words, you won't avoid as many test restores as you might hope!

Nevertheless, by incorporating this procedure into your automated backup testing routine, you can always be sure you are sampling enough backups to meet your required confidence level, no matter how your backup population grows.

Summary

From using them to populate test and development servers to safeguarding against disasters, a company relies on backups for its operation and survival. They are perhaps the most critical files DBAs work with. Give them the respect they deserve.

Performance Tuning with SQL Trace and Extended Events

Tara Kizer

We can gather information about activity on our SQL Servers in numerous ways, such as using Dynamic Management Views (DMVs), Performance Monitor, Extended Events and SQL Trace. Due to the level of detail it provides and its relative ease of use, the latter is one of my most-used tuning tools due to the level of detail it provides and its relative ease of use. SQL Trace allows us to collect and analyze data for different types of events that occur within SQL Server. For example, SQL Server acquiring a lock is an event, as is the execution of a statement or stored procedure, and so on. We can find our worst performing queries, see how often a query executes, check what exceptions and other errors are occurring, and much more.

The SQL Trace feature comes with a dedicated GUI called SQL Server Profiler, integrated into SSMS, which we can use for client-side tracing. We'll cover Profiler only briefly, mainly to explain the overhead associated with event data collection with this tool, and how this can degrade the performance of the server on which you're running the trace.

For this reason, I perform all my tracing server-side, using SQL Trace, accessing the tracing system stored procedures directly from scripts, rather than the GUI, and storing the event data to a file on the server. We'll dig into SQL Trace in detail, covering the SQL Trace system stored procedures, how to create, start, and stop a server-side trace, how to import the collected data, and some tips on how to analyze the collected data.

The chapter wraps up by offering a first "stepping stone" in the process of migrating from SQL Trace to Extended Events, the successor to SQL Trace. It summarizes some of the advantages of Extended Events and challenges, compared to SQL Trace, and demonstrates a way to migrate existing traces over to Extended Events.

Is SQL Trace Still Relevant?

Many DBAs will be aware that Microsoft deprecated SQL Trace in SQL Server 2012, serving notice that it will disappear from SQL Server at some point in the future. Its successor is a new event collection infrastructure called Extended Events. It can do almost all of what SQL Trace can do, it adds many new troubleshooting capabilities, and is designed to be a far more lightweight, low-overhead means of event data collection. With the release of SQL Server 2012, Microsoft introduced a UI for Extended Events, integrated into SSMS, to make the tool much more user friendly.

Nevertheless, SQL Trace is still in SQL Server 2012, and will be in SQL Server 2014, and I consider it a viable and valuable tool for performance diagnostics, at least over the next 3–4 years. I still find it one of the simplest diagnostic tools to use and, if you follow the practices in this chapter, you can minimize overhead to tolerable levels for a wide range of traces. In addition, SQL Trace is the only supported way to replay workloads (see HTTP://MSDN.MICROSOFT.COM/EN-US/LIBRARY/MS190995.ASPX) and, unlike Extended Events (currently at least), it integrates well with other tools such as PerfMon. With SQL Trace, we can synchronize a captured and saved trace with captured and saved PerfMon data.

Of course, in the meantime, we will need to start learning Extended Events and planning for the eventual migration of our existing tracing capabilities.

How SQL Trace Works

SQL Trace works by capturing events as they occur within the SQL Server engine. Though many activities generate events, SQL Trace captures only those events that are part of the current trace specification, and ignores the rest. Having captured an event, SQL Trace compares it to any filters defined on the active traces. If an event passes the filtering criteria, it passes it along to an internal buffer to await further processing. From this point, what happens depends on the type of trace.

If this is a server-side trace, SQL Trace writes the events from the buffer to the trace file. If this is a Profiler trace, SQL Trace sends the event information to the client application via Server Management Objects (SMO). It's even possible, using SMO, to develop our own client application to process these events.

Profiler: pros, cons, and best practices

SQL Server Profiler, or simply Profiler, is a graphical user interface for SQL Trace. It uses SQL Trace behind the scenes, but implemented visually in a client tool that makes it very easy to set up a trace. It allows us to choose our output destination, which events we want to capture, what information we'd like to know about each event, and any filters we'd like to apply.

Profiler provides templates that allow us to configure a trace with a predefined set of events based upon a category. For example, the **T-SQL_Tuning** template captures the events needed to investigate stored procedure and T-SQL batch execution. This template also provides a raw workload for the Database Engine Tuning Advisor (DTA), which will analyze the workload and make recommendations, such as adding, dropping or modifying indexes, though you should review and test its recommendations carefully, before implementation.

The downside of Profiler is that its use can cause the "observer effect," where the act of collecting diagnostic data to resolve a performance problem on a server, causes a performance problem on that server. The main problem is well documented (HTTP://SUPPORT.MICROSOFT.COM/KB/929728) but I'll summarize it briefly. SQL Server stores the event data temporarily in the trace buffers for the rowset I/O provider, from where the Profiler client consumes it. Each active SPID on the instance requires an exclusive latch to write the event data. The Profiler client often consumes the data at a slow rate, row by row, over a network. As a result, if a trace produces many events, queues can form as SPIDs wait for a latch, or simply some free space in the trace buffer, to write their event data, and this can affect the overall performance of the SQL Server instance.

We can minimize Profiler's impact by following these five rules or best practices:

1. **Never run Profiler on the database server** – run it on another machine that has the SQL client tools installed, making sure that this machine has a fast network connection.

2. **Save the trace data to a file, not a table** – writing the data to a table is much slower than to a file and simply compounds the previously described problem. In my early days, I once brought the performance of a SQL Server to its knees simply by running a Profiler trace that wrote directly to a table.

3. **Filter the results carefully, such as "`Duration > 1000`"** – events that fail to meet the filter will still fire, but we avoid the overhead of saving the data and writing it over to the client.

4. **Limit traces to only the most relevant events** – for example, when investigating slow queries, you may only need `SP:Completed` and `SQL:BatchCompleted`.

5. **Try to avoid collecting events that will fire a lot** – such as the lock- and latch-related events.

However, even if you follow all of these guidelines, the intrinsic overhead of writing event data to Profiler can still be too high and we can avoid it if, instead of using Profiler, we run a **server-side trace**. Rather than operating SQL Trace, and consuming the data through the GUI, we script out the trace definitions and run them directly on the server.

Of course, Profiler still has its uses. We can use it to generate the trace definitions quickly and easily and then export them to server-side traces that we can run on our production instances. Let's use Profiler to create a simple trace definition for capturing events relating to SQL batch and stored procedure execution that we can use to investigate slow and expensive queries. We'll script out and save the trace definition as a `.sql` file.

- Start Profiler and connect to the instance you wish to trace (using a login with sysadmin permissions).

  - From the Windows Start menu:
    - select **Program Files | Microsoft SQL Server 2008 R2 | Performance Tools**

    - select **File | New Trace** and connect to the target server.

  - From SSMS:
    - select **Tools | SQL Server Profiler**

    - connect to the target server.

- Set the required trace properties (**General** tab).

  - Give the trace a name, such as SlowQueries.

  - Choose the required template, the **Blank** template in this case.

  - Pick an output destination, if desired. This is not necessary in this case, but if you were planning to run this as a Profiler trace:

    - always choose a file destination, and set the properties as required (more on this in the next section)

    - always select the **Server processes trace data** box so that SQL Server rather than Profiler processes the trace data. This helps reduce trace overhead and avoids possible event loss when running Profiler on an already heavily loaded instance.

  - Check the **Enable trace stop time** box, but don't worry about its value right now (more on this in the next section). Setting a stop time allows us to schedule a trace to run via a job.

- Select the event classes (**Events Selection** tab).

  - In the **Stored Procedures** category, select the RPC:Completed event class.

  - In the **T-SQL** category, select the SQL:BatchCompleted event class.

  - Uncheck the **Show all events** box so Profiler displays only these two events.

- Select the data columns.

  - By default, the template will collect all available data columns for each of the event classes. To minimize the overhead of running the trace, collect only those columns that you really need to diagnose the problem. For the purpose of this trace, select only the following eight columns: CPU, Duration, LoginName, Reads, SPID (a required column), StartTime, TextData, Writes. I normally also add DatabaseName, ObjectName, ApplicationName, EndTime, and HostName, but I omitted those here for simplicity.

  - Uncheck the **Show all columns** box so Profiler displays only the selected columns.

Events	CPU	Duration	SPID	Start Time	Text Data	Reads	Login Name	Writes
Stored Procedures								
☑ RPC:Completed	☑	☑	☑	☑	☑	☑	☑	☑
TSQL								
☑ SQL:BatchCompleted	☑	☑	☑	☑	☑	☑	☑	☑

- Define trace filters.

  - Click on **Column Filters.**

  - Add a "greater than or equal 1000 [milliseconds]" filter to the Duration column.

- Capture and export the trace definition.

  - Click **Run** to start the trace and then stop it immediately (you do not need to wait for any events to appear in the trace).

  - In the **File** menu, click **Export**, **Script Trace Definition**, and then **For SQL Server 2005–2008 R2**.

  - Save the trace definition to a file (e.g. SlowQueries.sql) on the server that you wish to trace.

We're now ready to examine the trace definition, modify it as required, and run it as a server-side trace.

Server-side trace

Event data collection with server-side trace is still not "zero overhead." For example, the late-filtering problem hinted at in Rule 3 in the previous section means that SQL Server still incurs the overhead of firing an event, and collecting all the necessary event data, even if that event does not pass our trace's filter criteria. Extended Events (discussed towards the end of the chapter) addresses this overarching problem with the SQL Trace architecture.

However, if we use server-side tracing, and apply Rules 2–5 above, we can lessen the observer overhead dramatically. If you need further convincing, Linchi Shea has done some testing to prove this (HTTP://TINYURL.COM/33K489).

We implement a server-side trace using four system stored procedures, prefixed with **sp_trace_**:

- **sp_trace_create** – creates a new trace, defining the path to the trace file, maximum file size, the number of rollover files, and other options.

- **sp_trace_setevent** – adds an event to the trace, or a data column to an event. Our trace script must call this stored procedure once for every event and column combination; four events, with ten columns each, means we call it 40 times.

- **sp_trace_setfilter** – adds a filter to the trace; called once for every filter we wish to add.

- **sp_trace_setstatus** – sets the trace status (start, stop, close/delete).

We created the trace definition in the previous section so open the `.sql` file in SSMS and it should look as shown in Listing 1.

```
/**************************************************/
/* Created by: SQL Server 2008 R2 Profiler        */
/* Date: 08/10/2013   08:00:58 PM         */
/**************************************************/

-- Create a Queue
declare @rc int
declare @TraceID int
declare @maxfilesize bigint
declare @DateTime datetime

set @DateTime = '2012-08-10 21:00:34.207'
set @maxfilesize = 5

-- Please replace the text InsertFileNameHere, with an appropriate
-- filename prefixed by a path, e.g., c:\MyFolder\MyTrace. The .trc extension
-- will be appended to the filename automatically. If you are writing from
-- remote server to local drive, please use UNC path and make sure server has
-- write access to your network share

exec @rc = sp_trace_create @TraceID output, 0, N'InsertFileNameHere', @maxfilesize,
@Datetime
if (@rc != 0) goto error

-- Client side File and Table cannot be scripted

-- Set the events
declare @on bit
set @on = 1

exec sp_trace_setevent @TraceID, 10, 1, @on
exec sp_trace_setevent @TraceID, 10, 11, @on
exec sp_trace_setevent @TraceID, 10, 12, @on
exec sp_trace_setevent @TraceID, 10, 13, @on
exec sp_trace_setevent @TraceID, 10, 14, @on
exec sp_trace_setevent @TraceID, 10, 16, @on
exec sp_trace_setevent @TraceID, 10, 17, @on
exec sp_trace_setevent @TraceID, 10, 18, @on
exec sp_trace_setevent @TraceID, 12, 1, @on
exec sp_trace_setevent @TraceID, 12, 11, @on
exec sp_trace_setevent @TraceID, 12, 12, @on
exec sp_trace_setevent @TraceID, 12, 13, @on
```

```
exec sp_trace_setevent @TraceID, 12, 14, @on
exec sp_trace_setevent @TraceID, 12, 16, @on
exec sp_trace_setevent @TraceID, 12, 17, @on
exec sp_trace_setevent @TraceID, 12, 18, @on

-- Set the Filters
declare @intfilter int
declare @bigintfilter bigint

exec sp_trace_setfilter @TraceID, 10, 0, 7, N'SQL Server Profiler - 05332afa-db8c-
4ded-beca-38e2548e246b'

set @bigintfilter = 1000000
exec sp_trace_setfilter @TraceID, 13, 0, 4, @bigintfilter

-- Set the trace status to start
exec sp_trace_setstatus @TraceID, 1

-- display trace id for future references
select TraceID=@TraceID
goto finish

error:
select ErrorCode=@rc

finish:
go
```

Listing 1:   The SlowQueries trace definition.

Let's walk through the various sections of the script, focusing on those sections we need to modify to suit our requirements.

sp_trace_create section

We need to modify the script according to our requirements for the trace definition, as specified in the call to sp_trace_create.

```
set @DateTime = '2012-08-10 21:00:34.207'
set @maxfilesize = 5
...
exec @rc = sp_trace_create @TraceID output, 0, N'InsertFileNameHere', @maxfilesize,
@Datetime
```

We can skip past `@TraceID`, since SQL automatically assigns a value to this output parameter.

The second parameter is `@Options`, and we're currently using a value of 0, meaning that we're not specifying any of the available options, most significantly the number of trace rollover files. This means that SQL Server will only create one trace file, sized according to the value of `@maxfilesize`, and when the trace file reaches that size the trace will stop running. That's not usually the behavior I want, so I change the value of `@options` to 2, enabling the `TRACE_FILE_ROLLOVER` option. Other options are available, such as `SHUTDOWN_ON_ERROR`, but I typically don't use them (see Books Online for details, HTTP://TECHNET.MICROSOFT.COM/EN-US/LIBRARY/MS190362.ASPX).

Next, we come to the `@tracefile` argument, and this is the only part of the script that we *must* modify, in order to run it, supplying the path and name for the trace file, as indicated by `'InsertFileNameHere'` in the script. `'InsertFileNameHere'` can be a path and file name that is local or remote to the server. Ensure that you have sufficient free disk space at this location. How much space you'll need depends on your system and on what you select in the trace definition. Notice that we exclude the `.trc` extension from the file name because it is going to add it automatically. If you do add `.trc`, you'll end up with a file named `MyTrace.trc.trc`.

Next, we have the `@maxfilesize` argument, set to 5 MB by default. I set the `@maxfilesize` to 1024 for a maximum file size of 1 GB, but you should set this as appropriate for your system.

Finally, we come to the @stoptime argument, where we specify a specific time for the trace to stop running. Notice that the Profiler-generated script names the local variable @DateTime, rather than @stoptime and passes it to sp_trace_create via its input parameter position (5th). Profiler defaults to running a trace for an hour, but maybe we want it to run for a shorter or longer period, or maybe we want it to run until we stop it manually. In the latter case, we pass NULL to @DateTime. My servers are located in a different time zone to me, so I like to modify the script to use DATEADD instead, such as dateadd(hh, 1, getdate()).

Listing 2 summarizes all of these modifications.

```
set @DateTime = dateadd(hh, 1, getdate())
set @maxfilesize = 1024
...
exec @rc = sp_trace_create @TraceID output, 2, N'\\Server1\Share1\MyTrace',
@maxfilesize, @Datetime
```

Listing 2:   The modified sp_trace_create section of the SlowQueries trace definition.

There is one further input parameter, @filecount, that we didn't add to our script. It's the final argument for sp_trace_create and it allows us to specify the maximum number of trace files to maintain. We can only use @filecount if the script also specifies the value 2 (TRACE_FILE_ROLLOVER) for @options, as we did here. Once the specified number of rollover files exists, SQL Trace will delete the oldest trace file before creating a new one.

sp_trace_setevent and sp_trace_setfilter sections

Since we specified two events and eight columns, we have 16 calls to the sp_trace_setevent procedure. In each case, after the @TraceID argument, we have the @eventid and @columnid. You can find a full list of these values and their corresponding events and columns in Books Online, but for example the following line activates the Reads column (16) of the RPC:Completed (10) event.

```
exec sp_trace_setevent @TraceID, 10, 16, @on
```

In this example, we don't need to modify the events, columns, or filters that we set up in Profiler, so we don't need to touch the sp_trace_setevent and sp_trace_setfilter sections.

Setting up filters manually in a server-side trace can be tricky, so I would suggest letting Profiler handle that aspect for you. It's worth noting that, while in Profiler we could assign the Duration filter in milliseconds, SQL Server 2005 and later stores the data in microseconds, and we need to use microseconds in our server-side traces. Fortunately, Profiler helpfully converted the filter definition for us, supplying a value of @bigintfilter = 1000000. However, be aware that when you define a filter in milliseconds, in Profiler, the duration values you see in the event data will be in microseconds.

Starting the trace

We can now run the script. The command that actually starts the trace is sp_trace_setstatus with a value of 1 for the second parameter. Without that, all we've done is load the definition into SQL Server. The script will output the TraceId value, which you can note down to save you from having to look up the value when or if you need to stop the trace.

Tracing a workload

Having created the trace, we need to run it at a time, and for a period, that will enable us to capture the necessary workload. For a general performance problem we will need to run it over the period that will capture a representative workload for the server. If the problem is isolated to a specific user process, we can start the trace, ask the user to rerun the process to reproduce the problem, and then stop tracing.

In a development or testing environment, we may wish to simulate a realistic workload to evaluate performance and the impact of our query tuning efforts. Options here include the use of SQL Server Profiler's Replay Traces feature (HTTP://MSDN.MICROSOFT.COM/EN-US/LIBRARY/MS190995.ASPX), or the SQL Server Distributed Replay feature, for bigger workloads. Alternatively, various third party tools will allow us to simulate a workload on the server, for example Apache JMeter (HTTP://JMETER.APACHE.ORG/) or LoadRunner (HTTP://TINYURL.COM/9KZAT2T). For the purposes of this chapter, you might consider simply running a random workload against your `AdventureWorks2008R2` database (see, for example, Jonathan Kehayias's article at HTTP://TINYURL.COM/NMLOJWR).

Having captured the workload, we simply stop the trace. If the value of `@DateTime` (see Listing 2) is non-`NULL`, the trace will stop automatically when the system time on the server reaches that value. If we want to stop the trace earlier, or if we set `@DateTime` to `NULL`, then we need to stop and close/delete the trace manually. We can do this using `sp_trace_setstatus`, supplying the appropriate `TraceID` and setting its status to 0 (zero). If our user-defined trace is the only one running on the server, and assuming no one disabled the default trace, which has a `TraceID` of 1, then our trace will have a `TraceID` of 2.

The default trace

If you are unfamiliar with the default trace, it might be because Books Online documents it so poorly. You can find some better information about it here: HTTP://TINYURL.COM/PCU8LFP. *In Chapter 7, What changed? – Auditing Solutions in SQL Server, Colleen Morrow discusses its use for auditing purposes.*

We would use Listing 3 to stop, and then close and delete, our trace.

```
exec sp_trace_setstatus @TraceID = 2, @status = 0; --stop
exec sp_trace_setstatus @TraceID = 2, @staus = 2;  --close/delete
```

Listing 3:   Stopping a trace then closing it and deleting its definition.

We can restart a stopped trace with **sp_trace_setstatus** because its definition, events and filters are still stored. This might be handy if you plan to run the trace again, perhaps later in the day when the workload changes. Otherwise, you can close the trace and delete its definition (and simply recreate the trace from the script the next time you need it).

If there are several traces running and you failed to note the **TraceId** when you started a particular trace, you can look it up using the **fn_trace_getinfo** function, which accepts the **TraceID** as an argument, and returns a normalized view of the trace properties. If we pass it a zero, it'll return information about all traces defined on the system.

```
select * from fn_trace_getinfo(0)
```

Listing 4: Retrieving trace details with **fn_trace_getinfo**.

	traceid	property	value
1	1	1	2
2	1	2	F:\MSSQL.1\MSSQL\LOG\log_111543.trc
3	1	3	20
4	1	4	NULL
5	1	5	1
6	2	1	0
7	2	2	F:\DBA\MyTrace.trc
8	2	3	1024
9	2	4	2012-08-10 21:00:34.207
10	2	5	1

You should be able to recognize your **TraceId** from the result set as it contains information we passed to **sp_trace_create**, like the name of your trace file and a value of 1024.

Importing the trace for analysis

Now that we've stopped the trace, it's time to import it. We could use Profiler to do this, but that slows us down considerably, as it has to first read all of the trace files into the client's memory and then process them. Instead, we'll use `fn_trace_gettable`, which is a function that allows us to read a trace file and return its contents as a table.

It accepts two parameters, `filename` (the path to the trace) and `number_files`, the number of files that you want to import. It starts with the file you passed to the filename parameter and then continues reading the rollover files until it reaches the value of the `number_files` parameter. For example, we might have the initial trace file and four rollover files, as follows: `MyTrace.trc`, `MyTrace_1.trc`, `MyTrace_2.trc`, `MyTrace_3.trc` and `MyTrace_4.trc`.

```
USE MyDatabase
GO

--import the first file (MyTrace.trc)
SELECT  *
INTO    MyTrace
FROM    FN_TRACE_GETTABLE('\\Server1\Share1\MyTrace.trc', 1);

-- import all the files
SELECT  *
INTO    MyTrace
FROM    FN_TRACE_GETTABLE('\\Server1\Share1\MyTrace.trc', DEFAULT);

-- import a specific number of files
SELECT  *
INTO    MyTrace
FROM    FN_TRACE_GETTABLE('\\Server1\Share1\MyTrace.trc', 3);
```

Listing 5:   Importing trace data into a table.

You may have numerous files to import that total several gigabytes, and remember, these imports will create many log records in the transaction log, possibly causing it to grow considerably. If you have limited free space on the transaction log drive of the database, you may want to break up the import into multiple batches. Typically, I will import the trace data into a database that is using **SIMPLE** recovery model. However, if your database uses **FULL** or **BULK_LOGGED** recovery model, you will want to run a transaction log backup after each batch. In Listing 6, we break the import of 20 trace files into two batches of ten.

```
SELECT   *
INTO     MyTrace
FROM     FN_TRACE_GETTABLE('\\Server1\Share1\MyTrace.trc', 10)

INSERT   INTO MyTrace
SELECT   *
FROM     FN_TRACE_GETTABLE('\\Server1\Share1\MyTrace_10.trc', 10)
```

Listing 6:   Batching trace file imports.

If we specify a value for the `number_files` parameter that is higher than the number of trace files, it won't cause an error. The function is smart enough to read only the files that exist.

We can also use `fn_trace_gettable` to query the active trace file; we don't need to stop the trace to view or even import the data. This means we can view the trace data while the trace is running, just as we can in Profiler.

Analyzing the trace

Now that we have the data imported into a table, it's finally time to analyze it. This is where it gets fun! My first tool of choice for analyzing trace data is ClearTrace (HTTP://WWW.SCALESQL.COM/CLEARTRACE/). Of course, we can also perform custom analysis of the raw data simply by querying it from the table into which we imported it. We'll cover both options.

Using ClearTrace

I start my analysis at the summary level, using ClearTrace, a tool written by Bill Graziano that summarizes trace data information. Not only is it a great tool, it's free!

You don't even need to wait for the import to complete to run ClearTrace. `fn_trace_gettable` and ClearTrace can access your trace file(s) at the same time, which gives you an opportunity to start your analysis early. I sometimes even skip importing the data into a table because often ClearTrace has already revealed the problem.

After you've downloaded ClearTrace onto a client computer, double-click on the exe to launch it. You will need to specify a server and a database where it can store the summary data. Next, click the first **Browse** button next to the **First File** field and select the first file in your trace. By default, it will import all of the trace files in the sequence if you have multiple files. If you only want to import the first file, uncheck **Process All Trace Files in Sequence**. Click the **Import Files** button at the bottom for ClearTrace to start the import.

Depending on the size of your trace file(s), the import could take a few minutes. You can watch its progress in the **Import Status** tab. Once it has finished importing your trace file(s), it will show you the summarized results in the **Query the Imported Files** tab. It'll show you the top 15 summarized results, sorted by **CPU**. There are a lot of things we can change to see different results, but the most common things that I do is sort it by **Reads**, **AvgReads** and **Duration**.

Figure 1 shows sample output from our previous trace.

I selected the **Display Averages** option and, in the **Order By** drop-down, sorted the data by **AvgReads**. Note that ClearTrace strips all of the stored procedures of their parameters in order to group together the common SQL statements. The **CPU**, **Reads**, **Writes**, and **Duration** values are all cumulative. The **Average** columns show values averaged over the number of calls to the common SQL statement.

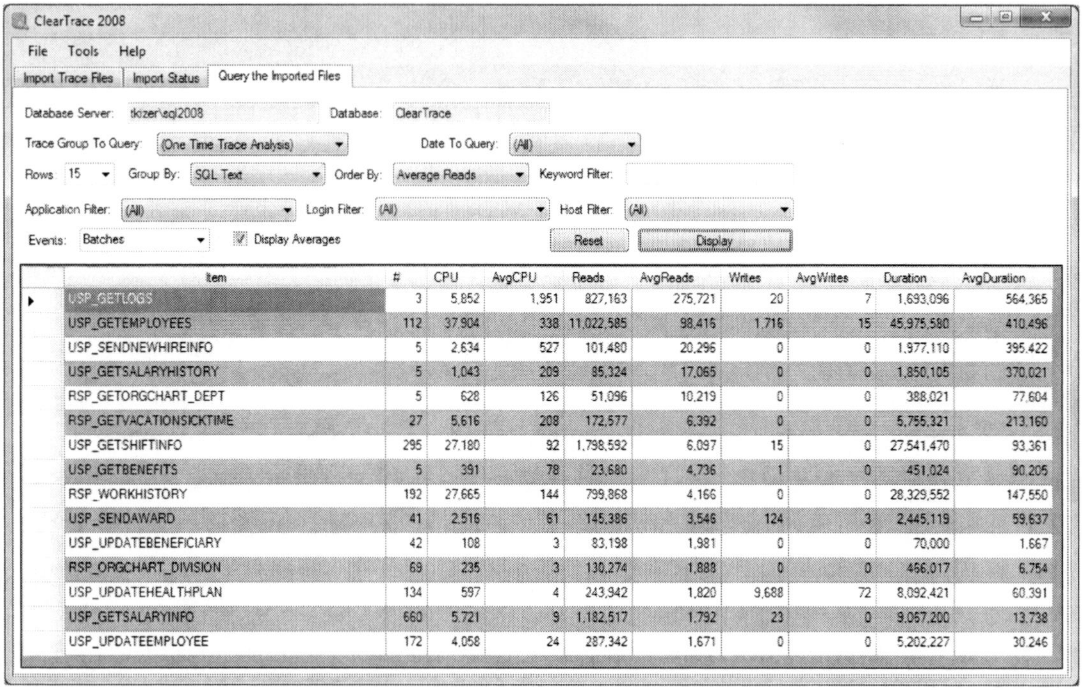

Item	#	CPU	AvgCPU	Reads	AvgReads	Writes	AvgWrites	Duration	AvgDuration
USP_GETLOGS	3	5,852	1,951	827,163	275,721	20	7	1,693,096	564,365
USP_GETEMPLOYEES	112	37,904	338	11,022,585	98,416	1,716	15	45,975,580	410,496
USP_SENDNEWHIREINFO	5	2,634	527	101,480	20,296	0	0	1,977,110	395,422
USP_GETSALARYHISTORY	5	1,043	209	85,324	17,065	0	0	1,850,105	370,021
RSP_GETORGCHART_DEPT	5	628	126	51,096	10,219	0	0	388,021	77,604
RSP_GETVACATIONSICKTIME	27	5,616	208	172,577	6,392	0	0	5,755,321	213,160
USP_GETSHIFTINFO	295	27,180	92	1,798,592	6,097	15	0	27,541,470	93,361
USP_GETBENEFITS	5	391	78	23,680	4,736	1	0	451,024	90,205
RSP_WORKHISTORY	192	27,665	144	799,868	4,166	0	0	28,329,552	147,550
USP_SENDAWARD	41	2,516	61	145,386	3,546	124	3	2,445,119	59,637
USP_UPDATEBENEFICIARY	42	108	3	83,198	1,981	0	0	70,000	1,667
RSP_ORGCHART_DIVISION	69	235	3	130,274	1,888	0	0	466,017	6,754
USP_UPDATEHEALTHPLAN	134	597	4	243,942	1,820	9,688	72	8,092,421	60,391
USP_GETSALARYINFO	660	5,721	9	1,182,517	1,792	23	0	9,067,200	13,738
USP_UPDATEEMPLOYEE	172	4,058	24	287,342	1,671	0	0	5,202,227	30,246

Figure 1: Sample output from the trace, viewed in ClearTrace.

The first row in this example shows that `USP_GETLOGS` (ClearTrace uppercases the data) was called three times and had 827,163 reads. Doing some math, we get 275,721 for the average reads which matches what ClearTrace shows.

When performance tuning at a high level, I start my analysis with the "worst performers," which I define loosely as those statements that average more than 5,000 reads per call, and investigate the possibility of missing indexes. Depending upon how well tuned your system is, your value for "high" may be different.

In this example, the top seven rows qualify as my "starting points" for analysis, but I'd look first at `USP_GETLOGS`, due to the very high average reads. This stored procedure also has the highest `AvgCPU`, as confirmed by sorting the results on this column.

Analyzing the raw trace data

Now that we've explored ClearTrace, let's look at the raw trace data that we imported into our **MyTrace** table. Depending on the size of the trace data, you may want to add indexes to speed up your queries. Immediately after importing the data, I added the three indexes shown in Listing 7, as I know I will be using these columns in my queries.

```
CREATE NONCLUSTERED INDEX idx_Duration ON MyTrace(Duration);
CREATE NONCLUSTERED INDEX idx_CPU ON MyTrace(CPU);
CREATE NONCLUSTERED INDEX idx_Reads ON MyTrace(Reads);
GO
```

Listing 7:   Indexing the **MyTrace** table.

Let's take a quick look at our trace data. The **fn_trace_gettable** function returns a table with all the columns that are valid for that specified trace. One such column is **EventClass**, which corresponds to the event IDs (see Listing 1). We can convert the event ID values to proper event names by joining to the **sys.trace_events**, a catalog view that lists the trace events, on the **trace_event_id** column. I always start my investigation by looking for the read-intensive queries.

```
SELECT TOP 1000
        e.name AS EventName ,
        TextData ,
        Reads ,
        CPU ,
        Duration / 1000 AS Duration_in_milliseconds ,
        Writes ,
        StartTime
FROM    MyTrace t
        INNER JOIN sys.trace_events e ON t.EventClass = e.trace_event_id
ORDER BY Reads DESC;
GO
```

Listing 8:   Read-intensive queries in our sample workload.

On an OLTP system, a high number of reads often indicates missing indexes, resulting in too many index or table scans. Therefore, I can frequently resolve performance issues just by looking at the **Reads** column and investigating tuning and indexing possibilities.

If you're analyzing a system that has queries taking a few seconds or longer, simply convert `Duration` to seconds (`Duration/1000000.0 as Duration`), rather than milliseconds. Use 1,000,000.0 instead of just 1,000,000 because the decimal points matter when dealing with seconds. There's a big difference between 1.01 seconds and 1.9 seconds and if you divide by 1,000,000, both values will display as 1.

Of course, it is easy to adapt Listing 8 as required. For example, to focus on specific events, we simply add the appropriate filter (e.g. `where e.name = 'RPC:Completed'`), or look for queries that breach a certain read or duration threshold (`where Reads > 5000` for example), and so on.

Listing 9 shows a different query that calculates the proportion of CPU usage attributable to each query in the workload (that has a duration of over 1,000 ms, since we added the filter to our trace).

```
SELECT TOP 1000
          ( CPU * 100 ) / ( ( SELECT   SUM(CPU)
                              FROM     MyTrace
                            ) * 1.0 ) AS PercentCPU ,
          TextData
FROM      MyTrace
ORDER BY PercentCPU DESC;
GO
```

Listing 9:   Which queries use the biggest proportion of CPU?

Unless a single process is hogging the CPU, this data may not be too interesting. It gets more exciting if we group together queries based on the object accessed. The easiest way to do this is if our system is using stored procedures for data access and can group by `ObjectName`.

```
DECLARE @TotalCPU BIGINT
SELECT  @TotalCPU = SUM(CPU)
FROM    MyTrace
SELECT TOP 1000
        ( CPU * 100 ) / ( @TotalCPU * 1.0 ) AS PercentCPU ,
        ObjectName
FROM    ( SELECT    SUM(CPU) AS CPU ,
                    ObjectName
          FROM      MyTrace
          GROUP BY  ObjectName
        ) t
ORDER BY PercentCPU DESC ;
```

Listing 10:   CPU by object accessed.

I broke out the total CPU time to make the query easier to read. For simplicity reasons, we didn't collect the ObjectName data column in our server-side trace. You will need to add it if you want to run the above query, or you can try parsing the procedure name out of the TextData column (see HTTP://TINYURL.COM/PF9KZMR for example).

If your system isn't using stored procedures for data access, then grouping isn't as easy unless you have the same queries running over and over again. You can try grouping by TextData, as shown in Listing 11, but the problem is that different query structures and hard-coded parameter values can make it hard to identify "similar" queries. We could normalize the data by stripping out the parameter values, but the T-SQL code becomes complex. It's easier to use ClearTrace, which does this automatically, in order to group together common queries.

```
DECLARE @TotalCPU BIGINT
SELECT  @TotalCPU = SUM(CPU)
FROM    MyTrace
SELECT TOP 1000
        ( CPU * 100 ) / ( @TotalCPU * 1.0 ) AS PercentCPU ,
        TextData
```

```
FROM     ( SELECT      SUM(CPU) AS CPU ,
                       TextData
           FROM      ( SELECT     CPU ,
                                  CONVERT(NVARCHAR(MAX), TextData) AS TextData
                        FROM      MyTrace
                      ) t1
           GROUP BY   TextData
         ) t2
ORDER BY PercentCPU DESC;
GO
```

Listing 11:   Grouping by `TextData`.

There may be times when the problem isn't related to high reads, duration or CPU alone but rather a combination of the duration of a statement and the number of executions of that statement. For example, a stored procedure that takes 5 minutes to run but is called only once per day is much less problematic than one that averages 200 milliseconds per execution but is called 50 times per second by multiple sessions. In the latter case, I'd certainly look for ways to tune the stored procedure to bring down the duration.

```
SELECT   COUNT(*) AS ExecCount ,
         ObjectName ,
         AVG(Duration / 1000) AS AvgDuration
FROM     MyTrace
WHERE    ObjectName <> 'sp_reset_connection' -- connection pooling
GROUP BY ObjectName
ORDER BY ExecCount DESC;
```

Listing 12:   Finding frequently executed queries.

You'll notice that I removed objects with a name of **sp_reset_connection** from the result set. If you have a system that is using connection pooling, you'll see a lot of these in your trace. You won't generally notice it for the other trace queries that we've run, but it might show up in a query like this where we are finding out how often things are being run. It doesn't provide anything useful here, hence the exclusion. You could also add this exclusion as a filter in the trace.

Resolution

Having identified through tracing the most problematic queries, our attention turns to resolution. It is not the intent of this chapter to discuss the details of query performance tuning; there are many whole books on this topic, but I will just review a few common causes from my own experience.

There are two broad reasons why code performs badly. Firstly, it could be bad code, for example, code that uses inefficient logic in calculations, contains non-SARGable predicates, or scans through the data more times than necessary, and so on. If so, we need to refactor the code, rewriting it to be more efficient.

If you're convinced the code is sound, then it could be that, for some reason, the SQL Server query optimizer is choosing a suboptimal execution plan. Let's review briefly some of the common causes of suboptimal plans.

Missing indexes

This is by far the Number One cause of performance issues in the environments that I support. Without the right index, queries will scan the clustered index or table, which will show up in our trace data as high reads. The most common resolution is to add an index, or to alter an existing index to make it a covering index and so avoid a key lookup.

If you have run a trace to identify the most expensive queries in your workload in terms of reads, duration, and frequency of execution, and so on, then you've already identified the ones most likely to benefit from a different indexing strategy. If not, then you can have Database Engine Tuning Advisor (DTA) analyze your workload. As discussed previously, you can use the Tuning template to create a workload that the DTA will then analyze to make index recommendations. Alternatively, and many DBAs prefer this route, you can use the missing indexes report (HTTP://TINYURL.COM/K8PALPB) to help you identify the "low-hanging fruit."

In either case, make sure that you analyze the suggested indexes. Don't just blindly create them, as each index comes with additional overhead, in terms of both space and the need for SQL Server to maintain each index in response to data modifications. I recommend Aaron Bertrand's article on what to consider before creating any "missing" indexes (see HTTP://TINYURL.COM/M9935UA).

Getting the right indexes on your system takes experience. For example, I recently had to drop an index to fix a bad execution plan problem. The query optimizer kept picking the "wrong" index for a table in a particular stored procedure, executed several times per second. We tried updating statistics and providing index hints, but it was still picking what we believed to be the wrong index. After reviewing other stored procedures that access the problem table, we realized that the "wrong" index was superfluous. We dropped it, and the query optimizer was now picking the "right" index and the stored procedure returned to running fast.

Out-of-date statistics

Statistics are metadata used by the query optimizer to "understand" the data, its distribution, and the number of rows a query is likely to return. Based on these statistics, the optimizer decides the optimal execution path. If the statistics are wrong, then it may make poor decisions and pick suboptimal execution plans. You need to make sure that for your SQL Server instances you've enabled both the `Auto Update Statistics` and `Auto Create Statistics` database options. For certain tables, especially large tables, you may in addition need to run a regular (such as daily) `UPDATE STATISTICS` job. Erin Stellato covers this topic in great length (HTTP://TINYURL.COM/PSF8G66).

Bad parameter sniffing

When the query optimizer chooses an execution plan, it uses the parameter values to look at the statistics and decide which plan to use and store for similar future calls. In some situations, the optimizer chooses a plan based on a parameter value that is non-representative of the majority of the data.

In other words, it might choose a plan based on a value that only returns a few rows, whereas many other values for that column will return hundreds of rows.

To fix this problem, you may just need to recompile the stored procedure or free the procedure cache, if you aren't using stored procedures. Alternatively, we can add the **WITH RECOMPILE** option, or the **OPTION(RECOMPILE)** query hint, to the stored procedure or query, instructing SQL Server not to store the execution plan and instead create a new one each time the procedure runs. There is an associated CPU cost, of course, so be careful setting this option if the stored procedure or query runs frequently.

Paul White has a good article on parameter sniffing, at HTTP://TINYURL.COM/MZ9GWJ4.

Preparing for Migration to Extended Events

I noted at the start of this chapter that in SQL Server 2012 Microsoft deprecated SQL Trace in favor of a new event collection infrastructure called Extended Events, and I explained why I believe SQL Trace is still a very valuable and viable diagnostic technique for the DBA. The learning curve for SQL Trace, over Extended Events, is undeniably shallower, allowing the DBA to start tracing quickly. In addition, with carefully designed server-side traces, avoiding the collection of too many events in a single trace and use of filtering, we can produce traces with relatively low I/O overhead.

Nevertheless, the mere fact of SQL Trace's deprecation means we must prepare to migrate to Extended Events over the next few years, and there are some good reasons why you might want to migrate sooner rather than later.

Extended Events is available only in SQL Server 2008 and later, and it is only in SQL Server 2012 that we have a built-in UI, allowing users to analyze the collected event data without recourse to XQuery and T-SQL, although it's possible to analyze SQL Server 2008 extended event data in the SQL Server 2012 UI.

Advantages of Extended Events for diagnostic data collection

Though there is a steeper learning curve to Extended Events over SQL Trace, there are many advantages in using Extended Events.

When configured in a manner described in this chapter, SQL Trace can be lightweight enough that it doesn't noticeably affect your server. However, "heavyweight" traces that produce many events can still have substantial overhead. Microsoft designed Extended Events to be even more lightweight (see, for example, HTTP://TINYURL.COM/D36MXT6) and much more extensible, in terms of the ease of adding new events.

The filtering capabilities in Extended Events are more flexible than SQL Trace. SQL Trace applies filters globally to all of the events in the trace. In Extended Events, we can apply specific filters to each event in our **event session** (roughly the equivalent of a trace). SQL Trace applies the filters only after the event has fired and the necessary data collected, so it incurs the event data collection overhead even for events that fail the filter criteria, and so our trace will filter out. Extended Events applies the filter (called **predicates**) much earlier, at the time the event fires, straight after collecting the minimal set of columns that comprise the event's **base payload**. After the first failed evaluation, event firing short circuits, and the engine collects no further data, and does not evaluate any further predicates.

For each event that fires, SQL Trace collects a set of global data (repeatable data), even if our trace does not need it. Extended Events also reduces the amount of data collected when an event fires, compared to SQL Trace. It collects in the base payload only data columns specifically required for that event. For many other data we wish to collect, we must add it to an event session definition, explicitly, as an **action**.

As well as global database columns, such as `session_id`, we can add to our events very useful actions such as:

- `query_hash` – (identifies queries with similar logic) and `query_plan_hash` (identifies similar plans); this saves us trying to parse the `TextData` column or using a tool such as ClearTrace, as we had to do with SQL Trace.

- `tsql_stack` – provides the `sql_handle` and offset information for each statement executed that led to an event firing.

Extended Events provides certain actions that invoke other tasks, or cause side-effects, such as a memory dump, when a particular event fires, much like a DDL or DML trigger. This is a lot harder to do with SQL Trace.

Extended Events also offers a lot more flexibility in terms of output **targets** for the event data. SQL Trace can only output to a file, to a table or to the GUI in SQL Profiler. As well as providing basic in-memory (`ring_buffer`) and file (`event_file`) targets, Extended Events offers a set of **advanced targets** that perform automatic aggregations. For example, an **Event Bucketizer** target that produces a histogram and an **Event Pairing** target that matches beginning and ending events. It can also output the SQL Server Error Log and the Windows Event Log.

There is no room in this chapter for more than this brief overview of just a few of the potential advantages of Extended Events. I highly recommend that you refer to Jonathan Kehayias's blog at HTTP://TINYURL.COM/OQ7OZ23 for much more in-depth coverage of this topic.

Creating event sessions in SSMS

To get a good feel for Extended Events, you'll want to start creating a few event sessions (the equivalent of a trace in SQL Trace). For basic event sessions, this is relatively simple to do using either the **New Session** dialog, or the **New Session Wizard**, in SSMS.

We'll take a brief look at how to use the former to create an event session that replicates as closely as possible our earlier SlowQueries trace. I do not even attempt to cover every detail and nuance of the UI. For further details refer to Books Online (HTTP://TECHNET.MICROSOFT.COM/EN-US/LIBRARY/GG471549.ASPX).

In SSMS Object Explorer, expand the Management folder and then the Extended Events folder. Right-click on the **Sessions** folder and select the **New Session** menu item. It will open up the New Session dialog. On the **General** Page, give the event session a name (such as SlowQueries) and then switch to the **Events** Page, where we can select the events we wish to include in our session.

To find an event, simply type the search text into the **Event library** search box. Add the relevant event to the session by clicking on it and hitting the > button. In this case, we want to add the rpc_completed and sql_batch_completed events (once added to the event session, an event disappears from the event library listing).

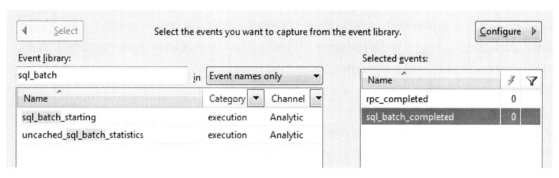

Figure 2:   Selecting events.

Click on the **Configure** button to move to the **Configure** view, which contains the configuration options for the selected events. We'll start with the **Event Fields** tab, which shows, for each event, the data columns that form part of its base payload. For example, Figure 3 shows the base payload for the sql_batch_completed event.

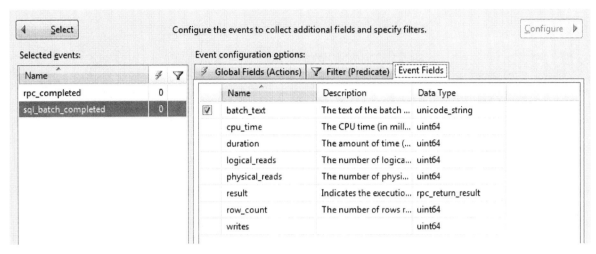

Figure 3:   The base payload columns for an event.

Notice that its base payload includes the equivalent of five out of eight of the data columns we included in the equivalent trace. The `batch_text` field is optional but included by default. Missing are the `SPID`, `LoginName` and `StartTime`.

Switch to the **Global Fields (Actions)** tab to see what data columns we can add as actions to our event session. In this case, we wish to add the `session_id` (equivalent to `SPID`) and `server_principal_name` (equivalent to `LoginName`) fields to both events. The `StartTime` column from SQL Trace is not available, though when the events fire, the event data will automatically include the collection time of the data.

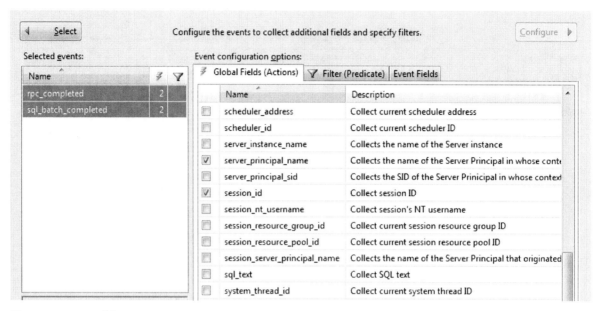

Figure 4:   Adding actions.

Finally, we want to add a filter, so move to the **Filter (Predicate)** tab. In Extended Events, unlike in SQL Trace, we can apply filters separately to individual events. We can create a filter on any event field or global field available to the event. For both our events, we want to add a filter on the **Duration** event field (which is common to both events), so **CTRL-click** to highlight both events, and define the filter as shown in Figure 5 (the duration is in microseconds).

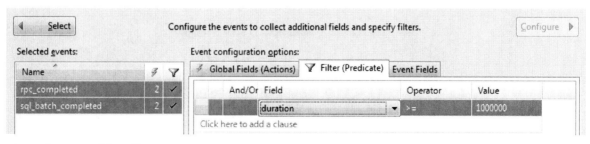

Figure 5:   Adding filters.

Next, move to the **Data Storage** page to define a target. To mimic our trace, we'll choose the event_file target with a maximum size of 1 GB.

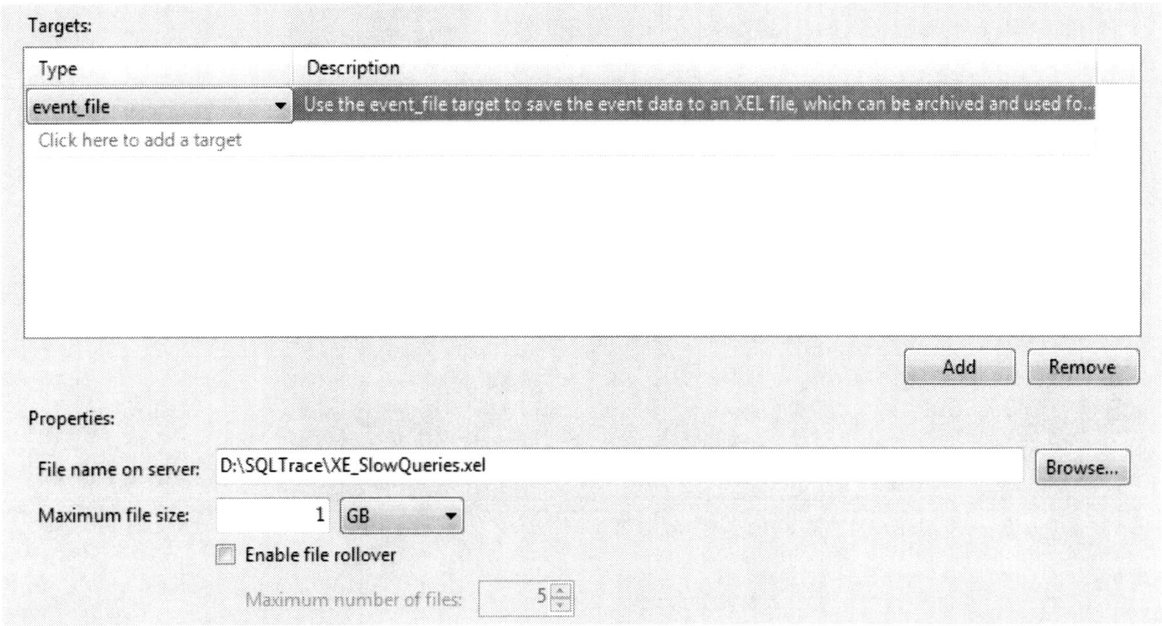

Figure 6:   Specifying a target.

Having done this, simply click **OK** to create the event session definition and then, in SSMS, right-click on the new event session to start the session. Run an appropriate workload and then right-click on the event_file target (under the SlowQueries event session) and select **View Target Data**, to see the event data collected.

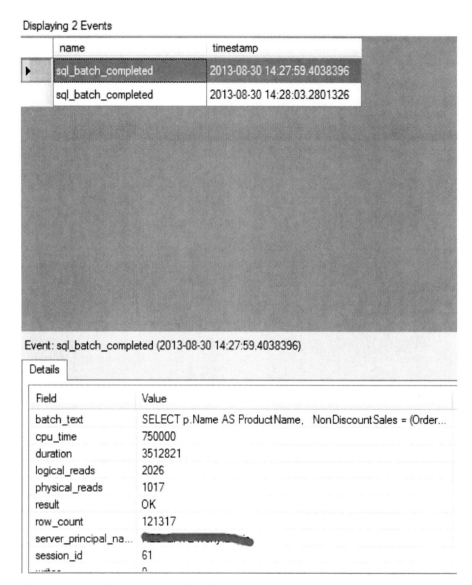

Figure 7: Viewing event data from the target.

Converting traces to Extended Events sessions

If you have a large catalog of existing SQL Trace definitions, then there are a few options to convert them from SQL Trace to Extended Events.

- **Convert an existing SQL Trace script to an Extended Events session** – this MSDN article provides a manual way to perform the conversion and shows how to map SQL Trace event classes and data columns to events and actions in Extended Events: HTTP://MSDN.MICROSOFT.COM/EN-US/LIBRARY/FF878114.ASPX.

- **Microsoft's Extended Events team provides a conversion utility through SQL CLR:** HTTP://TINYURL.COM/CPB5387.

- **Jonathan Kehayias's comprehensive converter:** HTTP://TINYURL.COM/O36HKAO.

Manually converting traces will be a lot of work if you have many traces. The SQL CLR converter sounds better, but you have to compile the assembly and then load it into your SQL instance. Jonathan Kehayias's converter uses a T-SQL stored procedure and works reliably. With his tool, I can convert my trace in a matter of minutes.

Download his converter and then open the script, which includes the code to create the stored procedure, and mark it as a system object, and to convert an existing trace. It will convert a specified server-side trace that is running, or whose definition is loaded into SQL Server.

Run the trace script from Listing 1 with the modifications from Listing 2 and then stop it (@status = 0 from Listing 3) but don't close it. We can now run the converter, as shown in Listing 13, supplying the value of @TraceID for the trace to be converted.

```
EXECUTE sp_SQLskills_ConvertTraceToExtendedEvents
    @TraceID = 2,
    @SessionName = 'XE_SlowQueries2',
    @PrintOutput = 1,
    @Execute = 1;
```

Listing 13:   Execute sp_SQLskills_ConvertTraceToExtendedEvents.

Specifying a value of 1 for @PrintOutput, the default value, prints out the T-SQL that creates the XE session. Listing 14 shows the output.

```
IF EXISTS ( SELECT  1
            FROM    sys.server_event_sessions
            WHERE   name = 'XE_SlowQueries2' )
    DROP EVENT SESSION [XE_SlowQueries2] ON SERVER;
GO
CREATE EVENT SESSION [XE_SlowQueries2] ON SERVER
    ADD EVENT sqlserver. rpc_completed
      ( ACTION
        ( sqlserver.server_principal_name -- LoginName from SQLTrace
        , sqlserver. session_id -- SPID from SQLTrace
          -- BinaryData not implemented in XE for this event
        ) WHERE ( duration >= 1000000 )
      ),
    ADD EVENT sqlserver.sql_batch_completed
      ( ACTION
        ( sqlserver. server_principal_name -- LoginName from SQLTrace
        , sqlserver. session_id -- SPID from SQLTrace
        ) WHERE ( duration >= 1000000 )
      )
    ADD TARGET package0. event_file
        ( SET filename = '\\MyDirectory\XE_SlowQueries2.xel',
              max_file_size = 1024,
              max_rollover_files = 0
        )
```

Listing 14: Output of sp_SQLskills_ConvertTraceToExtendedEvents.

You'll see the two events, **sqlserver.rpc_completed** and **sqlserver.sql_batch_completed** (sqlserver is the name of the parent package that contains these events). As noted previously, these events contain in their base payloads most of the event columns we defined in our server-side trace. The converter adds, as actions, the **sqlserver.server_principal_name** (equivalent to **LoginName**) and **sqlserver.session_id** (equivalent to **SPID**) global fields.

The filter (`"duration >= 1000000"`) applies to each event, individually. As noted earlier, this is a big difference between server-side traces and XE sessions. We can define multiple filters in a server-side trace, but they apply to all events in the trace that contain the filtered column. With XE, each event can have its own predicate.

The converter created the XE session, since we specified 1 for `@Execute`, but did not start it. We can start it from SSMS or via an **ALTER EVENT SESSION** command.

```
ALTER EVENT SESSION [XE_SlowQueries2] ON SERVER STATE = START;
```

Listing 15:   Start an event session.

Listing 16 will stop and delete the XE session.

```
ALTER EVENT SESSION [XE_SlowQueries2] ON SERVER STATE = STOP;

DROP EVENT SESSION [XE_SlowQueries2] ON SERVER;
```

Listing 16:   Stop and delete an event session.

Of course, it is never a good idea to convert code blindly, so we need to analyze the converted trace definition and test it. In this case, we can script out the event session we created manually in the previous section, and compare it to the converted trace definition.

Once we start to understand fully the Extended Events architecture, and how it works, we can start to build optimized event sessions.

Conclusion

Traces provide a wealth of information, including events that can help you diagnose a performance problem. By learning to perform a server-side trace instead of running a trace through Profiler, we can ensure that our traces do not impede performance on the server we are analyzing. Alongside this, we can also start to experiment with the migration of our existing trace portfolio over to Extended Events.

Windows Functions in SQL Server 2012

Dave Ballantyne

If you are a SQL Server 2012 developer, you may not be so interested in Always-on High Availability and "Big Data," the focus of the marketing hype for SQL Server 2012, but you'll love the enhancements to the SQL Windows functions. This is the real big-ticket item.

SQL Server 2005 ushered in the first ANSI-standard Windows ranking and aggregate functions, along with the OVER clause, which allowed us to apply the functions across each row in a specified window/partition of data. The use of OVER alongside the new Common Table Expressions (CTEs), made for a revolutionary change in the way that one could develop T-SQL solutions. Still, certain procedures, such as the rolling balance calculation, remained difficult and required the use of cursors or inefficient sub-selects.

SQL Server 2012 takes support for Windows functions to the next of many logical steps, by allowing us to use a true **sliding window** of data. With a sliding window, we can perform calculations such as the rolling balance using a faster, more efficient, and readable statement.

This chapter will walk through how to use the OVER clause and sliding windows, with aggregate and analytic functions. It will also demonstrate the performance overhead associated with different techniques for defining the frame extent of the window for our calculations.

Sliding Windows

Let's see what sorts of calculations are possible when using sliding windows. First, we need to generate some sample data from **AdventureWorks2012**, as shown in Listing 1.

```
USE AdventureWorks2012;
GO
SELECT  SALESPERSONID ,
        MIN(ORDERDATE) AS ORDERMONTH ,
        SUM(TOTALDUE) AS TOTALDUE
INTO    #ORDERS
FROM    SALES.SALESORDERHEADER SOH
WHERE   SOH.SALESPERSONID IS NOT NULL
GROUP BY SALESPERSONID ,
        DATEDIFF(MM, 0, ORDERDATE);
GO
```

Listing 1: Some sample Orders data.

In SQL Server 2005 and later, we can use the **OVER** clause to partition the data and perform calculations over the rows in each partition. For example, we can partition the data by **SALESPERSONID** in order to calculate the total sales attributable to each sales person, as shown in Listing 2. For each row (*i.e.* order) in each partition, it calculates the total sales for that sales person. This allows the developer to perform comparisons and calculations on the present row's value, relative to the total value (for example, calculate the percentage).

```
SELECT  * ,
        SUM(TOTALDUE) OVER ( PARTITION BY SALESPERSONID )
FROM    #ORDERS
ORDER BY SALESPERSONID;
```

Listing 2: Using OVER to calculate total sales per sales person.

In SQL Server 2012, we now have the means to look at specific rows within that partition of data relative to the "current" row i.e. to perform calculations across a sliding window of data. For example, Listing 3 calculates a simple rolling monthly balance for each sales person, simply by adding an ORDER BY clause to the OVER clause, and specifying that the order is ORDERMONTH.

```
SELECT  SALESPERSONID ,
        ORDERMONTH ,
        TOTALDUE ,
        SUM(TOTALDUE) OVER ( PARTITION BY SALESPERSONID ORDER BY ORDERMONTH )
                                            AS ROLLINGBALANCE
FROM    #ORDERS
ORDER BY SALESPERSONID ,
        ORDERMONTH;
```

Listing 3:   Using OVER with a sliding window to calculate a rolling monthly balance for each sales person.

By adding ORDER BY ORDERMONTH to the OVER clause, we changed the scope of the calculation from "totals sales value across the entire partition," as in Listing 2, to "total sales value for this row and every row preceding." However, watch out for missing data that can cause errors when we're trying, for example, to aggregate data over the previous financial quarter. If there has been no financial activity for a month within that financial quarter, then we will need a "blank" row to ensure that rows will still be equivalent to "months." Otherwise, there will be no entry for that month.

When using these functions, it is important to remember that the rows are relative to the current row within the partition, and the calculation is performed in the ORDER specified in the OVER clause. This order can be in an entirely different order to the order of the result set returned by the statement and, indeed, the order specified for any other window functions. All partitions and their ORDER BY clauses operate and calculate entirely independently of each other. In some cases, this can lead to suboptimal execution plans. For example, consider Listing 4, which uses two windowing functions, each establishing a different order for the ORDERMONTH column.

```
SELECT   SALESPERSONID ,
         ORDERMONTH ,
         TOTALDUE ,
         SUM(TOTALDUE) OVER ( PARTITION BY SALESPERSONID
                              ORDER BY ORDERMONTH ) AS ROLLINGBALANCE ,
         SUM(TOTALDUE) OVER ( PARTITION BY SALESPERSONID
                              ORDER BY ORDERMONTH DESC ) AS ROLLINGBALANCEDESC
FROM     #ORDERS
ORDER BY SALESPERSONID ,
         ORDERMONTH;
GO
```

Listing 4:   Windows functions with multiple sort orders.

The execution plan for Listing 4 contains three **Sort** operations, one for each of the windowing functions and then a third for the final ORDER BY clause of the statement. However, if we simply swap the positions of the ROLLINGBALANCE and ROLLINGBALANCEDESC calculations, the plan contains only two sorts; the final ORDER BY clause requires no sort because the previous sort guarantees the data is now in the required order.

The optimizer cannot change the sequence of functions, and therefore the sorting operations required, but it can exploit the fact that data is already guaranteed to be in the required order.

The OVER clauses in Listings 3 and 4 "hide" two default values, and are equivalent to:

```
OVER(PARTITION BY SALESPERSONID ORDER BY ORDERMONTH RANGE UNBOUNDED PRECEDING)
```

The first "hidden" default is use of the RANGE clause, and the second is UNBOUNDED PRECEDING, which defines the **window frame extent**. The use of RANGE means that, by default, the function works with each distinct value in the column used to order the rows, in each partition. The alternative is to specify ROWS, which means that the function works with each row in each partition. Use of UNBOUNDED PRECEDING simply means that, by default, the windows start with the first row in the partition.

However, we have other options to define the window frame extent. Let's look at these first, before investigating the behavioral and performance differences between using RANGE versus ROWS.

Defining the window frame extent

As discussed, our OVER clause from Listing 4 contained two "hidden" defaults, in terms of the type of clause, and the definition of the window frame extent.

Unless we specify otherwise, SQL Server uses the default option of UNBOUNDED PRECEDING for the window frame extent. Although that is perfectly valid syntax, the full option is BETWEEN UNBOUNDED PRECEDING AND CURRENT ROW, meaning that the frame starts at the first row in the partition and extends to the current row (if we're using ROWS) or current value (if we're using RANGE). However, other options are available that allow us to control the extent of the sliding window over our partition of data, in which we can do our aggregations.

The RANGE option supports only UNBOUNDED PRECEDING AND CURRENT ROW and CURRENT ROW AND UNBOUNDED FOLLOWING, the latter meaning simply that the window starts at the current value and extends to the last row of the partition. An attempt to use any other values will result in the following error message:

```
MSG 4194, LEVEL 16, STATE 1, LINE 1
RANGE IS ONLY SUPPORTED WITH UNBOUNDED AND CURRENT ROW WINDOW FRAME DELIMITERS.
```

If we're using ROWS, we have more flexibility. Continuing our #ORDERS example, Listing 7 specifies that we wish to SUM the TotalDue and get the MIN of OrderMonth for the present row and the four rows preceding it, inclusive, so five rows in total.

```
SELECT  * ,
        SUM(TOTALDUE) OVER ( PARTITION BY SALESPERSONID
                             ORDER BY ORDERMONTH ROWS 4 PRECEDING )
                                                        AS SUMTOTALDUE ,
        MIN(ORDERMONTH) OVER ( PARTITION BY SALESPERSONID
                               ORDER BY ORDERMONTH ROWS 4 PRECEDING )
                                                        AS MINORDERDATE
FROM       #ORDERS
WHERE      SALESPERSONID = 274
ORDER BY ORDERMONTH;
```

Listing 5:   Windows Frame Extent options when using ROWS.

Figure 1 explains the results obtained for the MIN(ORDERMONTH) calculation.

	SalesPersonID	OrderMonth	TotalDue	SumTotalDue	MinOrderDate
1	274	2005-08-01 00:00:00.000	23130.2957	23130.2957	2005-08-01 00:00:00.000
2	274	2005-09-01 00:00:00.000	2297.0332	25427.3289	2005-08-01 00:00:00.000
3	274	2005-11-01 00:00:00.000	7140.5866	32567.9155	2005-08-01 00:00:00.000
4	274	2006-02-01 00:00:00.000	68918.2404	101486.1559	2005-08-01 00:00:00.000
5	274	2006-03-01 00:00:00.000	20614.2427	122100.3986	2005-08-01 00:00:00.000
6	274	2006-04-01 00:00:00.000	37625.4303	136595.5332	2005-09-01 00:00:00.000
7	274	2006-06-01 00:00:00.000	55664.1342	189968.6342	2005-11-01 00:00:00.000
8	274	2006-07-01 00:00:00.000	4032.1579	186854.2055	2006-02-01 00:00:00.000

Figure 1:   Results of the MIN(ORDERMONTH) calculation.

Other variations on this theme for the ROWS option include:

- BETWEEN X ROWS PRECEDING AND Y PRECEDING – valid as long as X >= Y.

- BETWEEN CURRENT ROW AND UNBOUNDED FOLLOWING – we use FOLLOWING to look ahead a number of rows; it operates in exactly the same fashion as PRECEDING.

There are other ANSI standard options for defining the extent of sliding windows. For example, BETWEEN X MONTHS PRECEDING takes care of the earlier problem we discussed with discrepancies caused by missing data. However, this important functionality has yet to appear within SQL Server.

Behavioral differences between RANGE and ROWS

In our previous #ORDERS example, the values in the ORDERMONTH column, used to order the partitions, are unique. In such cases, our windowing function will return the same results regardless of whether we use ROWS or RANGE.

Differences between the two clauses arise when the values in the column specified in the ORDER BY clause of the OVER clause are not unique. If we use RANGE, then our windowing function will produce an aggregate figure for any rows in each partition with the same value for the ordering column. If we specify ROWS, then the windowing function will calculate row by row.

To appreciate these differences clearly, let's look at an example.

```
USE AdventureWorks2012;
GO
CREATE TABLE #SIMPLESALES
    (
        SIMPLESALESID INTEGER PRIMARY KEY ,
        SALEID INTEGER NOT NULL ,
        LINEID INTEGER NOT NULL ,
        SALES MONEY NOT NULL
    )
GO


INSERT  INTO #SIMPLESALES
        ( SIMPLESALESID, SALEID, LINEID, SALES )
VALUES  ( 1, 1, 1, 1 ),
        ( 2, 1, 2, 5 ),
        ( 3, 1, 2, 10 ),
        ( 4, 1, 3, 20 ),
        ( 5, 2, 1, 101 ),
        ( 6, 2, 2, 105 ),
        ( 7, 2, 2, 110 ),
        ( 8, 2, 3, 120 )
GO
```

Listing 6:   Create and load the #SimpleSales table.

The query in Listing 7 performs two SUM calculations, in each case partitioning the data by SALEID and ordering data within each partition according to LINEID. The only difference is that the first calculation uses RANGE and the second uses ROWS.

```
SELECT   SALEID ,
         LINEID ,
         SALES ,
         SUM(SALES) OVER ( PARTITION BY SALEID ORDER BY LINEID
                           RANGE UNBOUNDED PRECEDING ) AS UNBOUNDEDRANGE ,
         SUM(SALES) OVER ( PARTITION BY SALEID ORDER BY LINEID
                           ROWS  UNBOUNDED PRECEDING ) AS UNBOUNDEDROWS
FROM     #SIMPLESALES
ORDER BY SALEID ,
         LINEID
```

Listing 7:   Behavioral differences for RANGE versus ROWS.

	SaleID	LineID	Sales	UnboundedRange	UnboundedRows
1	1	1	1.00	1.00	1.00
2	1	2	5.00	16.00	6.00
3	1	2	10.00	16.00	16.00
4	1	3	20.00	36.00	36.00
5	2	1	101.00	101.00	101.00
6	2	2	105.00	316.00	206.00
7	2	2	110.00	316.00	316.00
8	2	3	120.00	436.00	436.00

Notice that for ROWS, for each row in each partition we get a running total for the current row and all previous rows in the window, in other words a row-by-row rolling balance. However, when we use RANGE, the function produces a single sales value for all rows within each partition that have the same value for LINEID. So for those rows where SaleID=1 and LineID=2, the UnboundedRange values for both are 16. Similarly for rows with SaleID=2 and LineID=2.

There are deep-underlying operational differences between ROWS and RANGE calculations, and this can lead to a considerable difference in performance. We'll look at this in more detail shortly, after a brief examination of options for defining the window frame extent.

Performance differences between RANGE and ROWS

As noted earlier, there are operational differences in the execution of RANGE versus ROWS queries. In both cases, you will see in their execution plans the new operator, **Window Spool**, but this is a "black box" and unfortunately, SQL Server does not expose the inner workings to the end-user.

The biggest difference, in terms of performance, is that when using RANGE, the **Window Spool** operator will always need to write to disk to complete its work. The ROWS option will only require the **Window Spool** operator to write to disk under certain conditions, and for most of the time it is able to work using an optimized in-memory spool rather than the slower, on-disk spool.

More specifically, ROWS will only cause the **Window Spool** to write to disk if we specify >= 10,000 rows (e.g. BETWEEN 9999 ROWS PRECEDING ROWS AND CURRENT ROW), or if we specify >4 ROWS and the aggregation is not cumulative (such as when using the MIN or MAX functions). However, if we specify UNBOUNDED with either PRECEDING or FOLLOWING, then SQL Server will be able to use the faster in-memory spool as the results are based upon a window with a fixed starting row and can accumulate to the current row.

Let's return to our #ORDERS example, and see what impact these operational differences might have on performance. The RANGE and ROWS queries in Listing 8 return identical results (due to the uniqueness of ORDERMONTH).

```
SELECT /* RANGE */ * ,
        SUM(TOTALDUE) OVER ( PARTITION BY SALESPERSONID ORDER BY ORDERMONTH )
FROM    #ORDERS;
GO
SELECT /* ROWS */ * ,
        SUM(TOTALDUE) OVER ( PARTITION BY SALESPERSONID ORDER BY ORDERMONTH ROWS
UNBOUNDED PRECEDING )
FROM    #ORDERS;
```

Listing 8:   Demonstrating performance difference between use of RANGE and ROWS.

If we were to examine the execution plans, we would see that SQL Server reports the **Query cost (relative to the batch)** as being an even 50/50 split, as shown in Figure 2.

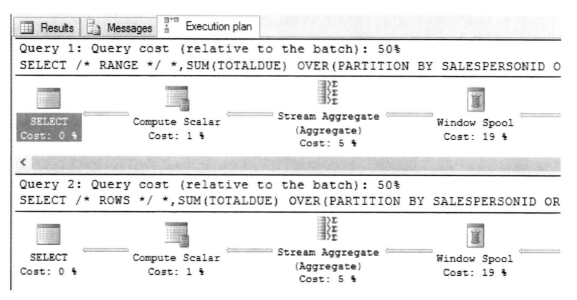

Figure 2:   Execution plans for "equivalent" RANGE and ROWS queries.

Unfortunately, this is simply not true. The correct phrasing should be *estimated* **query cost (relative to total** *estimate* **for batch)**; the cost figures used by the Optimizer are estimated costs, not actual costs. SQL Server estimates that the ROWS and RANGE operations cost the same in terms of I/O, though the actual execution costs are vastly different due to the **Window Spool** operator for the RANGE operation writing to disk but the one for the ROWS operation working with the faster in-memory spool.

The estimated I/O costs are only of use to the optimizer to enable it to pick between different candidate plans for a single query. For example, when joining two tables in a query, two candidate plans may be considered as viable, logically equivalent (*i.e.* they will produce the same output) alternatives. Let's say one of these plans uses a **Nested Loop** to join the tables, the other a **Hash Match** join. For each viable plan, the optimizer will calculate an estimated I/O figure and use it to make an educated choice as to the cheapest alternative.

However, to the optimizer, the **Window Spool** operator is a black box and in order to produce the user's expected results it has to execute it; there are no alternative execution plans that it can consider. In that context, it doesn't matter to the Optimizer that the estimated cost is unrepresentative of the actual execution cost.

A Profiler trace of the two queries highlights how much more expensive the RANGE query is over the ROWS query, and how wrong the estimate of a 50/50 split is.

EventClass	TextData	CPU	Reads	Writes	Duration
Trace Start					
SQL:BatchCompleted	/*RANGE */ select *, ...	16	4137	0	231
SQL:BatchCompleted	/* ROWS */ select *, ...	15	4	0	44

Figure 3:   Profiler Trace Results for RANGE versus ROWS.

There is, as you can see, a major difference between the reads and duration of the two, so you should always use ROWS unless you really need the functionality that RANGE offers. In light of this, it may seem odd that the default is RANGE but it is the ANSI standard and Microsoft is obliged to follow it.

Analytic Functions

SQL Server 2012 supports a collection of new analytic functions that we use with the OVER clause. These are LAG /LEAD, FIRST_VALUE / LAST_VALUE and then a set of functions for statistical analysis, PERCENTILE_CONT, PERCENTILE_DISC, PERCENT_RANK and CUME_DIST.

LAG and LEAD

We use the LAG function to return data from a single column from a row that is a specified number of rows behind the current row in the partition, according to the ORDER specified in the OVER clause.

The syntax for LAG is: LAG(<EXPRESSION>[,OFFSET[,DEFAULT]])

OFFSET and DEFAULT are both optional parameters. OFFSET is the number of rows behind the current row and its default value is 1, *i.e.* the prior row. DEFAULT specifies the value to return if the value of <EXPRESSION>, at the row indicated by OFFSET, is NULL, *i.e.* there is no valid value to return. The default value for the DEFAULT parameter is NULL.

Listing 9 shows how to use the LAG function to display OrderMonth from one row behind the present row, *i.e.* fetching the prior order month of the SalesPersonId.

```
SELECT  * ,
        LAG(ORDERMONTH, 1) OVER ( PARTITION BY SALESPERSONID
                                  ORDER BY ORDERMONTH ) AS LASTORDERMONTH
FROM    #ORDERS
ORDER BY SALESPERSONID ,
        ORDERMONTH;
GO
```

Listing 9:   Using the LAG analytic function.

	SALESPERSONID	ORDERMONTH	TOTALDUE	LASTORDERMONTH
1	274	2005-08-01 00:00:00.000	23130.2957	NULL
2	274	2005-09-01 00:00:00.000	2297.0332	2005-08-01 00:00:00.000
3	274	2005-11-01 00:00:00.000	7140.5866	2005-09-01 00:00:00.000
4	274	2006-02-01 00:00:00.000	68918.2404	2005-11-01 00:00:00.000
5	274	2006-03-01 00:00:00.000	20614.2427	2006-02-01 00:00:00.000
6	274	2006-04-01 00:00:00.000	37625.4303	2006-03-01 00:00:00.000
7	274	2006 05 01 00:00:00 000	55554 1242	2006 04 01 00:00:00 000

For the first row, there is no previous row, of course, so the LAG function attempts to reference a row outside of the partition boundary, and therefore returns the DEFAULT value.

Listing 10 shows the logically equivalent, and considerably more verbose, pre-SQL Server 2012 version.

```
SELECT  #ORDERS.* ,
        LASTORDERMONTH.ORDERMONTH AS LASTORDERMONTH
FROM    #ORDERS
        OUTER APPLY ( SELECT TOP ( 1 )
                             INNERORDERS.ORDERMONTH
                      FROM   #ORDERS INNERORDERS
                      WHERE  INNERORDERS.SALESPERSONID = #ORDERS.SALESPERSONID
                        AND INNERORDERS.ORDERMONTH < #ORDERS.ORDERMONTH
                      ORDER BY  INNERORDERS.ORDERMONTH DESC
                    ) AS LASTORDERMONTH
ORDER BY SALESPERSONID ,
         ORDERMONTH;
```

Listing 10:   The days before LAG.

Not only is the intent of the code harder to fathom, but performance is very poor in comparison to LAG.

The LEAD function is the mirror image of LAG and it works in exactly the same way with the same arguments, but processes rows ahead in the partition rather than behind.

FIRST_VALUE and LAST_VALUE

FIRST_VALUE is similar to LAG but rather than targeting a single row in relation to the present row, it is able to fully utilize the OVER clause to define a sliding window of data in which to operate. In particular, this allows easy reference to UNBOUNDED to find the absolute first row inside a partition.

Listing 11 shows how to use FIRST_VALUE to display the first OrderMonth for the sales person of the present row.

```
SELECT   * ,
         FIRST_VALUE(ORDERMONTH) OVER ( PARTITION BY SALESPERSONID
                                              ORDER BY ORDERMONTH )
FROM     #ORDERS
ORDER BY SALESPERSONID ,
         ORDERMONTH ,
         TOTALDUE;
GO
```

Listing 11:   Using FIRST_VALUE.

As discussed, the default of a windowing function is RANGE, so we can write the same query more formally by making the RANGE clause explicit.

```
FIRST_VALUE(ORDERMONTH) OVER
                        ( PARTITION BY SALESPERSONID
                          ORDER BY ORDERMONTH
                          RANGE BETWEEN UNBOUNDED PRECEDING AND CURRENT ROW )
```

As we saw earlier, there is a big performance difference between RANGE and ROWS, so if we change the previous query to use ROWS and then compare it to the RANGE query we can see a huge difference in the performance data, using Profiler.

```
FIRST_VALUE(ORDERMONTH) OVER
                         ( PARTITION BY SALESPERSONID
                           ORDER BY ORDERMONTH
                           ROWS BETWEEN UNBOUNDED PRECEDING AND CURRENT ROW )
```

EventClass	TextData	CPU	Reads	Writes	Duration
SQL:BatchCompleted	/*RANGE*/ ...	0	4137	0	28
SQL:BatchCompleted	/*ROWS*/ ...	0	4	0	1

As you can see, RANGE performs poorly compared to ROWS. Remember, though, that performance is not the only consideration in choosing between the two; as discussed earlier, they also behave differently if the ordering column in non-unique.

As long as the ordering column for the OVER clause is unique, as is the case with the #ORDERS table, FIRST_VALUE queries will return the same data, regardless of whether we use ROWS or RANGE. If it's not, then the sort order will be ambiguous and they may return different data.

Listing 12 for the #SIMPLESALES table uses FIRST_VALUE twice, once with RANGE and once with ROWS.

```
SELECT  * ,
        FIRST_VALUE(SALES) OVER ( PARTITION BY SALEID, LINEID ORDER BY LINEID
                        RANGE UNBOUNDED PRECEDING ) AS FIRSTVALUERANGE ,
        FIRST_VALUE(SALES) OVER ( PARTITION BY SALEID, LINEID ORDER BY LINEID
                        ROWS  UNBOUNDED PRECEDING ) AS FIRSTVALUEROWS
FROM    #SIMPLESALES
ORDER BY SALEID ,
        LINEID;
```

Listing 12:   Using FIRST_VALUE with ROWS and RANGE.

	SIMPLESALESID	SALEID	LINEID	SALES	FIRSTVALUERANGE	FIRSTVALUEROWS
1	1	1	1	1.00	1.00	1.00
2	2	1	2	5.00	5.00	5.00
3	3	1	2	10.00	5.00	5.00
4	4	1	3	20.00	20.00	20.00
5	5	2	1	101.00	101.00	101.00
6	6	2	2	105.00	105.00	105.00
7	7	2	2	110.00	105.00	105.00
8	8	2	3	120.00	120.00	120.00

In fact, the values returned are the same in each case, in this example, but only the use of ROWS guarantees those values. When using RANGE, for rows of equal LINEID values, such as the rows where SALEID=1 and LINEID=2, the FIRST_VALUE function, in theory at least, can return either 5.00 or 10.00. The fact that we ordered the partition by LINEID means that, in the case of ties (two rows with the same value), we do not care which value the function returns. If we do care then we need to make the sort order unambiguous by adding a "tie-breaker" to the sort; potentially, SIMPLESALESID would be a good choice. This is the only way to guarantee ROWS and RANGE will always return the same results.

Overall, it's easy to reach the conclusion that the RANGE functionality is rather super-fluous and can only serve to soak up some of our precious machine resources without adding any functional value.

LAST_VALUE is functionally similar to FIRST_VALUE, but returns data for the last row in the partition.

Statistical analysis functions

The remaining functions, PERCENTILE_CONT, PERCENTILE_DISC, PERCENT_RANK and CUME_DIST, are for statistical analysis of data.

CUME_DIST and PERCENT_RANK

CUME_DIST and PERCENT_RANK calculate the relative position of the value of the present row in relation to all the other rows within the specified partition (or the entire result set if we don't specify a partition). To put it another way, it answers the question, "How far through the set of data is this row?" For example, CUME_DIST for the second row in a 5-row result set returns 0.2, or "1 / (Total Rows / Present rows position)."

Listing 13 shows a query against the #SIMPLESALES to demonstrate this functionality.

```
SELECT  * ,
        CUME_DIST() OVER ( PARTITION BY SALEID
                           ORDER BY SALES ) AS CUME_DIST ,
        PERCENT_RANK() OVER ( PARTITION BY SALEID
                              ORDER BY SALES ) AS PERC_RANK
FROM    #SIMPLESALES
ORDER BY SALEID ,
         LINEID
```

Listing 13: Using CUME_DIST and PERCENT_RANK.

	SIMPLESALESID	SALEID	LINEID	SALES	CUME_DIST	PERC_RANK
1	1	1	1	1.00	0.25	0
2	2	1	2	5.00	0.5	0.333333333333333
3	3	1	2	10.00	0.75	0.666666666666667
4	4	1	3	20.00	1	1
5	5	2	1	101.00	0.25	0
6	6	2	2	105.00	0.5	0.333333333333333
7	7	2	2	110.00	0.75	0.666666666666667
8	8	2	3	120.00	1	1

Both functions return the relative position of the row within the partition, according to the order specified by the partition function's ORDER BY clause. The difference is that PERCENT_RANK returns 0 for the first row, and then evenly spaced values up to 1, for each partition, whereas the starting value for CUME_DIST is the step value.

If there are duplicate values in the dataset, then these functions return the same value for the duplicate rows, as demonstrated by Listing 14 and subsequent output, after rerunning Listing 13.

```
INSERT  INTO #SIMPLESALES
        ( SALEID, LINEID, SALES )
VALUES  ( 1, 2, 5 )
```

Listing 14:   INSERT duplicate values into #SIMPLESALES.

SIMPLESALESID	SALEID	LINEID	SALES	CUME_DIST	PERC_RANK
1	1	1	1.00	0.2	0
2	1	2	5.00	0.6	0.25
9	1	2	5.00	0.6	0.25
3	1	2	10.00	0.8	0.75
4	1	3	20.00	1	1
5	2	1	101.00	0.25	0
6	2	2	105.00	0.5	0.333333333333333
7	2	2	110.00	0.75	0.666666666666667
8	2	3	120.00	1	1

We see that for the rows WHERE SIMPLESALESID IN(2,9), each of the functions returns the same values.

PERCENTILE_CONT and PERCENTILE_DISC

PERCENTILE_CONT and PERCENTILE_DISC look at the same problem but approach it from a different angle. Rather than answering the question *"How far through...?"* they will answer *"What value is x% through the partition?"*

The PERCENTILE_DISC function returns a value that exists in the result set, but PERCENTILE_CONT will return a calculated value that is exactly the specified percentage through the result set. The value may exist in the result set, but only by chance.

Listing 15 uses each function to return the value that is .5 (or 50%) of the way through the data, partitioned by SALEID and ordered by SALES.

```
SELECT   *  ,
     PERCENTILE_DISC
         ( 0.5 )
         WITHIN GROUP ( ORDER BY SALES )
         OVER ( PARTITION BY SALEID ) AS PERC_DISC ,
     PERCENTILE_CONT
         ( 0.5 )
         WITHIN GROUP (  ORDER BY SALES )
         OVER (PARTITION BY SALEID ) AS PERC_CONT
FROM    #SIMPLESALES
ORDER BY SALEID ,
         LINEID;
```

Listing 15:   Using PERCENTILE_CONT and PERCENTILE_DISC.

SIMPLESALESID	SALEID	LINEID	SALES	PERC_DISC	PERC_CONT
1	1	1	1.00	5.00	5
2	1	2	5.00	5.00	5
9	1	2	5.00	5.00	5
3	1	2	10.00	5.00	5
4	1	3	20.00	5.00	5
5	2	1	101.00	105.00	107.5
6	2	2	105.00	105.00	107.5
7	2	2	110.00	105.00	107.5
8	2	3	120.00	105.00	107.5

Notice how, as there are an even number of rows for SALEID 2, the PERC_CONT function returns a value midway between the two middle values (107.5), which is not a value that exists in the result set.

Performance of analytic functions

How do the analytic functions actually perform? We already know that there is a big enough performance difference between ROWS and RANGE to make it wise to use ROWS wherever possible. However, are the new analytic functions any better performing than an equivalent statement written with 2005 syntax?

To investigate, we need to scale up our data. After executing Listing 16 our #ORDERS table should contain 237,056 rows, so just about enough data for performance testing. We also add a supporting index.

```
DECLARE @MAXSALESID INTEGER
SELECT TOP ( 1 )
        @MAXSALESID = SALESPERSONID
FROM    #ORDERS
ORDER BY SALESPERSONID DESC


INSERT  INTO #ORDERS
        SELECT  SALESPERSONID + @MAXSALESID ,
                ORDERMONTH ,
                TOTALDUE
        FROM    #ORDERS;
GO 9


CREATE UNIQUE CLUSTERED INDEX idxOrder ON #Orders(SalesPersonId,OrderMonth);
GO
```

Listing 16:   Scaling up the data in #ORDERS.

In the test in Listing 17, we have two logically equivalent statements that return all of the orders along with the value of the first order made by the relevant sales person. The first statement uses a 2005-and-later compatible CROSS APPLY clause, and the second uses the new FIRST_VALUE analytic function.

I use **SELECT INTO** simply to suppress the returning of results to SSMS. In my experience, the time it takes SSMS to consume and present results can skew the true performance testing results (an often-overlooked factor in performance testing).

```
DROP TABLE #1;
DROP TABLE #2;
GO

-- CROSS APPLY
DECLARE @T1 DATETIME = GETDATE()
SELECT  #ORDERS.* ,
        FIRSTORDERVALUE.TOTALDUE AS FIRSTTOTDUE
INTO    #1
FROM    #ORDERS
        CROSS APPLY ( SELECT TOP ( 1 )
                             INNERORDERS.TOTALDUE
                      FROM   #ORDERS INNERORDERS
                      WHERE  INNERORDERS.SALESPERSONID = #ORDERS.SALESPERSONID
                      ORDER BY  INNERORDERS.ORDERMONTH
                    ) AS FIRSTORDERVALUE
ORDER BY SALESPERSONID ,
        ORDERMONTH ;

SELECT  DATEDIFF(MS, @T1, GETDATE()) AS 'CROSSAPPLY TIME';
GO

--FIRST_VALUE
DECLARE @T1 DATETIME = GETDATE()
SELECT  #ORDERS.* ,
        FIRST_VALUE(TOTALDUE) OVER ( PARTITION BY SALESPERSONID
                                     ORDER BY ORDERMONTH ROWS UNBOUNDED PRECEDING )
                                                            AS FIRSTTOTDUE
INTO    #2
FROM    #ORDERS
ORDER BY SALESPERSONID ,
        ORDERMONTH;

SELECT  DATEDIFF(MS, @T1, GETDATE()) AS 'FIRSTVALUE TIME (ROWS)';
```

Listing 17:   Comparing logically equivalent CROSS APPLY and FIRST_VALUE queries.

	CROSSAPPLY TIME
1	696

	FIRSTVALUE TIME (ROWS)
1	830

If we were to make a naïve judgment based only on these figures, we'd conclude that FIRST_VALUE runs a little slower and so, in terms of duration at least, there seems little reason to use it. However, don't leap to any conclusions because we've yet to gain the full performance picture. Let's start a profiler trace and then rerun Listing 17.

EventClass	TextData	CPU	Reads	Writes	Duration	SPID
SQL:BatchCompleted	DROP TABLE #1 DROP TABLE #2	16	232	0	4	53
SQL:BatchCompleted	/* CROSS APPLY */ DECLARE @T1 DA...	2141	788391	1024	695	53
SQL:BatchCompleted	/* FIRST_VALUE */ DECLARE @T1 DA...	812	2262	1032	811	53

Figure 4:   Profiler trace results for CROSS APPLY versus FIRST_VALUE.

Although the duration of the FIRST_VALUE query exceeds that for the CROSS APPLY query, the number of reads for CROSS APPLY is vastly greater. You'll see, as well, that the CPU time is much greater than the duration in the case of the CROSS APPLY query.

What's happened here is that the CROSS APPLY query exceeded SQL Server's cost threshold for parallelism threshold and so the optimizer has produced a **parallel plan**. However, SQL Server did not parallelize the FIRST_VALUE query, simply because the threshold cost was not crossed. Accidentally comparing parallel and serial plans is another common problem in performance tests, and it complicates the answer to the question "which is faster?"

If you run this test on a system with only one available CPU, or with parallelism disabled, you should see that FIRST_VALUE query is at least twice as fast. Ultimately, which one will perform better at scale with many concurrent requests of this and other queries? The answer is FIRST_VALUE.

Summary

With support for sliding windows of data, SQL Server 2012 offers a way to perform complex analytical calculations in a more succinct and high-performance fashion. I hope that this chapter offers you some ideas for how we can exploit them to solve more business problems within the SQL Server engine than has ever previously been possible.

SQL Server Security 101

Diana Dee

In theory, SQL Server security sounds simple. We grant permissions to the people and processes that need access to our SQL Server instances and databases, while controlling which data they can access and what actions they can perform.

However, behind this simple statement lies much complexity. In practice, it is easy for the novice database administrator (DBA) to get lost in the hierarchy of *principals*, *securables* and *permissions* that comprise the SQL Server security architecture. The most common result is the path of least resistance, where people end up with "too many privileges." They can access data they shouldn't be able to see; they can perform actions they have no need to perform. Most people may be unaware of their over-privileged status. However, if an illegitimate person gains access to their credentials, it will, of course, compromise the security and integrity of your databases and their data.

My primary goals in this chapter are to provide a simple, concise description of how the SQL Server permission hierarchy works, and then to demonstrate, step by step, how to implement the "Principle of Least Privilege" in securing SQL Server. According to this principle, any person or process that we allow to access a SQL Server instance, and any database in it, should have just enough privileges to perform their job, and no more.

Any DBA tasked with implementing basic security within a SQL Server instance should refer first to their written security plan to find a detailed specification of who should be allowed to do what. After reading this chapter, they should then be able to implement that plan, ensuring access to only the necessary objects, and the ability to perform only essential actions, within that instance and its databases.

Securing SQL Server, the Bigger Picture

You need only glance through the *Securing SQL Server* topic in Books Online to understand just what's involved in the task of making sure our SQL Server machines, instances and databases are secure from unauthorized access. Starting at the "outside" and working in, we need to consider:

- **Securing the physical hardware and the network** – network firewalls, Windows Firewall on the computer hosting the SQL Server instance (hereinafter referred to as the "computer host"), and restricted-access server rooms.

- **Securing the Windows operating system on the computer host** – careful account and permission management at the Windows level, plus application of all service packs, security fixes, and so on.

- **Auditing of actions and object access within the SQL Server instance** – government regulations mandate many of these auditing requirements.

- **Encrypting certain data, or entire databases, as necessary** – never store or transmit personal and sensitive data in plain text form.

- **Protecting backups from unauthorized access** – unless we encrypt the backup file directly or use transparent data encryption, then someone can read it.

- **Securing the SQL Server instance** – granting permissions to perform actions or access objects.

This chapter covers only the very last of those bullet points.

SQL Server Security Architecture, a Brief Overview

Security architecture for SQL Server consists of a hierarchical collection of resources, called **securables**, which we can secure with **permissions**. We grant these permissions to **principals**. The permissions that we can grant depend on the securable. The principal to which we can grant permission depends on where we are in the securable hierarchy.

We'll discuss the securable and principal hierarchies in more detail as soon as we've nailed down the definitions of these key terms.

- A **principal** is an *authenticated identity* to which we may grant a permission, allowing the principal to access a securable, or perform a certain action on that securable. Examples of principals include a **Windows user**; a **SQL Server login**; a **database user**, or a **database role.**

- A **securable** is a *resource* to which the SQL Server authorization system controls access. Associated with each securable are a set of permissions we can grant to a principal (depending on where we are in the securable hierarchy). Examples of securables include a **database**; a **table.**

- A **permission** *controls the access* of a principal to a securable. Within SQL Server, permissions are implicitly denied; that is, a principal does not have a permission unless we explicitly grant it. Examples of permissions include **CREATE**, **SELECT**, and **EXECUTE**.

We can think of the SQL Server Security hierarchy as a set of nested containers, similar to a folder hierarchy in Windows Explorer, or similar to a city block containing buildings, which in turn contain rooms, which in turn contain objects, or "content." Books Online provides a good illustration of this hierarchy, which I reproduce here. For the original, see: HTTP://TECHNET.MICROSOFT.COM/EN-US/LIBRARY/MS191465.ASPX.

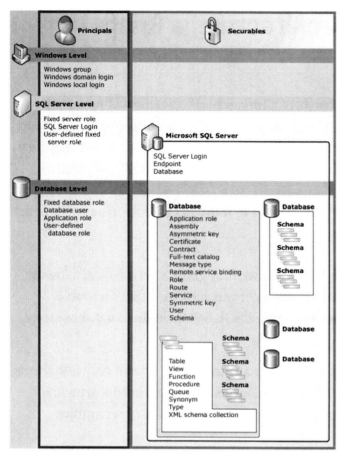

Figure 1:   The permission hierarchies.

Imagine that the city block represents the Windows operating system, the outermost level of the hierarchy. On the city block sits a building that represents the SQL Server instance (an installation of SQL Server). A principal needs permission to enter the building. Within the building's walls are a few objects, and the principal may be granted permissions on these objects.

The building also contains rooms that represent databases, and a principal needs permission to enter each room. Within each room, there exist objects, organized into a set of containers. This is the database level of the hierarchy and a principal who can enter a database may be granted permission on the database and/or its schema and objects.

The hierarchy of principals

The outermost container in the principal hierarchy is the Windows operating system (OS), on the computer host. Principals at the OS container level are:

- Windows local groups and users.

- Active Directory groups and users (if the computer host is in an Active Directory domain).

Within this hierarchy, a SQL Server instance is an application installed within the Windows operating system. A SQL Server instance, referred to as "the server," is a complete database environment created by one installation of SQL Server. At the SQL Server instance or server container level, the principals are:

- **SQL Server login** – there are two types of login, a *SQL-authenticated login* within the server, associated with a single SQL Server principal, or a *Windows login* based on a Windows operating system principal (Windows group or Windows user).

- **Server-level role** – a collection of SQL Server logins. Each member of a role receives all of the server-level permissions granted to that role.

Figure 2 shows the server-level principles in the SQL Server Management Studio (SSMS) Object Explorer.

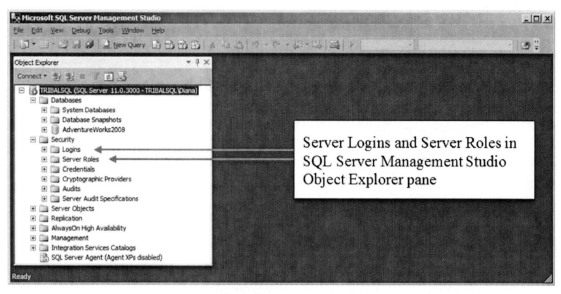

Figure 2:   Logins and server roles in SSMS.

Contained within the server are databases. The principals within a database are:

- **A database user** – an account defined within a specific database, and usually associated with a SQL Server login. Certain database user accounts appear by default in every database (though many are disabled by default). We can also create our own database users.

- **A database role** – a collection of database users. Each member of a database role receives all of the permissions granted to that role, for that database. SQL Server provides a number of fixed database roles that exist in every database, as well as the ability to create user-defined database roles.

- **An application role** – after an application connects to a database using a login mapped to a user, the application may change context to the application role by supplying the name of the role and its password. After that, the connection to the database has the permissions of the application role, and can connect to any another database only as the guest user in the other database. Application roles are not covered in further detail; see Books Online, *Application Roles*, for more information.

Figure 3 shows the database-level principals in SSMS object explorer, under the **Security** folder of the AdventureWorks2012 database.

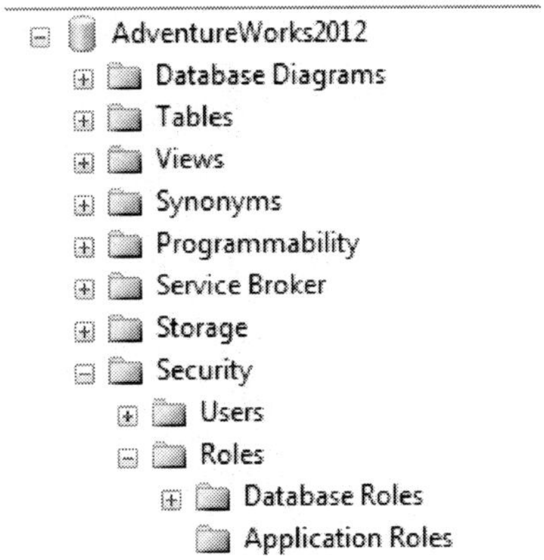

Figure 3:   Users and roles in SSMS.

The hierarchy of securables

In a similar fashion, we have a hierarchy of resources to which the database engine can regulate access, using permissions. From the perspective of the DBA, these securables start at coarse-grained (server-level and database-level) down to fine-grained (individual objects within a database).

Windows OS-level securables

Windows OS securables are Windows registry keys and folders. Certain Windows users that act as "service accounts" in SQL Server get automatic permissions to certain registry keys. We'll discuss service account security in more detail later. However, DBAs normally do not need to be concerned with granting permissions on Windows registry keys.

Within the SQL Server instance (the server), the securable hierarchy follows the four-part SQL Server object naming convention:

server.database.schema.object

We will refer to each level ("nested container") within the hierarchy as a "level". Books Online refers to the first three levels as "scopes." Each of these four levels forms the major focus of this chapter. We assign permissions at each level.

Granting permissions in the hierarchy

Server-scoped securables offer server-level permissions, which we can grant only to server-level principals. Likewise, database-scoped securables have associated database-level permissions, which we can grant only to database-level principals. At the schema scope and object level, there are various schema- and object-level permissions, which we can grant to database-level principals.

For example, SQL Server logins may connect to the server and be granted permissions at the server level, or be placed in a server-level role. Examples of server-level permissions include **ALTER TRACE** and **CREATE ANY DATABASE**. Database users may connect to their database and be granted permissions, such as **CREATE TABLE** and **SELECT** at the database, schema, or object level, or be placed in a database role.

However, we can't grant permissions to logins, a server-level principal, at the database scope. For example, **BACKUP DATABASE** and **BACKUP LOG** are database-scope permissions and we must grant them to a database user in the database; we cannot grant them to a login. To put it another way, if we have a login called **TribalSQL\SQL Users** and an associated database user called **SQLUsers**, we must grant permissions on database scope securables, and all contained securables, to **SQLUsers**, not to **TribalSQL\SQL Users**.

All contained schema or objects inherit a permission granted at the database scope, and below, in the hierarchy. For example, granting `EXECUTE` permission on the database will, in effect, grant `EXECUTE` permission on every stored procedure, user-defined function, and user-defined data type in the database.

Although we may grant permissions to a principal on each individual object, if the principal needs the same permission on more than one object, it is easier to group those objects in a **schema**. If we grant, to a principal, permissions at the schema scope, then that principal inherits the same permissions on all relevant objects in the schema. For example, granting `SELECT` permission on a schema to a principal will, in effect, grant `SELECT` permission on every table and view in that schema to the principal.

The three permission keywords

As noted earlier, the SQL Server security model denies permission by default; we have to assign explicitly the appropriate permission, using the `GRANT` keyword. There are cases where we might grant, to a database user, permission at the database scope that we wish to deny at the schema scope, or on a particular object, in which case we can use the `DENY` keyword.

- **GRANT** – allows a principal to perform the action relating to the permission granted.

- **DENY** – denies an action; overrides a `GRANT` that the principal may have from a role membership or from an inherited `GRANT` at a higher scope.

- **REVOKE** – removes a `GRANT` or a `DENY`. Think of `REVOKE` as an eraser, removing the `GRANT` or `DENY` permission. This is the same as unchecking a box in the GUI.

Applying the Principle of Least Privilege

Instead of granting too much privilege, the DBA should take care to grant privileges so that all people or processes accessing the SQL Server will be able to perform the tasks they need to, and no more.

Following is the step-by-step methodology for following the Principle of Least Privilege, which we'll work through over the coming sections of this chapter, followed by some end-to-end examples. The existence of the principal and securable hierarchies should inform your understanding of why these steps are necessary.

1. Create a Windows group to contain Windows users who need the same privileges within SQL Server.

2. Create a login to SQL Server for that group. If a SQL Server-authenticated login is required (because a login from Windows cannot be used), create it.

3. Grant or deny server-level permissions, as required by the security plan, or place the login in a server-level role having appropriate permissions, if appropriate to meet security plan requirements.

4. Map the login to a user in the relevant database(s).

5. Grant/deny permissions to the database user, or place the user in a fixed or administrator-defined database role, as appropriate.

Creating SQL Server logins

A SQL Server login ("login") allows a person or application to authenticate to, and connect to, the server. A login is a server-scope principal.

There are two main types of logins: a **Windows login** ("login from Windows"), created from a Windows security principal, and a **SQL-authenticated login** ("SQL login"), created in the SQL Server instance. We can also create a login from a certificate or asymmetric key but we will not cover those login types in this chapter.

SQL Server autocreates some logins during installation (take a look at the **Logins** folder in Object Explorer). We'll describe some of these later, in the section, *Auto-created logins and sysadmin*.

Login from Windows

SQL Server recognizes Windows groups and Windows user accounts, both on the computer host and in the Active Directory domain of which the computer host is a member.

It is a best practice to create a login from a Windows group, as opposed to one login for each individual Windows user. This allows permission control by adding or removing Windows users from the Windows group.

Following are instructions for creating a login from Windows for SQL Server, in SSMS Object Explorer. In these instructions, angle brackets < > indicate a place for you to enter a value; the angle brackets are not typed.

Expand the server's **Security** folder, right-click **Logins** and then select **New Login** to bring up the **Login – New** dialog. In the **Login name** box, either:

- Type the Windows group name in the format <domain>\<group>. The domain is either the Active Directory domain or the name of the computer host (to use the local computer's security database).

- Alternatively, click the **Search** button to the right of the **Login name** box to find the appropriate, recognized Windows group through the **Select User or Group** dialog. Ensure that **Object Types** includes **Group**. In **Locations**, choose the domain or the local computer. In the **Enter the object name to select** box, type the group name, and then click the **Check Names** button. If the group is recognized, the name will appear in <domain>\<group> format with an underline. Click **OK** to have the <domain>\<group> item placed into the **Login Name** box of the **Login – New** dialog. The resulting dialog should look as shown in Figure 4.

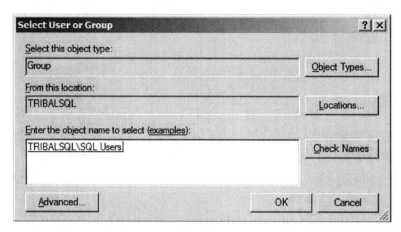

Figure 4:   Creating a login from a recognized Windows group.

Back at the **Login – New** dialog, we're obviously going to use Windows authentication, and we can leave all the other options at their default settings.

At the bottom of Figure 5, you'll see that the default database is master. The login will connect automatically to this database when it establishes a connection to the server. We may choose any user-defined database as the login's default database, but keep in mind that the login must be mapped to a user in that database in order for the login to successfully connect to the server. The master database allows guest access and so we don't need to map the login to a user in master.

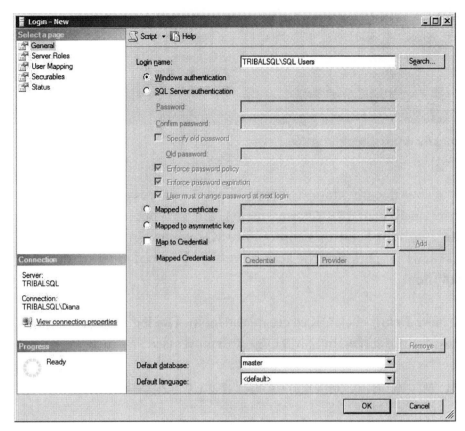

Figure 5:   The Login – New dialog for the `TribalSQL/SQL Users` Windows group.

Before clicking **OK** to create the login, click the **Script** button to capture the CREATE LOGIN script to a new query window.

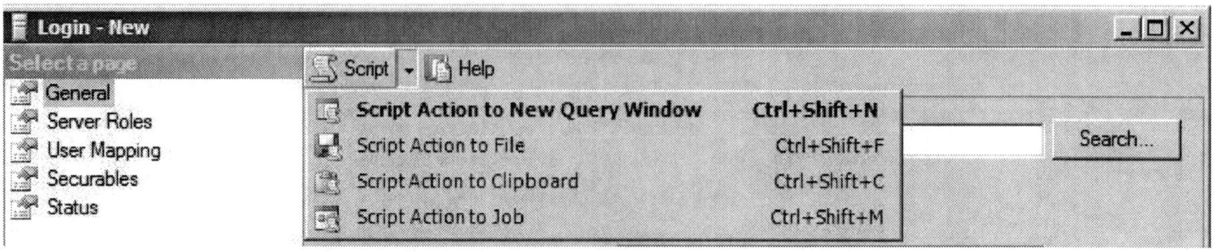

Figure 6:   Script options for documenting an action.

Save the query as part of your documentation. Alternatively, if you are creating a Solution in SSMS to contain all your **CREATE** statements, you can choose **Script Action to Clipboard** and paste it into the Solution's appropriate SQL script window. The Transact-SQL (T-SQL) code that performs the action can then be saved together in a Project within the Solution.

Finally, in the **Login – New** dialog, click **OK** to create the login. The login name will appear under the **Logins** for the server, in SSMS Object Explorer (see Figure 2).

Alternatively, of course, we can create the login directly from T-SQL code, as demonstrated in Listing 1.

```
CREATE LOGIN [TribalSQL\SQL Users] FROM WINDOWS
WITH DEFAULT_DATABASE = [master];
GO
```

Listing 1:   Create a login for a Windows group named SQL Users, in a domain named TribalSQL.

When a Windows user logs on to Windows, whether using Kerberos or NTLM authentication, an access token is created and attached to the user's Windows process. This access token contains the security identifier (SID) of the user, the SIDs of all the groups of which the user is a member, the SIDs of any groups nested with those groups, and so on.

When the Windows user attempts to connect to a SQL Server instance (think of the **Connect to Server** dialog you see when you open SSMS), the Windows user's access token is presented to the server. If any of the SIDs match a login from Windows, the user will successfully connect to the server.

SQL Server "trusts" the authentication of the Windows user that Windows performed; thus, a Windows connection to a SQL Server is a trusted connection and therefore the Windows user does not have to present a user name and password to the SQL Server.

SQL-authenticated logins

A login created within the SQL Server instance is a **SQL-authenticated login** ("SQL login"), because the server creates and stores a user name and a (hashed) password for that login. A SQL login is a "singleton" and not a group login.

We can only use SQL logins to connect to a server that is using "SQL Server and Windows Authentication mode." The other server authentication mode is "Windows Authentication mode" and is more secure, as it allows only trusted connections. However, it may be necessary to allow SQL Server-authenticated connections, because some front-end applications can use only SQL logins to connect. We can change the server authentication mode on the Security page of the Server Properties window. Restart the SQL Server service for the change to take effect.

To create a SQL login, use the **Login – New** dialog as explained for Windows logins, but select the SQL Server authentication radio button and enter a name for the login and the password details.

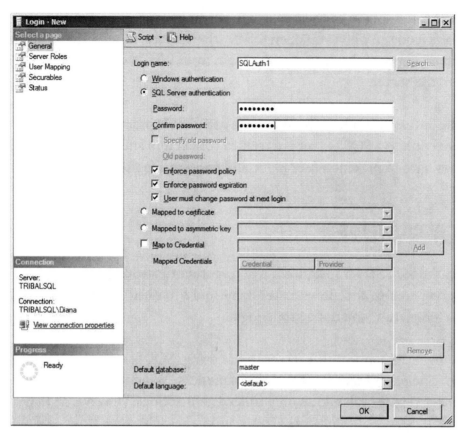

Figure 7:   Login – New dialog for a SQL login.

SQL logins in SQL Server 2005 or later can use one of three password enforcement options. These enforcement options may be used if the computer host's operating system is Windows Server 2003 or later, or Windows Vista or later. The password enforcement options take the Windows account policies that apply to the computer host and apply them to the SQL login, according to which password enforcement policies are selected for the login.

- **Enforce password policy** (T-SQL: CHECK_POLICY=ON) enforces settings of the following Windows Account Policy settings: Password must meet complexity requirements; Minimum password length; Minimum password age; Enforce password history.

- **Enforce password expiration** (T-SQL: CHECK_EXPIRATION=ON) enforces the following account policies: Maximum password age; Account lockout threshold; Account lockout duration; Reset account lockout counter after. CHECK_POLICY must be ON to enable this option.

- **User must change password at next login** (T-SQL: MUST_CHANGE) enforces the Windows user account property of that name. CHECK_EXPIRATION must be ON to enable this option.

If the computer host is a member of a Windows Active Directory domain, the Windows account policy settings linked to the Organizational Unit (OU) to which the computer host belongs will take precedence over the settings in any parent OUs. Those, in turn, will take precedence over any policy settings linked to the domain, which will take precedence over any policy settings set on the local computer. If the computer host is not a member of a domain, the policy settings set on the local computer will be in effect. You can find a good explanation of all Windows Account Policies at: HTTP://TECHNET.MICROSOFT.COM/EN-US/LIBRARY/DD349793(V=WS.10).ASPX.

Details for the default database for the login are as described previously, and we can script out the login creation. Listing 2 creates the login named SQLAuth1 with a password of Pa$$w0rd, and enables the three password policy options.

```
USE [master]
GO
CREATE LOGIN [SQLAuth1]
  WITH PASSWORD=N'Pa$$w0rd'
       DEFAULT_DATABASE=[master],
       CHECK_EXPIRATION=ON,
       CHECK_POLICY=ON,
       MUST_CHANGE;
GO
```

Listing 2:   T-SQL for creating a SQL login.

When a person or application wants to connect to the server with SQL authentication, the login name and password must be presented to the SQL Server instance. If the connection is over a network, this information is sent in clear, unless the transmission is encrypted.

Fixed server-level roles

There are several built-in, or fixed, server-level roles and any member inherits all permissions assigned to that role. A login may be placed in a server-level role when the permissions the role has are appropriate for the login.

It is all too common that a login is placed in the **sysadmin** server-level role, in a situation in which the login does not need the privileges that role provides. Be aware of the privileges each role provides; do not place a login in a server-level role unless the login needs all the privileges of the role.

The Books Online topic, Permissions of Fixed Server Roles (Database Engine) lists all the built-in server-level roles, and the permissions granted to each role, but here are a few of the more significant roles:

- **sysadmin** – members can perform any action in the SQL Server instance. Granting CONTROL SERVER permission to an individual login is almost equivalent to sysadmin membership; the difference is that DENY permissions will apply (whereas DENY permissions to a sysadmin member are ignored).

- **securityadmin** – members can manage logins. Members can grant server-level and database-level permissions. Note: a security admin member may grant CONTROL SERVER permission to a login other than itself.

- **dbcreator** – members can create, alter, drop, and restore databases.

With the exception of `public`, we cannot change the permissions granted to a built-in server-level role. Starting with SQL Server 2012, we can create additional, **user-defined server-level** roles.

Every login is automatically a member of the `public` server-level role, introduced in SQL Server 2008; permissions assigned to the `public` role apply to all logins. By default, the `public` role has the `VIEW ANY DATABASE` permission, meaning that any login may see all the databases that exist on the server (although not what is in them).

Windows Administrators group and sysadmin

Through SQL Server 2005, but not in SQL Server 2008 and later, SQL Server automatically created a login based on the computer host's local Administrators group, `BUILTIN\Administrators`, and added it to the `sysadmin` server role.

If the computer host is a member of a Windows domain, the domain's `Domain Admins` global group is automatically a member of the computer's `BUILTIN\Administrators` group. For SQL 2005 and earlier, any Windows user who is a `Domain Admins` member can connect to and perform any action in the server. This is an important security consideration. In SQL 2005, or earlier, the DBA should make sure the appropriate logins exist and are in `sysadmin`, and then remove the `BUILTIN\Administrators` group as a login.

SQL Server service accounts and sysadmin

Each SQL Server component runs on Windows as a Windows service and each service runs in the context of a Windows user account. That Windows user account appears as a login and is often a member of **sysadmin**. As a DBA, you need to know about these accounts so you don't delete them. The accounts usually have all the permissions they need within SQL Server, but you may need to grant a permission in the operating system, for example to enable SQL Server to connect to a network share being used to receive SQL Server backups.

The database engine runs as the SQL Server service. Other services include:

- SQL Server Agent service

- SQL Server Integration Services (IS) service

- SQL Server Browser service

- Full-text Filter Daemon Launcher service

- A service for each of the other components, if installed (Analysis Services, Reporting Services).

Except for Browser and IS services, each installed SQL Server instance has its own set of services, and these services are said to be "instance aware." For example, the database engine service for a default instance of SQL Server is `MSSQLSERVER`, whereas for an instance named `DBENGINE2`, the database engine service is `DBENGINE2`.

When running SQL Server 2005 or later, you can see all the SQL Server-related services running on the server using SQL Server Configuration Manager tool (**Start** > **All Programs** > **Microsoft SQL Server nnnn** > **Configuration Tools** > **SQL Server Configuration Manager**).

Select **SQL Server Services** in the left pane and a list of services will appear on the right. A service for the default instance of SQL Server will have `(MSSQLSERVER)` at the end of its name whereas a named instance will have `(instance_name)`.

Name	State	Start Mode	Log On As	Process ID	Service Type
SQL Server Integration Services 11.0	Running	Automatic	NT Service\MsDtsServer110	1136	
SQL Full-text Filter Daemon Launch...	Running	Manual	NT Service\MSSQLFDLauncher	724	
SQL Server (MSSQLSERVER)	Running	Automatic	.\SQL_Server	1540	SQL Server
SQL Server Browser	Stopped	Other (Boot, Sy...	NT AUTHORITY\LOCALSERVICE	0	
SQL Server Agent (MSSQLSERVER)	Stopped	Manual	.\SQL_Agent	0	SQL Agent

Left pane:
- SQL Server Configuration Manager (Local)
  - SQL Server Services
  - SQL Server Network Configuration (32bit)
  - SQL Native Client 11.0 Configuration (32bit)
  - SQL Server Network Configuration
  - SQL Native Client 11.0 Configuration

Figure 8:   SQL Server services as shown in SQL Server Configuration Manager.

The **Log On As** column reveals the Windows user account under which the service is running.

The two most important Windows user accounts are those for the SQL Server and SQL Server Agent services. In SQL Server 2008, the SQL Server installation process creates the following two Windows groups on the local "host" computer (the groups may have different names in SQL Server 2005):

- `SQLServerMSSQLUser$`**`computer`**`$MSSQLSERVER` – for the SQL Server service

- `SQLServerMSSQLAgentUser$`**`computer`**`$MSSQLSERVER` – for the SQL Server Agent service.

The character string **computer** will be the name of the computer host. A named instance will have the instance name at the end of the group name, instead of `MSSQLSERVER`.

The Windows user account for the SQL Server service is placed into the `...MSSQLUser...` group; the Windows user account for the SQL Server Agent service is placed into the `...MSSQLAgentUser...` group.

SQL Server automatically creates a login based on each of these Windows groups and places them into the `sysadmin` role, meaning that the service Windows user accounts are granted `sysadmin` privileges within the SQL Server instance.

SQL Server 2012 assigns new account types to the SQL Server services. In a Windows domain, a **Managed Service Account** should be created in Active Directory (AD) prior to installation, with the name having the format: `DOMAIN\ACCOUNTNAME$`. If a computer is not a member of a Windows AD domain, a Virtual Account is automatically created, with the name `NT SERVICE\<SERVICENAME>`. For example, for the default instance database engine: `NT SERVICE\MSSQLSERVER` will be the SQL Server service account, and `NT SERVICE\SQLSERVERAGENT` will be the SQL Server Agent service account.

Follow these steps to implement "least privileges" security for the service accounts:

- If possible, use different Windows user accounts for the SQL Server and SQL Server Agent services. There are more circumstances requiring the SQL Server Agent s ervice account to be a Windows administrator than there are for the SQL Server service account.

- Preferably, make the accounts in the AD domain. Make the accounts on the local computer host if the computer does not belong to an AD domain.

- Set the account property **Password never expires** – an expired password for the service's Windows user means the service will not start!

- Use complex passwords and store them securely.

- Create the Windows user accounts that will run the services before installing the SQL Server instance that will use them.

- Do not place the Windows user accounts that will run the services in any group, to avoid the account having privileges it does not need. The SQL Server installation process (or changing the account using SQL Server Configuration Manager) will give the account appropriate privileges.

- Never allow a real person to use the Windows user accounts for the SQL Server services.

Auto-created logins and sysadmin

SQL Server creates the following logins and makes them members of the `sysadmin` server-level role, by default:

- **sa** – This is a special SQL Server-authenticated login. If using Windows authentication mode, we don't have to specify a password for **sa** during installation. If using Windows and SQL Server authentication mode (or subsequently switching to this mode), assign a strong password to the **sa** login, or disable it by denying **CONNECT** permission.

- **The Windows user account that installs the SQL Server instance** – this Windows user account can be "provisioned" as a login during installation and is placed into sysadmin.

- **A Windows user account under which a service runs** – as explained previously. Use SQL Server Configuration Manager, not the Windows Services applet, if you need to change this account.

Server-level permissions

Following are the types of securable on which we may assign server-level permissions:

- The server instance.

- Endpoints – connection points to SQL Server; not discussed further.

- Logins.

- Server role (SQL Server 2012 only).

- Availability groups (SQL Server 2012 only).

To see a list of permissions that apply to the server, see the Books Online topic, *Permissions (Database Engine)*. For SQL Server 2012, you can find this at HTTP://MSDN.MICROSOFT.COM/EN-US/LIBRARY/MS191291.ASPX.

Within this reference, scroll down to the table labeled *SQL Server Permissions*. Within this SQL Server Permissions table, scroll down to the point at which the first column has the value SERVER. The second column will show all the permissions for the base securable SERVER. The table also shows possible permissions for endpoints, logins, and server roles.

Formatting tip for the SQL Server Permissions table

If you want to copy the Permissions table to Excel, set the page to landscape and, before the copy, pre-set the first five column widths to: 25.22, 33.22, 8.11, 17.00, and 34.44.

It may not be easy to discover what permissions you need to grant at the server level to conform to the Principle of Least Privilege. Sometimes, permissions granted to a fixed server role might allow more actions than you want to permit the login to perform.

If you look up, in Books Online, the Transact-SQL (T-SQL) command of an action you want to grant a principal permission to perform, the Permissions section of that command will tell you what permissions are required for that action. For example, the **CREATE DATABASE** action requires us to grant either **CREATE ANY DATABASE** or **ALTER ANY DATABASE** server-level permission to the login that needs to create databases. As another example, the **ALTER TRACE** permission is required to set up and run a trace in SQL Profiler.

To grant a server-level permission in SSMS Object Explorer, right-click on the server (the securable), select **Properties** and select the **Permissions** page. In the upper **Logins or roles** pane, select the login or role to which you want to grant the permissions. In the lower pane, on the **Explicit** tab, which show the explicitly-granted permissions, select the check box in the **Grant** column, opposite each permission required (the **Effective** tab shows the accumulated permissions from role membership, plus explicit permissions).

Notice that the **Connect SQL** permission is already granted to the selected login. Capture the script for documentation, and then click **OK**.

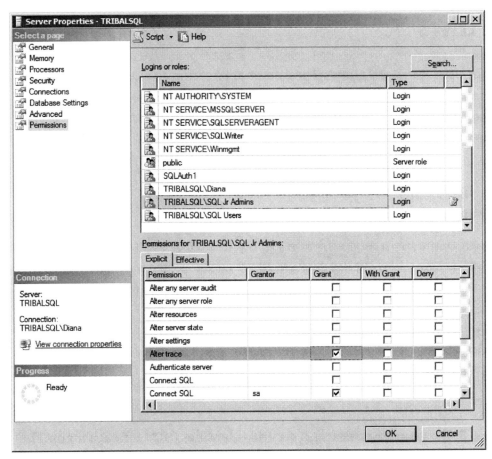

Figure 9: Granting ALTER TRACE permission to the SQL Jr Admins login.

We can grant and deny server-level permissions with Transact-SQL code, as demonstrated in Listing 3.

```
GRANT ALTER TRACE TO [TribalSQL\SQL Jr Admins];

DENY VIEW ANY DATABASE TO [TribalSQL\SQL Users];
```

Listing 3: Granting and denying server-level permissions.

Database users

A database user (or user, for short) allows a person or application to authenticate to, and connect to, the database in which the user is defined. The database user type primarily described in this chapter is one that is mapped from a login (CREATE USER...FOR LOGIN). We'll cover the special case of a contained database, introduced in SQL Server 2012, a little later.

Users without logins and users created from a certificate or key

There are other users, created from a certificate or from a key (e.g. CREATE USER...FOR CERTIFICATE), or users created without logins, using CREATE USER...WITHOUT LOGIN. We won't cover these user types in this chapter but Raul Garcia's blog, Quick Guide to DB users without logins in SQL Server 2005, explains how to use a WITHOUT LOGIN user for impersonation:
HTTP://BLOGS.MSDN.COM/B/RAULGA/ARCHIVE/2006/07/03/655587.ASPX.
Note that a user without login may not connect to a database, but must be used via execution context switching after a connection is made.

SQL Server stores, in the master database, a security identifier (SID) for each login. The SID of a login from Windows is the same as the SID for the Windows group (or Windows user) stored in the Windows operating system. Therefore, a login from a particular Windows group (or user) on any SQL Server instance in the domain will have the same SID for the login. On the other hand, the SID for a SQL-authenticated login will be random, because it is created within the SQL Server instance. Two SQL-authenticated logins named Bob on two different instances with have two different SIDs.

When we map a login to a user in a database, SQL Server stores the SID of the login in the database, as the SID of the user created from that login. In other words, the login SID and the database user SID match (we'll deal with cases where they don't, called *orphaned users*, a little later).

Default database users

SQL Server creates certain users in every database, by default:

- **dbo** – this is an acronym for "database owner." Members of the `sysadmin` server-level role are mapped to this user, by default. This user is a member of the `db_owner` database role and can perform any action on or in the database.

- **guest** – this user is disabled by default. With the **guest** user enabled (by granting it `CONNECT` permission for the database), any login not explicitly mapped to a user in the database may connect to the database as `guest`.

- **sys** – this user owns the `sys` schema, and is disabled by default.

- **INFORMATION_SCHEMA** – this user owns the `INFORMATION_SCHEMA` schema, and is disabled by default.

If you want a user to appear in every database created on (not restored to) a server, create the user in the `model` database.

Creating database users

To create a user in SSMS (for any database except a contained database – see later), expand the **Security** folder, right-click the **Users** folder, and then click **New User** to bring up the **Database User – New** dialog. Enter the details as shown in Figure 9 (using the ellipsis button to search for the correct, associated login). Notice that the user name does not have to be the same as the login name.

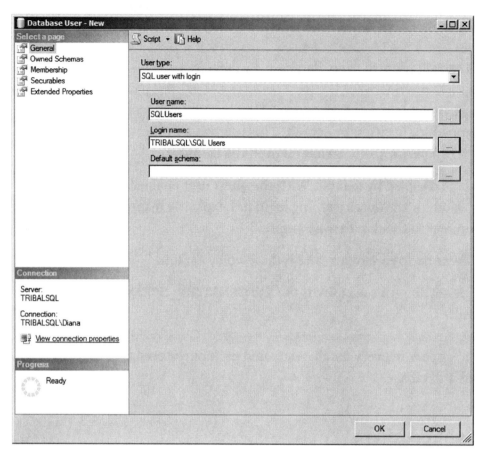

Figure 10: Create a SQLUsers database user for the TribalSQL\SQL Users login.

Listing 4 shows the equivalent T-SQL script for creating this user (be sure you are connected to the appropriate database).

```
CREATE USER [SQLUsers] FOR LOGIN [TribalSQL\SQL Users];
```

Listing 4: T-SQL to create the SQLUsers user.

To see more of the CREATE USER command syntax, see the Books Online topic, *CREATE USER (Transact-SQL)*.

The problem of orphaned users

As noted earlier, when we create a user from a login, the SID of the user and associated login will match, allowing the user to connect to the server and thence to the database.

However, the situation can arise where these SIDs do not match. For example, when we restore a database backup from one SQL Server instance to a different target instance, we'll also restore, with that database, any associated users. Therefore, we might restore to the target a database user called Bob but the new instance might have no login for Bob, or there might be an existing login called Bob on the target instance, but its SID will not match the SID for the restored user. In such cases, Bob is what we call an "orphaned" user.

There are a couple of useful catalog views for exploring login and user SIDs, shown in Listing 5.

```
-- logins (execute within any database)
SELECT    name ,
          principal_id ,
          sid ,
          type ,
          type_desc
FROM      sys.server_principals
WHERE     name NOT LIKE '##%';

-- users (execute within databas of interest)
SELECT    name ,
          principal_id ,
          sid ,
          type ,
          type_desc
FROM      sys.database_principals
WHERE     name NOT LIKE 'db_%'
```

Listing 5:   Scripts for determining SIDs.

We can synchronize the user's SID (user Bob in our example) to the login's SID by executing Listing 6, when connected to the database on the target instance.

```
ALTER USER Bob WITH LOGIN = Bob;
```

Listing 6:   Synchronizing an orphaned user with a login.

Alternatively, we can use the sp_change_users_login stored procedure to discover orphaned users and synchronize login and user SIDs, although beware that Microsoft has that procedure on the deprecated list, so it will be removed from a future version.

If you need many logins on another instance, you can use the Integration Services Transfer Logins task.

Database users for contained databases

SQL Server 2012 introduced a new kind of database, called contained databases, although the term "partially contained" might be more accurate since certain related objects, such as jobs that connect to the database, are not contained in the database.

In a contained database, we can create users that the database, rather than the SQL Server instance, authenticates. Therefore, we don't have to map these users to a login.

We can back up a contained database and restore it to a different instance without worrying about synchronizing user and login SIDs, therefore solving the orphaned user problem. This helps, for example, in moving or copying a database from test to production, or from a production version to other members of an Always On Availability Group. A user that authenticates at the contained database may connect directly to that database.

For a contained database, the Principle of Least Privilege steps are as follows:

1. Create a Windows group to contain Windows users who need the same privileges within the database.

2. Create a user in the contained database for that group. If a database-authenticated user is required (because a Windows principal cannot be used), create it.

3. Grant/deny permissions to the database user, or place the user in a fixed or administrator-defined database role, as appropriate.

Database roles

A **database role** is a database-level principal that we use to group together database users who need the same permission or permission set.

Every database has several "fixed" database roles that exist by default. Permissions assigned to a fixed database role (except **public**) cannot be altered. Some of the key fixed database roles are:

- **db_owner** – Members can perform any action in the database and can drop the database. This is equivalent to CONTROL DATABASE permission. Members of **sysadmin** map to the dbo user in every database, and are thus a member of this database role.

- **db_backupoperator** – Members can back up the database.

- **db_datareader** – Members can SELECT data from all tables and views.

- **db_datawriter** – Members can INSERT, UPDATE, and DELETE data from all user tables and views. Note that UPDATE and DELETE statements usually target one or more specific rows, requiring a WHERE clause. A WHERE clause requires SELECT permission!

- **public** – All users are automatically members of this database role. Permissions granted to this role apply to all users in the database.

When a fixed database role does not have the permission set that fits the need (too little or too much permission), we can create a user-defined database role.

To add a user (or another database role) to a database role in SSMS, open the **Properties** window for that role and click the **Add** button near the bottom, to browse and select from the list of database users and roles. This method is best if you want to select multiple users/roles to add to the role.

If you have the **Properties** window for a user open, you may select a role to which to add the user. Be careful! The upper pane has a list of **Owned Schemas** that are named the same as database roles. Selecting one of these will give the user ownership of the schema. This is probably not what you want. Use the lower list, **Database role membership**, to select the role to which to add the user.

If you prefer the T-SQL route, Listing 7 provides the script to add the SQLUsers user to the db_datareader role.

```
EXEC sp_addrolemember N'db_datareader', N'SQLUsers'; -- through SQL 2008 R2

ALTER ROLE db_datareader ADD MEMBER SQLUsers; -- SQL Server 2012
```

Listing 7:   Adding a user to a database role.

Granting Least Privileges in the database: schema: object hierarchy

The goal of the Principle of Least Privilege is to grant the minimum permissions necessary so the person or application connecting to a database can accomplish their necessary tasks, and no more.

Sometimes though, this is easier to say than do. Books Online can be quite intimidating; the table in previously referenced *Permissions (Database Engine)* article lists about 200 individual permissions. How do we know exactly which permissions we need to perform a specific task? The approach I use is to create a document listing the required tasks and against them research and list the permissions required for each.

Sometimes this is relatively straightforward. For example, let's say our task is to allow one database user to create other database users (from logins that already exist). The first thing to do is search for the task "create database user" in Books Online. On that page, you'll find a *Permissions* section stating that this requires the ALTER ANY USER permission on the database.

Likewise, if the task is "Create a table," navigate to that task page and, in the *Permissions* section, it states that this will require CREATE TABLE permission on the database and ALTER permission on the schema in which we're creating the table. If you examine the SQL Server Permissions table in the previously referenced *Permissions (Database Engine)* topic, and scroll down to the SCHEMA / ALTER row, you'll see that this permission is inherited from DATABASE / ALTER ANY SCHEMA. Therefore, an alternative to granting ALTER permission on the schema is to grant ALTER ANY SCHEMA permission on the database, allowing table creation in any schema in that database. Also note that there is no CREATE TABLE permission at the schema level.

Remember that the security hierarchy is **Server > Database > Schema > Object**. At the server scope, permissions are granted to logins (or server roles). The server/database boundary represents a security boundary, because at the database scope and below, permissions are granted to users (or database roles). A login does not have any privileges within an existing database (unless the login is a sysadmin or has CONTROL SERVER permission).

At the database scope and below, a permission granted at a higher-level scope is inherited by all contained, lower-level scopes and objects in this hierarchy.

Schemas are incredibly useful for implementing the Least Privilege approach. For example, if a user needs UPDATE and DELETE permission on certain tables, we can create a schema, place the tables into that schema, and grant to that user UPDATE, DELETE, and SELECT permissions on that schema. If more than one user needed those permissions on those objects, we would create a database role, place the users in that role, and grant to that role those permissions on the schema.

Likewise, we can use a schema to prevent users from viewing objects containing sensitive data. For example, in the sample AdventureWorks database that models a mythical bicycle company, assume that the HumanResources schema contains tables and views with confidential information about employees. For users of the database who should not be allowed to view the confidential employee information, we can grant SELECT permission on the database, but deny SELECT permission on the HumanResources schema. Those permissions would allow the ability to read any table or view in the database except those in the HumanResources schema.

Granting permissions in SSMS

The process of granting permissions at each of the database, schema and object levels is very similar, and there are two ways to do it in each case. We can use either the **Permissions** page of the securable's **Properties** dialog, or the **Securables** page of the Properties dialog for the principal to which we wish to apply permissions.

Through the securable

In SSMS Object Explorer, open the **Properties** window for the database, or schema (under the **Security** folder in the database), or object and select the **Permissions** page. A list of database users and roles will appear in the **Users or roles** window. An existing database role or user will appear in the **Users or roles** window if it has already been granted a permission on the securable whose Properties window is open. Otherwise, add the user or role using the **Search** button.

Select the appropriate principal in that upper list and then select the permissions to grant or deny from the list below. Figure 11 shows an example of applying schema-level permissions to the SQLUsers user. Remember to capture the T-SQL script before clicking **OK**.

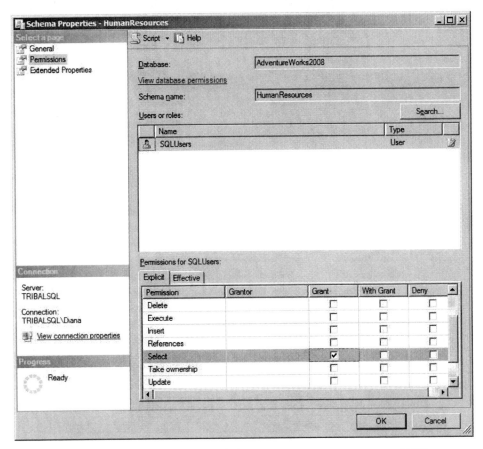

Figure 11:   Granting SELECT permission on HumanResources to SQLUsers.

Through the principal

Navigate to the **Securables** page of the principal's **Properties** window. The **Search** button is used to locate the object. Select **Specific objects**, then select the object type and select the desired object(s) from a list. Once you get the object into the **Securables** pane, you can use the lower pane to assign the permission(s) on that object.

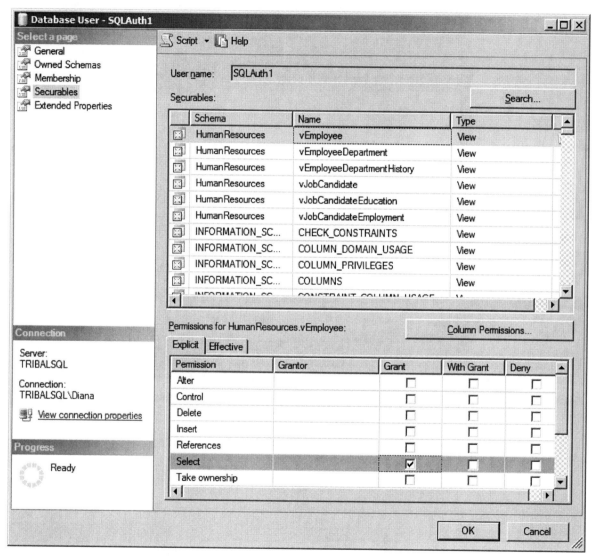

Figure 12: Granting `SELECT` permission on `vEmployees` to `SQLAuth1`.

Granting permissions in T-SQL

Using T-SQL to grant permissions might be easier. Listing 8 shows some examples.

```
/*Database scope*/
GRANT SELECT TO [SQLUsers];

/*Schema Scope*/
DENY SELECT ON SCHEMA::[HumanResources] TO [SQLUsers];

/*Object level*/
GRANT SELECT ON [HumanResources].[vEmployee] TO [SQLAuth1];
```

Listing 8:   Granting SELECT on a database, schema, or object.

The two colons following SCHEMA make SCHEMA:: a "scope identifier." This tells SQL Server that the [HumanResources] object is a schema.

Testing permissions

To test permissions for a Windows user, have the Windows administrator create a Windows user and place that user in the appropriate Windows group. Use **Run As** (or Switch user) to open SQL Server Management Studio as that Windows user, and connect to the server using Windows authentication.

You can also use the SQLCMD application to check permissions. The following command line code demonstrates a good way to open a command prompt window as another Windows user. It will show the Windows user (Alice, in this example), in the command prompt window title bar:

runas /noprofile /user:Alice cmd

You would then run SQLCMD as a "trusted" user in this command prompt window.

For a SQL Server-authenticated login, in SSMS, simply make a connection to the SQL instance using SQL Server authentication. In a command prompt window, use the —U option of SQLCMD.

Another way of checking permission is to switch execution context using EXECUTE AS.

Taking the "Least Privileges" Challenge

In this section, I'll describe two examples where you need to apply to principals the "least privileges" required to perform the stated task. I hope that you'll devise your own solutions before looking at the answers!

As a reminder, here is the permission assignment methodology given at the beginning of this chapter:

1. Create a Windows group to contain Windows users who need the same privileges within SQL Server.

2. Create a login to SQL Server for that group. If a SQL Server-authenticated login is required (because a login from Windows cannot be used), create it.

3. Grant or deny server-level permissions, if required by the security plan, or place the login in a server-level role having appropriate permissions.

4. Map the login to a user in relevant database(s).

5. Grant/deny permissions to the database user, or place the user in a fixed or administrator-defined database role, as appropriate.

Example 1

Assume that the **AdventureWorks** company is running a Windows domain named **AW**. Assume the computer host for the production SQL Server instance, **SQL1**, is a member of the **AW** domain.

The requirement in your permission plan is that a group of Windows users will be responsible for creating new databases and backing up all user databases.

Example 2

In the **AW** domain, on the test SQL Server instance, **SQLT1**, whose computer host is a domain member, a group of Windows users will be responsible for creating and testing stored procedures in the **AdventureWorks** database.

Answer 1

- Create a domain global group, **AW\SQLMaintenance**, and place the appropriate Windows users into this group.

- Create a login on the **SQLT1** production instance from the Windows group **AW\SQLMaintenance**.

- Place that login into the server-level role **dbcreator**. This will satisfy the requirement for the capability of creating new databases.

- Map that login to a user named **SQLMaintenance** in each user database.

- In each database, make the **SQLMaintenance** user a member of the **db_backupoperator** database role.

- The last two steps will satisfy the requirement for the capability to back up all user databases. If the same task is to be performed in many databases, consider using the undocumented sp_MSforeachdb procedure. (See, for example: HTTP://WEBLOGS.SQLTEAM.COM/JOEW/ARCHIVE/2008/08/27/60700.ASPX.)

Answer 2

[Hint: CREATE PROCEDURE requires CREATE PROCEDURE permission in the database and ALTER permission on the schema in which the procedure is being created.]

- Create a domain global group, AW\SQLDevelopers, and place the appropriate Windows users into this group.

- Create a login on the SQLT1 test instance from the Windows group AW\SQLDevelopers.

- Map that login to a user named SQLDevelopers in the AdventureWorks database.

- On the AdventureWorks database, grant CREATE PROCEDURE permission to SQLDevelopers.

- Create a schema, Procedures, to hold all of the created stored procedures.

- Grant ALTER and EXECUTE on the Procedures schema to the SQLDevelopers user. This allows both creation and testing of the stored procedures.

Note

If a member of sysadmin, *mapped to the* dbo *user in the database, creates a schema, that schema is, by default, owned by the* dbo *user. Objects created in the schema are, by default, owned by the schema owner. When a stored procedure owned by* dbo *is executed, the default execution context is the* dbo *user. Any action performed by the stored procedure will be allowed.*

Further exercise for the reader: How would you modify the above answer if `AdventureWorks` were a partially contained database and the Test server is running SQL Server 2012?

Summary and Next Steps

Now that you understand the securable and principal hierarchies, how to determine what permissions are required for an action and how to grant them, you have the knowledge you need to grant people and processes only the permissions they need, and no more.

Once you feel comfortable with the material presented in this chapter, consider expanding your knowledge and skills in the following areas:

- Execution context switching (**EXECUTE AS**).

- Transparent database encryption.

- Column-level encryption.

- Creating logins and users from certificates, used for code signing.

Further reading

- **SQL Server Books Online** (for whatever version you are using).

- ***Securing SQL Server, Second Edition***, Cherry, Denny (2012) Waltham, MA: Elsevier, Inc. ISBN: 978-1-59749-947-7

- ***SQL Server 2012 Security Best Practice Whitepaper***: HTTP://TINYURL.COM/6VXFH67

- *Context Switching (Database Engine)*, and subtopics:
  HTTP://TECHNET.MICROSOFT.COM/EN-US/LIBRARY/MS188268(V=SQL.105).ASPX

- *Transparent Data Encryption (TDE)*:
  HTTP://TECHNET.MICROSOFT.COM/EN-US/LIBRARY/BB934049.ASPX

- *Encrypt a Column of Data*:
  HTTP://TECHNET.MICROSOFT.COM/EN-US/LIBRARY/MS179331.ASPX

- Creating logins and users from certificates for the purpose of module signing:

  - *SQL Server 2005: procedure signing demo*, Laurentiu Cristofor, 2005:
    HTTP://BLOGS.MSDN.COM/B/LCRIS/ARCHIVE/2005/06/15/429631.ASPX

  - *Module Signing (Database Engine)*:
    HTTP://MSDN.MICROSOFT.COM/EN-US/LIBRARY/MS345102.ASPX

- *Giving Permissions through Stored Procedures
  (Ownership chaining, Certificates, and ... EXECUTE AS)*:
  Erland Summerskog, 2011:
  HTTP://WWW.SOMMARSKOG.SE/GRANTPERM.HTML

- Catalog views to list permissions, principals, and role members:
  See *Security Catalog Views (Transact-SQL)*:
  HTTP://TECHNET.MICROSOFT.COM/EN-US/LIBRARY/MS178542.ASPX

What Changed? Auditing Solutions in SQL Server

Colleen Morrow

Picture this: it's a beautiful morning. The sun is shining; big, fluffy clouds dot the sky. Perhaps it's early autumn and a light breeze is rustling the newly-changing leaves. Traffic is light on your commute, so you arrive at work early enough to swing by Starbucks for a non-fat latte. You feel great.

Until you arrive at your desk. Help Desk personnel and the odd manager or two are circling like a pack of jackals. The *WhatsIt* application is performing dog-slow and users are complaining. On top of that, the *WhosIt* application is suddenly throwing an error every time a user tries to save a new record. They all look at you and ask, *"What changed?"* (because, *of course*, it's the database, silly!).

If you're not auditing your databases, that can be a tough question to answer, especially if "what changed" was that someone dropped a database object. However, with a DDL audit in place, a quick scan of the results will allow you to explain the situation, calmly. The *WhatsIt* application is slow because John dropped a critical index, meaning that a very common query is now performing a full table scan. The application error is due to a syntax error in a new `insert` trigger that Mary added to the *SuchAndSuch* table in the *WhosIt* database. Recreate the index, fix the trigger bug, and you're free to enjoy your latte.

Whether it's to log DDL changes, record who's logging in to a server, or track what users are accessing sensitive data, there comes a time in just about every DBA's career when we need to perform some sort of audit (or wish we had auditing in place). It's important to know what options are available and the pros and cons of each, because they are not all created equal.

SQL Server provides many ways to audit activity on your instances. In this chapter, we'll focus on the following tools, discussing how each one works, along with their strengths and weaknesses:

- **SQL Trace** – familiar, easy to implement, and available in all Editions.

- **SQL Audit** – robust, first-class auditing tool offering a wide range of covered events.

- **DIY auditing solutions using triggers and event notifications** – when an out-of-the-box solution won't cut it, why not develop your own?

Auditing Options Not Covered

The tools I cover in this chapter are good, generally easy-to-use options for DDL and security event monitoring, which is the chapter's focus. However, as noted above, SQL Server offers many other auditing options, and I'll review a few of them here, just briefly, with references for further reading.

C2 auditing

C2 is a security standard established by the National Computer Security Center (NCSC) and intended for high-security environments. A C2 audit records every single event that occurs in your SQL instance and logs it to an audit file in your default data directory. It is not configurable in any way, except to turn it on or off, which requires an instance restart. So what you have is *a lot* of audit information being written to your default data directory. If that directory were to fill up, SQL Server would shut down and would not start until it could write to the audit file again. To put it bluntly, don't enable C2 auditing unless you absolutely need to, and if you need to, you'll know.

Policy Based Management

First introduced in SQL Server 2008, Policy Based Management (PBM) is a system for defining, implementing and enforcing enterprise-wide standards, across all instances and databases. For example, your organization may have a security policy stating that xp_cmdshell should always be disabled. With PBM, it's easy to enforce such a rule and create audit reports showing whether a particular instance is in compliance. In fact, you can use PBM in conjunction with Central Management Server, also available in SQL Server 2008 and above, to audit multiple instances simultaneously.

For more information on Policy Based Management, please see Books Online (BOL) at HTTP://TECHNET.MICROSOFT.COM/EN-US/LIBRARY/BB510667.ASPX.

Change Data Capture and Change Tracking

If you need to audit DML, then SQL Server offers Change Data Capture (CDC) and Change Tracking. With Change Tracking, SQL Server will record the details of modifications to rows in a specified user table, including the DML operation, and the affected column(s). However, it will not record the original or any intermediate values of the changed data. For that level of auditing, you'll want to use CDC. Often used by ETL (Extract-Transform-Load) applications, CDC uses the SQL Server transaction log to find changes to a tracked table and record those changes to a change table.

Both these solutions work without any modifications to the underlying tables. For more information on Change Tracking and Change Data Capture, see the Track Data Changes section of BOL at HTTP://TECHNET.MICROSOFT.COM/EN-US/LIBRARY/BB933994.ASPX.

The Basis of Auditing: Events and Event Classes

The Oxford English Dictionary defines an **event** as:

...a thing that happens or takes place, especially one of importance.

Just about everything of any significance that happens inside the SQL Server engine generates an event. Logging in to the instance? That's an event. Creating a table? Event. Even issuing a `SELECT` statement generates an event. Events aren't confined to just user-related activities. Internal processes such as locking and allocating disk space also generate events.

An **event class** is the definition of an event, including all of its related information. An event is an instantiation of an event class. An analogy that works for me is that an event class is a table and all its columns. It defines what data is stored inside. An event would be a row inside that table. If you're more developer-minded, you might liken an event class to a *struct* definition in a language like C (did I just date myself there?) and the event itself to declaring a variable based on that *struct*.

Each event class has a different set of information that's relevant to that class. For example, the `Data File Auto Grow` event class contains the column `Filename`, which stores the name of the data file that auto-expanded. The `Object:Created` event class however, doesn't contain this column; it simply doesn't make sense for that event. On the other hand, `Object:Created` *does* include columns like `IndexID` and `ObjectID`, which are relevant to that event.

When we perform an audit in in SQL Server, we're essentially recording relevant events. To get an idea just what events are available for auditing in SQL Trace, and the information they provide, we can interrogate the SQL Trace catalog views, as shown in Listing 1.

```
SELECT   cat.name AS CategoryName ,
         e.name AS EventName ,
         col.name AS ColumnName
FROM     sys.trace_categories AS cat
         JOIN sys.trace_events AS e ON e.category_id = cat.category_id
         JOIN sys.trace_event_bindings AS b
             ON b.trace_event_id = e.trace_event_id
         JOIN sys.trace_columns AS col
             ON col.trace_column_id = b.trace_column_id
ORDER BY cat.name ,
         e.name ,
         col.trace_column_id
```

Listing 1:   SQL Trace – event categories, events and data columns that comprise each event.

That's quite a list, to be sure, with twenty-one event categories containing 180 event classes. For auditing purposes, our primary focus will be on those events in the **Objects** and **Security Audit** event categories. To help make sense of it all, BOL provides the following resources:

- A description of all the event classes:
  HTTP://MSDN.MICROSOFT.COM/EN-US/LIBRARY/MS175481.ASPX

- A description of available columns:
  HTTP://MSDN.MICROSOFT.COM/EN-US/LIBRARY/MS190762.ASPX

The new Extended Events framework, introduced in SQL Server 2008, which forms the basis for the SQL Audit tool, exposes even more events. We can query the Extended Events metadata, stored in various Dynamic Management Views (DMVs) for the Extended Events packages, and the 600+ events they contain (see, for example, HTTP://TINYURL.COM/M6FU384). However, many of the auditing events are not available to the Extended Events DDL, only through the SQL Audit tool (more on this shortly).

Now that we know a little more about what we'll be auditing, let's look at some of the tools we can use.

SQL Trace

SQL Trace, first introduced in SQL Server 6.5, is the oldest audit method still available in SQL Server. The 6.5 version was limited in scope; we could monitor what a client was executing or what stored procedures it was calling, but that was about it. SQL Server 7.0 improved matters (and introduced Profiler), enabling us to gather much more information about what was going on with regard to locking, blocking, and activity on our database instances.

SQL Trace is now a mature and robust tool. Furthermore, as described in detail in Chapter 4, as long as we perform server-side traces, rather than using Profiler, and we adopt general good practices in our trace definitions, we can capture traces with minimal performance impact on even the most heavily loaded server.

Most DBAs use SQL Trace to monitor and troubleshoot performance issues in SQL Server, but we can also use it as a tool for auditing activities in the database. Chapter 4 covers how to create trace definitions in Profiler, export them, and run server-side traces, so refer there for those details. Here, I'll focus on:

- creating a simple server-side trace for DDL auditing

- using the default trace for auditing.

Server-side trace for DDL auditing

Open Profiler, and we'll create a very simple trace definition to capture event data every time a user creates, deletes, or modifies an object in the AdventureWorks database.

For auditing purposes, there isn't really a system-defined trace template to suit our needs, but that's OK as it's easy to define our own trace templates for reuse. For now, select the "Blank" template. On the **Events Selection** tab, expand the **Objects** group and click the check boxes for the `Object:Altered`, `Object:Created` and `Object:Deleted` event classes. The data columns define all of the data that SQL Trace can capture for event classes. Not every data column applies to every event. Any columns that don't apply to our selected events, such as `ColumnPermissions` and `FileName`, appear in gray and aren't available for selection.

To hide irrelevant events and columns uncheck the **Show all events** and **Show all columns** check boxes.

Events	Application Name	Bigint Data 1	Client Process ID	Database ID	Database Name	Event Sequence	Event SubClass	GroupID	
Objects									
☑ Object:Altered	☑	☑	☑	☑	☑	☑	☑	☑	
☑ Object:Created	☑	☑	☑	☑	☑	☑	☑	☑	
☑ Object:Deleted	☑	☑	☑	☑	☑	☑	☑	☑	

Figure 1:   SQL Trace – auditing ALTER, CREATE and DROP events.

By default, Profiler will collect 27 data columns for each of these event classes. If there are any you don't require, it's good practice to deselect them, in order to reduce the trace overhead. However, for simplicity here, we'll capture them all.

We want to audit DDL changes in the `AdventureWorks` database only, so click on the **Column Filters** button, select the `DatabaseName` column, expand the **Like** group and enter `AdventureWorks`. Wildcards are also acceptable here.

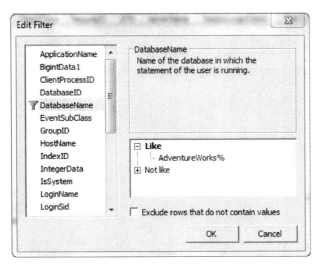

Figure 2:   SQL Trace – adding a filter to the `DatabaseName` data column.

Having done this, click **Run** to start the trace, and verify that it's working as expected, by running the DDL in Listing 2.

```
USE [AdventureWorks2008R2];
GO
CREATE TABLE MyAuditTable
    (
        FirstName VARCHAR(20) ,
        LastName VARCHAR(20)
    );
GO
```

Listing 2:   SQL Trace – creating `MyAuditTable`.

We should see that event recorded in our Profiler session. We see two rows for the creation of our table, one each for the start and end of the transaction that created it. If desired, we could add an `EventSubClass = 1` filter to the trace definition to limit the output to just the commit records.

EventClass	ApplicationName	BigintData1	ClientPr...	DatabaseID	DatabaseName	EventSubClass	E
Trace Start							
Object:Created	Microsoft...		3872	16	AdventureWorks2008R2	0 - Begin	
Object:Created	Microsoft...	4975065	3872	16	AdventureWorks2008R2	1 - Commit	

Figure 3: SQL Trace – trace results viewed in Profiler.

Stop the trace. If we want to save this trace definition as a template, we can simply select **Save As | Trace Template**, give it a name, such as AdventureWorksDDLAudit, and the next time we need to create a trace, it will appear as a custom template at the bottom of the list of available templates.

Having configured our audit trace using Profiler, we want to export the trace definition to a file so that we can run it as a server-side trace. Navigate **File | Export | Script Trace Definition | For SQL Server 2005–2008 R2** and save the .sql file with an appropriate name and location.

Open the .sql file in SSMS to see the trace definition, and modify it as necessary, as shown in Listing 3. The full script, available in the code download, contains 81 calls to sp_trace_setevent, one for each combination of 3 events and 27 data columns.

```
-- Create a Queue
DECLARE @rc INT
DECLARE @TraceID INT
DECLARE @maxfilesize BIGINT
SET @maxfilesize = 5
EXEC @rc = sp_trace_create @TraceID OUTPUT, 2,
    N'D:\SQL2008\Audit\AdventureWorksDDLAudit.trc', @maxfilesize, NULL
IF ( @rc != 0 )
    GOTO error
-- Set the Events
DECLARE @on BIT
SET @on = 1
EXEC sp_trace_setevent @TraceID, 164, 7, @on
EXEC sp_trace_setevent @TraceID, 164, 8, @on
EXEC sp_trace_setevent @TraceID, 164, 24, @on
--<...further events ommitted for brevity...>
```

```
-- Set the Filters
DECLARE @intfilter INT
DECLARE @bigintfilter BIGINT
EXEC sp_trace_setfilter @TraceID, 35, 0, 6, N'AdventureWorks'
-- Set the trace status to start
EXEC sp_trace_setstatus @TraceID, 1
-- Display Trace ID for Future References
SELECT   TraceID = @TraceID
GOTO finish
error:
SELECT   ErrorCode = @rc
finish:
go
```

Listing 3:   SQL Trace – scripting the auditing trace definition.

Execute the script to start the server-side trace. Once started, it will continue to run until a predefined stop time (we did not define one here), or until it is explicitly stopped with a call to `sp_trace_setstatus`, or until the SQL Server instance is stopped. Usually, we want our audit trace to run continuously and to resume on startup. To make this happen, use the `sp_procoption` stored procedure (see Books Online for more information on this procedure).

A server-side trace has only one output option, a trace (`.trc`) file. Once we have the audit trace up and running, we can simply open that trace file in Profiler to view the output. However, for security or DDL auditing purposes, we'll want to be able to process the output and report on it. For this, we use the `fn_trace_gettable` function.

```
SELECT   *
FROM     FN_TRACE_GETTABLE('D:\SQL2008\Audit\AdventureWorksDDLAudit.trc',
                           NULL);
GO
```

Listing 4:   SQL Trace – reading trace output using `fn_trace_gettable`.

This built-in function allows us to treat the trace file as a table, *i.e.* joining it with other tables, sorting, grouping, filtering, and so on (see Chapter 4 for further details).

Using the default trace

Often overlooked is the fact that SQL Server performs DDL and security auditing out of the box in the form of the default trace. Enabled unless explicitly disabled, the default trace includes all of the events from the `Object` event category and many from the `Security` event category, in addition to many others. For a full list of the events and columns included in the default trace, run the query in Listing 5.

```
SELECT  tcat.name AS EventCategory ,
        tevent.name AS EventClassName ,
        tcolumn.name AS ColumnName
FROM    sys.traces AS t
        CROSS APPLY FN_TRACE_GETEVENTINFO(t.id) AS tdef
        JOIN sys.trace_events AS tevent
            ON tdef.eventid = tevent.trace_event_id
        JOIN sys.trace_categories AS tcat
            ON tcat.category_id = tevent.category_id
        JOIN sys.trace_columns AS tcolumn
            ON tcolumn.trace_column_id = tdef.columnid
WHERE   t.is_default = 1 --default trace
        AND t.status = 1 --running
ORDER BY EventCategory ,
        EventClassName ,
        ColumnName;
GO
```

Listing 5: SQL Trace – event categories, events and data columns that comprise the default trace.

While certainly useful for investigating what just happened on an instance, the default trace has some limitations that make it less than ideal for a rigorous auditing solution. The default trace comprises five rollover files, each 20 MB in size. Unfortunately, we cannot modify this configuration. Considering the number of events captured by the default trace, you can imagine how quickly the oldest file might be aged out. When auditing for later reporting purposes, you'll need to implement a procedure for saving the trace data to a permanent repository on a regular basis in order to prevent audit data loss (see, for example, HTTP://TINYURL.COM/KGB27U2).

SQL Trace: pros and cons

SQL Trace is a powerful tool for auditing, familiar to most DBAs, and reasonably light-weight if used with care. However, there are some caveats to keep in mind when using SQL Trace for auditing. The biggest of these is the limited information set that SQL Trace collects. Not all data columns are available for all events. Depending on what events we wish to capture, SQL Trace can't always record all of the data we need. Take our DDL Audit trace, for example, recording object creations, deletions and changes in a database. One of the data columns missing from these events is the SQL text executed (`TextData`). This isn't really a problem when a user creates or deletes an object, but is more of a factor in object modifications. Is it enough to know simply that an object was changed, or do we also need to know *how* it was changed? If this information is critical for an audit, we need to consider one of the other auditing solutions SQL Server has to offer.

SQL Audit

SQL Server 2008 introduced the SQL Audit feature, for the first time making Audit objects first-class objects, meaning we can manage them via DDL statements, rather than through stored procedures.

SQL Audit is built on the Extended Events framework, also introduced in SQL Server 2008. I can't delve into the details of Extended Events here but suffice it to say that using Extended Events allows for synchronous or asynchronous processing of event data with minimal performance overhead, even less than SQL Trace.

You can find further information on Extended Events in Chapter 4 of this book, and in Books Online, which includes a query that provides a correlation of SQL Trace event classes to Extended Events (HTTP://TINYURL.COM/KXNZHPH). If you run it, you'll notice that while some of the auditing events in which we're interested, such as the object modification events, and a few of the security audit events, are available in the Extended Events `sqlserver` package, many others are "missing." These events migrated to the `SecAudit` package, which is for exclusive use by SQL Audit (see HTTP://TINYURL.COM/KSKEJWJ).

SQL Audit: how it works

What makes SQL Audit unique among auditing solutions is that events are recorded, not when they actually happen, but rather when the permissions check for the event occurs. To an auditor, this means that we know when a user *attempted* to access certain data, or *attempted* to modify an object, whether or not that attempt was successful. This makes it easier to see when people or applications are trying to perform unauthorized activities. Tracing based on permissions checks also means that the audit can capture indirect activities on an object, such as a stored procedure or view that references a table we happen to be auditing.

SQL Audit: terminology

Before creating a SQL Audit, we should familiarize ourselves with two basic components:

- **SQL Server `Audit` object** – describes the general configuration of the audit, including the name of the audit, properties and destination of the target (output file), whether SQL Server writes the data to the target synchronously or asynchronously, and so on. This object contains no information on what events we're auditing; it simply defines where that information goes.

- **Audit Specification object** – belongs to a SQL Server `Audit` and describes which events we wish to audit. There are two kinds of audit specification:

  - **`Database Audit Specification`** – audits events at the database level. For example, selecting from a certain table (or all tables), altering a stored procedure, and so on.

  - **`Server Audit Specification`** – captures events at the instance level, such as logging in, adding principals to server roles, and so on.

An audit specification, server or database level, can be associated with only one SQL Server `Audit` object. However, any SQL Server `Audit` object can have one or more audit specifications assigned to it (in other words, we can have one server audit specification and one database audit specification per database). Think of it as a separation of duties. The audit specifications are data collectors gathering audit information, which they send on to the audit object for formatting and output.

SQL Audit: creating the audit

A SQL Server `Audit` object (termed the `Audit` object from here on) describes the general configuration of the audit, so we have some fundamental choices when creating it. We can create an `Audit` via DDL statements or through the SSMS graphical user interface.

In the SSMS Object Explorer (at the server level), expand the **Security** directory, right-click the **Audits** folder and choose **New Audit**. Figure 4 shows the **General** page, completed for our example, similar to our previous server-side trace for auditing DDL actions on the `AdventureWorks` database, but more fine-grained.

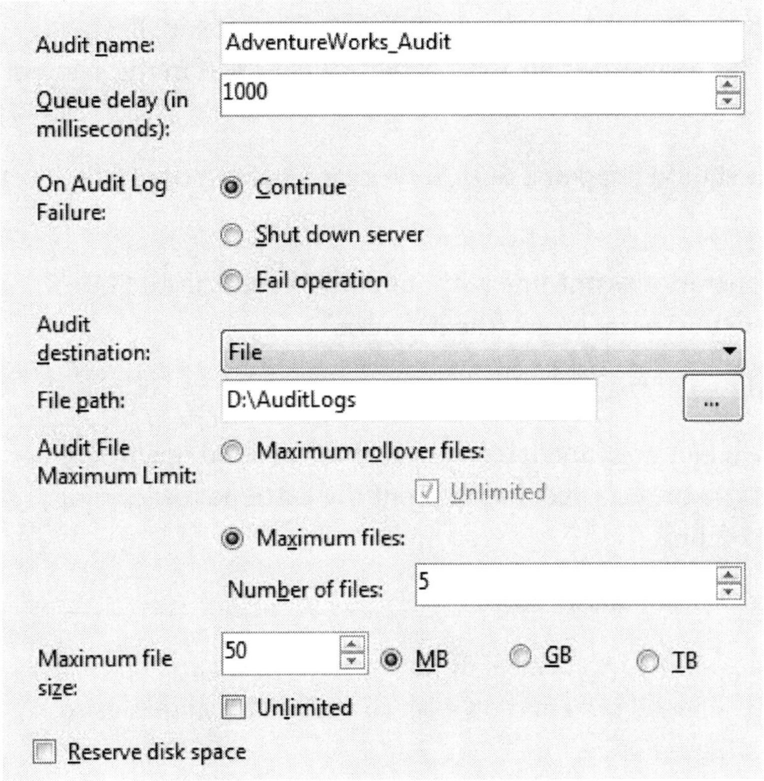

Figure 4: SQL Audit – creating the SQL Server Audit object.

A brief description of each of the options follows:

- **Audit name** – choose a relevant name, AdventureWorks_Audit in this case.

- **Queue delay** – when an event occurs, SQL Server writes audit records to a temporary buffer location. Within a certain time, as specified by the QUEUE_DELAY parameter, SQL Server must harden the audit records to the designated output.

  - QUEUE_DELAY > 0 – this is an *asynchronous* audit and is the default option, with a delay of 1 second. User processing of auditable transactions continues as soon as SQL Server writes the audit record to buffer. Minimal impact on performance but audit records may be lost in the event of a system failure.

- **QUEUE_DELAY** = 0 – this is a *synchronous* audit. Auditable transactions cannot complete until SQL Server hardens the audit records to the target. More likely to impact user performance but guarantees no audit activity will be lost in the event of a system failure.

- **On Audit Log Failure** – what should happen if SQL Server can't harden the audit records for some reason?

  - **CONTINUE** – SQL Server operations continue without audit records until SQL Server is able to resume writing to the target (the default).

  - **SHUTDOWN** – force a shutdown of the server.

  - **FAIL_OPERATION** – SQL Server 2012 and later only. Fail the audited operation, ensuring no audited events go unrecorded, but without the extreme measure of taking the entire instance off line.

- **Audit destination** – the target for the audit records.

  - **File** – a user-designated file, ideally in a central directory (encrypted and restricted access) on a network available to all systems you wish to audit. This allows us to query and process all audit files at once.

  - **Security log** – the Windows Security log. High security; writing to the Security log is a privileged operation and requires "Generate Security Audit" rights on the server.

  - **Application log** – the server's central Windows Application Log.

- **Target file properties** (relevant only if **FILE** is selected for Audit destination).

  - **File path** – we specify a path, but SQL Server will automatically generate a file name using the audit name and GUID, a sequential number and a time-stamp.

  - **Audit File maximum limit** – maximum number of rollover files to create in response to current file reaching maximum size. Keep in mind that multiple smaller files are easier to manage than a single large file.

  - **Maximum file size** – maximum size for the file.

In SQL Server 2012, there is also a **Filter** page, where we can add a filter to the `Audit` object, in the form of a predicate. The type of filter we want to create might depend on whether we intend to use a database- or server-level audit specification. In the former case, we might want to limit the audit to just the `Customers` table, in which case we could add an `object_name='Customers'` predicate to the `Audit` object definition. For a server-level audit, we might want to add a predicate to limit it to specific databases, or exclude certain databases. Our audit specification, later, will ensure we only audit events on the required database, so there's no need to define a filter here, in this case.

We can now select **Script | New Query Edit Window** to view the underlying definition of our `Audit` object.

```
USE [master]

GO

CREATE SERVER AUDIT [AdventureWorks_Audit]
TO FILE
(    FILEPATH = N'D:\AuditLogs'
    ,MAXSIZE = 50 MB
    ,MAX_FILES = 5
    ,RESERVE_DISK_SPACE = OFF
)
WITH
(    QUEUE_DELAY = 1000
    ,ON_FAILURE = CONTINUE
)
GO
```

Listing 6:   SQL Audit – creating the SQL Server `Audit` Object.

Either run this script, or click **OK** in the **Create Audit** window, to create the `Audit` object.

SQL Audit: creating the audit specification

Now we get to the good stuff: specifying what we want to audit. To create a server audit specification, right-click on the **Security | Server Audit Specifications** folder. Alternatively, we create a database audit specification by right-clicking on the **Security | Database Audit Specifications** folder, for the relevant database.

We're going to create a database audit specification for the AdventureWorks2012 database. First, we specify a name for the new audit specification (AuditEmployees) and associate it with its parent Audit object (AdventureWorks_Audit). So far so good, but now things can get intimidating.

Explore the drop-down box under **Audit Action Type** and you'll find all sorts of options for auditing. Note that, in the context of SQL Audit, an "action" is simply an event you'd like to audit. Some of the options refer to individual actions, such as DELETE, EXECUTE, and REFERENCES. Others refer to groups that encompass numerous actions. The BACKUP_RESTORE_GROUP, for example, contains the BACKUP, BACKUP LOG, and RESTORE actions at the database level.

It's not always evident which option will record the event, or action, you wish to audit. For example, when I first started working with SQL Audit, I wanted to audit DDL events, so I chose the DATABASE_OBJECT_CHANGE_GROUP. It made sense to me. After all, I was auditing changes to database objects, right? Not exactly. When I tested my audit by creating and dropping a table, what I saw in my audit log was not a table being created and dropped, but rather a schema being modified. What I *really* wanted to audit was the SCHEMA_OBJECT_CHANGE_GROUP.

Fortunately, the sys.dm_audit_actions view contains a row for every auditable action (name) and the group to which it belongs (containing_group_name). We can combine that with sys.dm_audit_class_type_map to see the parent group for any action on any object type.

```
SELECT   a.name AS Audited_Action ,
         m.class_type_desc AS SQL_Object ,
         a.class_desc ,
         a.containing_group_name
FROM     sys.dm_audit_class_type_map m
         JOIN sys.dm_audit_actions a ON m.securable_class_desc = a.class_desc
WHERE    a.name <> a.containing_group_name
ORDER BY a.name ,
         m.class_type_desc
```

Listing 7:   SQL Audit – listing the parent group for all actions on all object types.

If I'd known about these views when I started, I would have seen that the `"CREATE"`
action of a `"TABLE"` object falls in the SCHEMA_OBJECT_CHANGE_GROUP. By adding a
simple `WHERE` clause to this query we can see every action associated with this group.

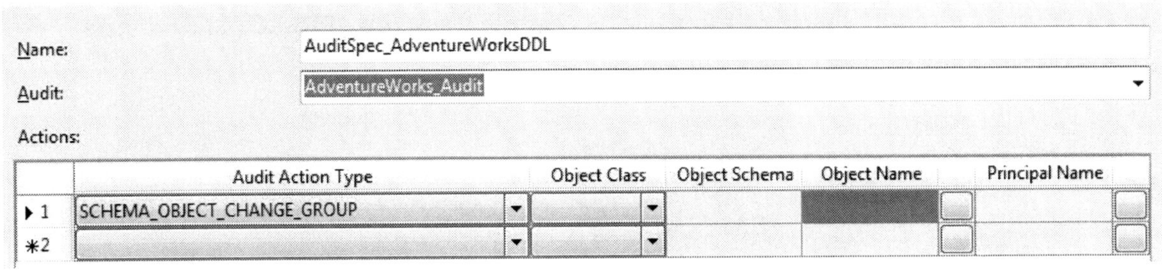

Figure 5:   SQL Audit – creating the database audit specification.

You will find that for some action types the other columns (`Object Class`, `Object
Schema`, and so on) are sometimes configurable and sometimes not. In general, if we're
specifying a group as an **Audit Action Type**, we won't be able to narrow it down to specific
objects. In this example, we can't audit events in the SCHEMA_OBJECT_CHANGE_GROUP
for a particular object within the database, such as a table. If we script out our audit specification, it looks as shown in Listing 8.

```
USE [AdventureWorks2012]
GO

CREATE DATABASE AUDIT SPECIFICATION [AuditSpec_AdventureWorksDDL]
FOR SERVER AUDIT [AdventureWorks_Audit]
ADD (SCHEMA_OBJECT_CHANGE_GROUP)
GO
```

Listing 8:   SQL Audit – creating the database audit specification.

Create the audit specification by running this script, or from the dialog. This specification will mean that we'll audit all actions on all objects in the **AdventureWorks** database. This is where a filter on the **Audit** object comes in handy, as discussed earlier, if we wish to limit auditing to particular objects.

If we specify individual actions, like **UPDATE** or **SELECT** in the **Audit Action Type**, then we can refine our audit specification to, for example, track only **SELECT** statements issued on the **Employees** table by any user.

	Audit Action Type	Object Class	Object Schema	Object Name		Principal	
▶ 1	SELECT	OBJECT	HumanResources	Employee	...	public	...
*2							

Figure 6:   SQL Audit – creating a database audit specification for a specific object.

Listing 9 shows the corresponding script (don't try to create this additional specification; remember there can be only one database audit specification per database for a given **Audit** object).

```
USE [AdventureWorks2012]
GO

CREATE DATABASE AUDIT SPECIFICATION [AuditSpecEmployees]
FOR SERVER AUDIT [AdventureWorks_Audit]
ADD (SELECT ON OBJECT::[HumanResources].[Employee] BY [public])
GO
```

Listing 9:   SQL Audit – creating a database audit specification for a specific object.

Having created both our `Audit` object and a database audit specification we can enable them by right-clicking on each one in SSMS Object Explorer, and selecting the **Enable** option. To test the audit, simply recreate our `MyAuditTable` (Listing 2) n the `AdventureWorks2012` database.

SQL Audit: viewing audit output

If we write the audit data to a file, there are two ways we can view the output. The first method is via the Log Viewer in SSMS. Right-click on the `Audit` object, and select **View Audit Logs**. You'll see the most recent 1,000 audit records.

Figure 7:   SQL Audit – viewing the audit output in Log Viewer.

Scroll right and you'll see that the audit data includes a lot more detail than SQL Trace, including the text of the SQL statement executed.

To view more than 1,000 records, or to carry out more sophisticated operations on the audit data, use T-SQL and the fn_get_audit_file function. This built-in function accepts three parameters: the file pattern, the path and file name of the first audit file to read, and the starting offset within that initial file.

Listing 10 will return the contents of all audit files for the AdventureWorks_Audit.

```
SELECT   *
FROM     fn_get_audit_file('D:\AuditLogs\AdventureWorks_Audit*', DEFAULT,
                           DEFAULT)
```

Listing 10:   SQL Audit – viewing the audit output using fn_get_audit_file.

Listing 11 will return the contents of all audit files for the AdventureWorks_Audit starting with a certain file and offset.

```
SELECT   *
FROM     fn_get_audit_file('D:\AuditLogs\AdventureWorks_Audit*',
                           'D:\AuditLogs\AdventureWorks_Audit_C3D7D531-0A9C-40FB-
B07B-E315BD72174D_0_129745881197320000.sqlaudit',
                           1024)
```

Listing 11:   SQL Audit – viewing audit output beginning at a specific location within a file.

This option is handy if you've already processed some records and just want to pick up where you left off.

SQL Audit: pros and cons

For many DBAs, the biggest limitation of SQL Audit is the fact that it is not available in 2008/2008 R2 Standard Edition, and only basic auditing is available in 2012 Standard Edition. What's "basic auditing," you ask? According to BOL:

> *All editions of SQL Server support server level audits. Database level auditing is limited to Enterprise,*
> *Developer, and Evaluation editions.*

The bottom line is that, if you're running Standard Edition, you'll need to find another way to audit DDL.

If you do work with a SQL Server edition that supports the full SQL Audit feature, then it offers some great benefits. By making audit objects first-class objects, SQL Audit offers a very holistic approach to auditing that really hasn't been available until now. The solution is less susceptible to tampering. The audit output records all changes to the audit definition. We can send audit output to the Windows Security log or to a directory with very restricted access. There's also the option to shut down the instance in the event that SQL Server can't write the audit output.

However, there are also limitations even with the full SQL Audit feature. In SQL Server 2008, we have the ability to include specific objects in some audit specifications, but it's difficult to exclude objects or events. An example of this would be the `SCHEMA_OBJECT_CHANGE_GROUP`. It will certainly record all `CREATE`, `ALTER`, and `DROP` statements we issue on database objects, but it will also record `UPDATE STATISTICS` statements, which you may not want to include in your audit. The problem is that there is no choice in the matter. Nor can we choose to audit DDL on a specific object or in a specific schema. Certainly, we can filter out unwanted events when reading the audit file, but this can create a lot of "noise" cluttering the audit files.

SQL Server 2012 improved this situation somewhat with the introduction of the filter functionality, but even that isn't perfect. If we only have a handful of exclusions, we can list them out easily enough, but this soon becomes cumbersome and difficult to maintain. It would help to be able to store filter criteria in a table and refer to that table in the filter predicate. Unfortunately, that's not an option at present.

Develop Your Own Audit: Event Notifications or Triggers

Looking to get back in touch with your inner developer? Are the built-in auditing methods offered by SQL Server not meeting your needs? Think you can do better? You can always code your own audit using event notifications or triggers. If you're willing to do a little more work up front, each of these methods offers some advantages over traditional solutions.

Event notifications: how it works

SQL Server 2005 heralded the arrival of event notifications, which works in conjunction with SQL Server Service Broker. A detailed description of the Service Broker architecture is outside the scope of this discussion, but it helps to think of Service Broker as like email, a way to send messages back and forth. When a monitored event occurs in the engine, SQL Server sends an XML message to the Service Broker service. That message waits in the Service Broker queue (think Inbox) until it is processed. How that message is processed is where you come in. You create a stored procedure to read messages from the Service Broker queue and process them in any manner you see fit, within the capabilities of the T-SQL language. Unlike SQL Trace and SQL Audit, not only can you record the audit data, but you can also perform an action, such as sending an email to the DBA, in response to an event.

Being the author of your own auditing program gives you a lot of flexibility. For example, I once had to provide a list of SQL logins along with the time they were last used, for all instances across the enterprise. Any one of the auditing options covered in this chapter will record login events, but that would have produced quite a bit of output and required additional processing to produce a list of logins and last login dates. By using an event notification with the AUDIT_LOGIN event, I was able to maintain a table of logins, their last login date, and the application that used the login.

Event notifications respond to a wide variety of SQL Trace and DDL events, at both the instance and the database level. The biggest advantage is that they execute asynchronously, outside the scope of the transaction that caused the event. This means that the end-user process doesn't have to wait for the audit processing to complete.

Event notifications: creating an event notification

The first thing to decide when designing an event notification is the scope. Do you want to audit events at the server level or at the database level? For some events, such as login or logout events, there is no decision to make, since those events only exist at the server level. But what about DDL statements like CREATE TABLE? Technically, that event happens at the database level, but with event notifications comes the ability to audit that event for all databases by creating the event notification at the server level. If there is a need to audit activity across a number of databases in a particular SQL Server instance, we don't have to create a separate event notification for each one.

The second decision to make is what to audit. Event notifications respond to a number of events. We can track individual events, such as CREATE_TABLE or ALTER_PROCEDURE, or we can track predefined groups, such as DDL_DATABASE_LEVEL_EVENTS, which will capture any database-level DDL event. The sys.event_notification_event_types system catalog view offers a complete listing of available events, or we can refer to Books Online (HTTP://TINYURL.COM/2CV27CG).

Before creating an event notification, we need to configure a Service Broker service, including a queue, route, and service. We also need to create a service program to read messages from the queue and process them. That service program is where the magic happens. Don't let the term "service program" intimidate you; it's just a regular stored procedure and we assign it to a Service Broker queue to process messages, automatically.

Let's look at an example. I've created a new database, called `Audit`, to serve as a permanent repository for my audit objects and the audit output. The stored procedure in Listing 12 reads (or receives) messages from the `auditQueue` Service Broker queue. The messages are in XML format, so it helps to be familiar with XML. I don't want to record events such as index maintenance or update statistics, so I'm checking each message for those events before I insert the record into my `auditLog` table.

```
-- make sure broker is enabled
IF EXISTS ( SELECT   *
            FROM     sys.databases
            WHERE    name = 'Audit'
                     AND is_broker_enabled = 0 )
    ALTER DATABASE Audit SET ENABLE_BROKER;
GO

USE Audit
GO


CREATE TABLE auditLog (
    LoggingID INT IDENTITY(1,1) PRIMARY KEY CLUSTERED,
    SQLInstance VARCHAR(100),
    DatabaseName VARCHAR(100),
    EventTime DATETIME,
    EventType VARCHAR(100),
    LoginName VARCHAR(100),
    DatabaseUser VARCHAR(100),
    ClientHostName VARCHAR(100),
    NTUserName VARCHAR(100),
    NTDomainName VARCHAR(100),
    SchemaName VARCHAR(100),
    ObjectName VARCHAR(100),
```

```
        ObjectType VARCHAR(100),
        Success INT,
        FullSQL varchar(max),
        FullLog XML,
        Archived BIT NOT NULL
)
GO
ALTER TABLE dbo.auditLog ADD CONSTRAINT
DF_auditLog_Archived DEFAULT 0 FOR Archived
GO

CREATE PROCEDURE [dbo].[auditQueueReceive_usp]
AS
    BEGIN
        SET NOCOUNT ON;
        SET ARITHABORT ON;
        DECLARE @message XML ,
            @messageName NVARCHAR(256) ,
            @dialogue UNIQUEIDENTIFIER;


        BEGIN TRY

--Continuous loop
        WHILE ( 1 = 1 )
            BEGIN
                BEGIN TRANSACTION;
        --Retrieve the next message from the queue
                SET @dialogue = NULL;
                WAITFOR (
        GET CONVERSATION GROUP @dialogue FROM dbo.auditQueue
            ), TIMEOUT 2000;
                IF @dialogue IS NULL
                    BEGIN
                        ROLLBACK;
                        BREAK;
                    END;
                    RECEIVE TOP(1)
        @messageName=message_type_name,
        @message=message_body,
        @dialogue = conversation_handle
        FROM dbo.auditQueue
        WHERE conversation_group_id = @dialogue;
```

```
                  IF ( @message.value('(/EVENT_INSTANCE/EventType)[1]',
                                  'VARCHAR(100)') )
                                  NOT LIKE '%STATISTICS%'
              AND (
                  @message.value('(/EVENT_INSTANCE/TSQLCommand)[1]',
                                  'VARCHAR(2000)') )
                                  NOT LIKE 'ALTER INDEX%REBUILD%'
              AND (
                  @message.value('(/EVENT_INSTANCE/TSQLCommand)[1]',
                                  'VARCHAR(2000)') )
                                  NOT LIKE 'ALTER INDEX%REORGANIZE%'
              BEGIN
                  INSERT  INTO auditLog
                          ( SQLInstance ,
                            DatabaseName ,
                            EventTime ,
                            EventType ,
                            LoginName ,
                            DatabaseUser ,
                            ClientHostName ,
                            NTUserName ,
                            NTDomainName ,
                            SchemaName ,
                            ObjectName ,
                            ObjectType ,
                            Success ,
                            FullSQL ,
                            FullLog
                          )
                  VALUES  (
        ISNULL(@message.value('(/EVENT_INSTANCE/SQLInstance)[1]',
                            'VARCHAR(100)'),
              @@SERVERNAME) ,
        ISNULL(@message.value('(/EVENT_INSTANCE/DatabaseName)[1]',
                            'VARCHAR(100)'),
              'SERVER') ,

        @message.value('(/EVENT_INSTANCE/PostTime)[1]',
                    'DATETIME') ,
        @message.value('(/EVENT_INSTANCE/EventType)[1]',
                    'VARCHAR(100)') ,
```

```
                    @message.value('(/EVENT_INSTANCE/LoginName)[1]',
                                'VARCHAR(100)') ,
                    @message.value('(/EVENT_INSTANCE/UserName)[1]',
                                'VARCHAR(100)') ,
                    @message.value('(/EVENT_INSTANCE/HostName)[1]',
                                'VARCHAR(100)') ,
                    @message.value('(/EVENT_INSTANCE/NTUserName)[1]',
                                'VARCHAR(100)') ,
                    @message.value('(/EVENT_INSTANCE/NTDomainName)[1]',
                                'VARCHAR(100)') ,
                    @message.value('(/EVENT_INSTANCE/SchemaName)[1]',
                                'VARCHAR(100)') ,
                    @message.value('(/EVENT_INSTANCE/ObjectName)[1]',
                                'VARCHAR(50)') ,
                    @message.value('(/EVENT_INSTANCE/ObjectType)[1]',
                                'VARCHAR(50)') ,
                    @message.value('(/EVENT_INSTANCE/Success)[1]',
                                'INTEGER') ,
                    @message.value('(/EVENT_INSTANCE/TSQLCommand)[1]',
                                'VARCHAR(max)') ,
                    @message
                                );
                END
            COMMIT;
        END
END TRY
BEGIN CATCH
    DECLARE @errorNumber INT ,
        @errorMessage NVARCHAR(MAX) ,
        @errorState INT ,
        @errorSeverity INT ,
        @errorLine INT ,
        @errorProcedure NVARCHAR(128)
    SET @errorNumber = ERROR_NUMBER();
    SET @errorMessage = ERROR_MESSAGE();
    SET @errorState = ERROR_STATE();
    SET @errorSeverity = ERROR_SEVERITY();
    SET @errorLine = ERROR_LINE();
    SET @errorProcedure = ERROR_PROCEDURE();
    IF NOT ( XACT_STATE() = 0 )
        ROLLBACK;
```

```
            RAISERROR('%s:%d %s (%d)',
                    @errorSeverity,@errorState,@errorProcedure,@errorLine,
                    @errorMessage,@errorNumber) WITH log;
        END CATCH
    END
GO
```

Listing 12:   Event notifications – creating the Service Broker service program.

Once we have the service program in place, we can create the rest of the Service Broker
objects. For a detailed description of these objects and the syntax used to create them,
please refer to Books Online.

```
USE Audit
GO
--CREATE QUEUE
CREATE QUEUE auditQueue
WITH ACTIVATION (
STATUS = ON,
PROCEDURE_NAME = audit.dbo.auditQueueReceive_usp ,
MAX_QUEUE_READERS = 2, EXECUTE AS SELF)
GO

--CREATE SERVICE
CREATE SERVICE auditService
ON QUEUE [auditQueue]
([http://schemas.microsoft.com/SQL/Notifications/PostEventNotification])
GO

--CREATE ROUTE
CREATE ROUTE auditRoute
WITH SERVICE_NAME = 'auditService',
ADDRESS = 'Local'
GO
```

Listing 13:   Event notifications – creating the Service Broker queue, service, and route.

Finally, we can create the event notification itself. Here, we're creating an event notification at the server level (so across all databases), tracking all database-level DDL events, and we're sending that information to the `auditService` service we just created.

```
CREATE EVENT NOTIFICATION ddlDatabase_event
ON SERVER
FOR DDL_DATABASE_LEVEL_EVENTS
TO SERVICE 'auditService', 'current database'
GO
```

Listing 14: Event notifications – creating the event notification.

We've attached our service program to the `auditQueue`, so that it will process messages as they arrive. Alternatively, by not attaching the procedure to the queue and simply executing it manually or via a job, we could process messages in batches, at scheduled intervals. This is sometimes preferred to save processing for a period when the server isn't as busy.

Before we move on, take a last look at the **CREATE ROUTE** statement above and notice the **ADDRESS** clause. In this example, we're specifying `Local`, meaning the target service is located on the local instance. We could also send messages to a remote service by specifying the DNS name or IP address of that server here. By doing this, we can potentially log audit information from many servers to a central audit database.

Let's see our event notification in action. Run the statements in Listing 15 to produce some audit output.

```
USE AdventureWorks2012
GO

CREATE TABLE EventNotificationTest ( name VARCHAR(20) );
GO
```

```
INSERT  INTO EventNotificationTest
VALUES  ( 'Noelle' ),
        ( 'Tanner' ),
        ( 'Colin' ),
        ( 'Parker' ),
        ( 'Conner' )
GO

SELECT  name
FROM    EventNotificationTest
WHERE   name = 'Conner';
GO

CREATE INDEX i_name_idx ON EventNotificationTest (name);
GO

UPDATE STATISTICS EventNotificationTest WITH FULLSCAN;
GO

DROP TABLE EventNotificationTest;
```

Listing 15:   Event notifications – testing the event notification.

Now, we can view the audit data by reading from the **auditLog** table.

```
USE Audit
GO

SELECT  EventTime ,
        DatabaseName ,
        EventType ,
        LoginName ,
        SchemaName ,
        ObjectName ,
        ObjectType ,
        FullSQL
FROM    dbo.auditLog;
GO
```

	EventTime	DatabaseName	EventType	LoginName	SchemaName	ObjectName	ObjectType	FullSQL
1	2013-09-03 19:06:58.623	AdventureWorks2012	CREATE_TABLE	AW_DBO	dbo	EventNotificationTest	TABLE	CREATE TABLE EventNotificationTest (name varchar...
2	2013-09-03 19:06:58.670	AdventureWorks2012	CREATE_INDEX	AW_DBO	dbo	i_name_idx	INDEX	CREATE INDEX i_name_idx on EventNotificationTest.
3	2013-09-03 19:06:58.780	AdventureWorks2012	DROP_TABLE	AW_DBO	dbo	EventNotificationTest	TABLE	DROP TABLE EventNotificationTest.

Listing 16:   Event notifications – viewing the event notification output.

You should see three rows, one recording the creation of the table, one for the index creation, and one for dropping the table. We don't see a record for the **UPDATE STATISTICS** command, nor for the statistics that SQL Server automatically created when we ran the **SELECT** statement, because we filtered out **STATISTICS** commands in our service program.

DDL and Logon triggers: how they work

Another way to handle audits programmatically is to use triggers. DML triggers have been available in SQL Server for a long time, but it wasn't until SQL Server 2005 that we also got DDL and Logon triggers.

Similar to event notifications, triggers respond to events in the SQL engine using custom procedural code. Unlike event notifications, however, triggers respond to a more limited range of events and they execute synchronously, meaning that DDL or Logon triggers execute within the scope of the firing transaction, and could affect the performance of that transaction. Of course, we can turn this potential drawback into a benefit, if the intention is to prevent unwanted activities, like preventing a user from dropping a table.

Oftentimes, we use generic application logins in our databases, logins that a number of individuals might share. These shared logins make it more difficult to track DDL changes, or other audited activities, back to a real person. However, synchronous execution has another advantage: it captures the client information of the firing connection, so we can see the client host name or network login of the person who performed the activity. That's something that SQL Audit and event notifications can't provide.

DDL and Logon triggers: creating triggers

Just like with event notifications, we must define the scope and the events to audit, and the same DDL events and event groups apply. DDL and Logon triggers, however, use the EVENTDATA() function to extract information about the event. This function returns data in an XML format (another reason to brush up on XML). The schema of the XML produced varies depending on the firing event. The EventData topic in Books Online (HTTP://TINYURL.COM/P9ELNWS) provides a link to a description of the schema returned from each type of event.

In the example in Listing 17, we're auditing all CREATE, DROP, and ALTER PROCEDURE events in the AdventureWorks2012 database, and logging those events to a ChangeLog table in our Audit database (provided with the code download, but not shown here).

```
USE AdventureWorks2012;
GO

CREATE TRIGGER [tr_ddlchanges] ON DATABASE
  FOR CREATE_PROCEDURE, ALTER_PROCEDURE, DROP_PROCEDURE
AS
  SET nocount ON
  DECLARE @data XML
  DECLARE @WorkStation VARCHAR(50)

  SET @data = EVENTDATA();
  SELECT  @WorkStation = HOST_NAME();

  INSERT  INTO Audit.dbo.Changelog
          ( SQLInstance ,
            databasename ,
            WorkStation ,
            eventtype ,
              objectschema ,
            objectname ,
            objecttype ,
            sqlcommand ,
            loginname
          )
```

```
  VALUES ( @@SERVERNAME ,
          @data.value('(/EVENT_INSTANCE/DatabaseName)[1]', 'varchar(256)') ,
          @WorkStation ,
          @data.value('(/EVENT_INSTANCE/EventType)[1]', 'varchar(50)') ,
          @data.value('(/EVENT_INSTANCE/SchemaName)[1]', 'varchar(256)') ,
          @data.value('(/EVENT_INSTANCE/ObjectName)[1]', 'varchar(256)') ,
          @data.value('(/EVENT_INSTANCE/ObjectType)[1]', 'varchar(25)') ,
          @data.value('(/EVENT_INSTANCE/TSQLCommand)[1]', 'varchar(max)') ,
          @data.value('(/EVENT_INSTANCE/LoginName)[1]', 'varchar(256)')
          )
GO
```

Listing 17: DDL triggers – creating a DDL trigger in the `AdventureWorks2012` database.

We can test our trigger by creating a simple stored procedure in `AdventureWorks2012`, as shown in Listing 18.

```
USE AdventureWorks2012;
GO

CREATE PROCEDURE dbo.TribalSQL_usp
AS
    BEGIN
        SELECT  'Wow! Auditing is awesome!'
    END
GO
```

Listing 18: DDL triggers – testing the DDL trigger.

Viewing the audit output is as easy as querying the `changeLog` table (see Listing 19).

Although, in this example, we're logging our audit data to a local database, we could also send this information to a remote database by using Service Broker. People often forget this possibility in the context of triggers, because triggers don't go hand-in-hand with Service Broker in the way that event notifications do.

```
USE Audit;
GO

SELECT  EventDate ,
        DatabaseName ,
        EventType ,
        Workstation ,
        LoginName ,
        ObjectSchema ,
        ObjectName ,
        ObjectType ,
        SQLCommand
FROM    ChangeLog
GO
```

	EventDate	DatabaseName	EventType	Workstation	LoginName	ObjectSchema	ObjectName	ObjectType	SQLCommand
1	2013-09-03 19:45:43.967	AdventureWorks2012	CREATE_PROCEDURE	ASUS	ASUS\Colleen	dbo	TribalSQL_usp	PROCEDURE	CREATE PROCEDURE dbo.TribalSQL_usp AS BEGI...

Listing 19:   DDL triggers – viewing the audit output.

Event notifications and triggers: pros and cons

Ultimately, any self-made auditing solution is only as good as your coding abilities. However, as long as you're comfortable writing your own T-SQL procedures, then event notifications and DDL/Logon triggers offer a great alternative or supplement to conventional auditing methods. It's easy to filter out unwanted events before they make it to our target destination, and we have the option of writing to a database table, rather than having to deal with external audit or trace files.

It's not all rainbows and unicorns, however. If the intention is to audit user access on a particular table, we can't do that using either of these methods. They also won't record failed events, in the manner of SQL Audit. Also, a word of warning: a busy system generating many events, combined with an inefficient service program, can quickly overwhelm a Service Broker queue. A poorly designed trigger can directly affect users. Unless you're prepared to take ownership of the entire auditing process, perhaps one of the other audit methods would be a better choice.

Third-party Solutions

If your boss is willing to open the purse strings, there are a number of third-party auditing solutions on the market. The best ones require little or no change to your existing SQL Server environment, and have minimal impact on overall performance. Idera's SQL Compliance Manager, for example, uses a lightweight agent to capture SQL Trace events. Other options are IBM Guardium and Imperva SecureSphere.

Third-party auditing solutions offer some distinct advantages over homegrown audits. The biggest of these is scalability. If you have to audit many SQL Server instances, then third-party products generally make it very easy to deploy and manage multiple audits from a central location. You're also off the hook when it comes to supporting the audit code. And keep in mind that, whereas you as a DBA probably have a number of responsibilities, the folks that produce this software have one: auditing. They know it inside and out, and are much more likely to produce a thorough and efficient solution.

Just know that licensing such software can quickly become an expensive proposition.

Conclusion

So there you have it: SQL Trace, SQL Audit, event notifications, and triggers; four viable options for auditing many different activities in your SQL Server database. Each offers its own unique set of benefits and comes with its own limitations. Which one you choose will depend on what actions you want to audit, what data you want to capture, and how you want to handle the output. Obviously, personal preference will be an important factor, too. And don't think your options end here, either. Though I don't go into it in this chapter, with the increased exposure of Extended Events in SQL Server 2012, we get yet another opportunity to develop our own basic auditing solutions. Indeed, with so many different options available, there's really no excuse for not knowing who dropped that index.

SQL Injection: How It Works and How to Thwart it

Kevin Feasel

Imagine waking up one morning and, while surfing the Internet at breakfast, seeing news articles describing how a hacker stole your company's proprietary data and put it up on Pastebin. Millions of customer records, perhaps Protected Health Information, credit card numbers, or even names of sources or undercover agents, all out there for the world to see. This may be roughly the time when you crawl back into bed and start planning that long-dreamed-of trip to the Australian outback to start a new life as a nomad.

Before you reach the point where you are trying to explain to an interviewer the circumstances behind your sudden departure from your previous employment, perhaps I should divulge the single most pernicious résumé-updating experience (security flaw division) out there: SQL injection.

In September of 2011, Imperva's *Hacker Intelligence Initiative* released a report stating that SQL injection was responsible for 83% of successful data breaches from 2005 through to the report's release (HTTP://TINYURL.COM/PY8LTLF). It should be no surprise that the Open Web Application Security Project (OWASP) rated injection attacks, and especially SQL injection, as the number one threat vector in 2010 (HTTP://TINYURL.COM/PZKRLDS).

In every instance of SQL injection, the flaw is the same: an attacker injects SQL code in a manner the application's developers did not anticipate, allowing the attacker to perform unexpected and unauthorized actions. For a very simplistic example of this, imagine a basic web page with a search box on it. The web page developer expects users to search for a product and look up rows in a table based upon the contents of that search box.

If the developer is not careful, the user may be able to craft a search string that returns all products – or something much worse, like returning a list of all of the tables in the database, or a list of patients' medical records in another database.

Now that we have a common understanding of the gravity of the problem, as well as a basic definition of SQL injection, the rest of this chapter will go into further detail on how to perform SQL injection attacks, how to defend against them, and how to keep your Chief Information Security Officer from appearing on the nightly news.

My First SQL Injection Attack

If you know the enemy and know yourself, you need not fear the result of a hundred battles. If you know yourself but not the enemy, for every victory gained you will also suffer a defeat. If you know neither the enemy nor yourself, you will succumb in every battle.

Sun Tzu, The Art of War (HTTP://GUTENBERG.ORG/CACHE/EPUB/132/PG132.HTML)

You cannot truly defend against a threat you do not understand, so the first step in defending against a SQL injection attack is to understand precisely how one works. Before I begin, some standard provisos. Firstly, don't perform a SQL injection attack on any application without express, written permission. Second, don't put known unsafe code on a production machine. Finally, don't put your testing code in a publicly accessible location, as some bad person somewhere will probably find it eventually.

With that out of the way, the first example will be a very simple web page on top of the ubiquitous AdventureWorks database, specifically an ASP.NET web forms application talking to a SQL Server 2008 instance, but SQL injection is relevant across all application and database platform combinations.

Imagine a very basic grid showing a list of product subcategories from the `Production.ProductSubcategory` table in `AdventureWorks`. In addition to this list, we have a name filter in which a user can type a partial, with a grid that displays matching items. The SQL for such a query could look as shown in Listing 1.

```
DECLARE @Filter NVARCHAR(50);
SET @Filter = 'Bike';
SELECT   ProductSubcategoryID ,
         ProductCategoryID ,
         Name
FROM     Production.ProductSubcategory
WHERE    Name LIKE '%' + @Filter + '%'
```

	ProductSubcategoryID	ProductCategoryID	Name
1	1	1	Mountain Bikes
2	2	1	Road Bikes
3	3	1	Touring Bikes
4	26	4	Bike Racks
5	27	4	Bike Stands

Listing 1:   A filtered list of product subcategories.

The query returns rows of products that include "Bike" in their name. This is the expected behavior, and all is well. To simulate a SQL injection attack, we can try changing the filter value from `'Bike'` to `'Bike'' OR 1=1--'`. Our goal as attackers is to get "outside" the bounds of the parameter, at which point we can manipulate the query itself or run some completely different SQL statement. In this particular case, our goal is to extend the search surreptitiously, to return rows where the `Name` is like "%Bike" or all of the results (because 1 equals 1 is always true). We then comment out the rest of the query to prevent any syntax errors.

Running this first attempt at an attack will show no results, meaning our attack failed. The reason is that we were not able to get "outside" of the parameter, so instead of searching for "%Bike" or where 1=1, we are actually searching for a product subcategory whose name is like "Bike' OR 1=1--" and naturally, there are no product subcategories which match that name.

What we did was attempt to perform SQL injection against a static SQL query, which simply is not possible. SQL injection is only possible against dynamic SQL, either through an ad hoc statement put together by an application, which communicates with SQL Server, or through SQL Server's built-in dynamic SQL capabilities. Listing 2 constructs a basic dynamic SQL query that returns the same results as Listing 1, when used as intended.

```
DECLARE @Filter NVARCHAR(MAX);
SET @Filter = 'Bike';

DECLARE @sql NVARCHAR(MAX);
SET @sql = N'select ProductSubcategoryID, ProductCategoryID, Name
             from Production.ProductSubcategory where Name like ''%'
    + @Filter + N'%'''
EXEC(@sql);
```

Listing 2:   Returning a filtered list of product subcategories using dynamic SQL.

However, try the same attack (substituting in SET @Filter = 'Bike'' OR 1=1--';), and we see very different results. The query returns all of the subcategories, including entries such as Handlebars and Brakes. This is certainly not something that the procedure writer expected, and can have considerable negative ramifications. For example, if we change the filter as shown on Listing 3, we can see all of the table schemas and names.

```
DECLARE @Filter NVARCHAR(MAX);
SET @Filter = 'I do not care''
   UNION ALL
   select 1, 1, TABLE_SCHEMA + ''.'' + TABLE_NAME
    from INFORMATION_SCHEMA.TABLES --';

DECLARE @sql NVARCHAR(MAX);
SET @sql = N'select ProductSubcategoryID, ProductCategoryID, Name
             from Production.ProductSubcategory where Name like ''%'
    + @Filter + N'%'''
EXEC(@sql);
GO
```

Listing 3:   Using SQL injection to view table schemas and names.

From there, we can perform reconnaissance on various tables and even do entirely unexpected things like inserting our own product subcategories or, even worse, dropping tables. In Listing 4, we take advantage of our reconnaissance work to insert a new product subcategory. We know that a product subcategory has four non-nullable, non-identity attributes: `ProductCategoryID` (of type `integer`), `Name` (a `varchar`), `rowguid` (a `uniqueidentifier`), and `ModifiedDate` (a `datetime`). The code in Listing 4 fills in all four columns with appropriate values, so that our malicious insert statement succeeds.

```
declare @Filter nvarchar(max);
set @Filter = 'i do not care'';
    insert into Production.ProductSubcategory(ProductCategoryID, Name,
    rowguid, ModifiedDate)
    values(4, ''Evil Subcategory'', newid(), current_timestamp);--';
```

Listing 4: Using SQL injection to add an "evil" subcategory.

If the account running the query has elevated privileges, it could possibly have access to other databases, allowing an attacker to collect information far more valuable than product subcategories.

Attacking Websites

In the previous section, we envisioned a basic site. In this section, we will build the site and attack it directly, applying what we learned in Management Studio. The full code for this project is available in .zip format, as part of the code download for this book.

Our website will be a rather simple ASP.NET web forms application. Listing 5 shows the base HTML.

```
<div>
   <asp:TextBox ID="txtSearch" runat="server" Text="Enter some text here." />
   <asp:Button ID="btnClickMe" runat="server" Text="Click Me" OnClick="btnClickMe_
Click" />
</div>
<br />
<div>
  You searched for: <asp:Label ID="lblSearchString" runat="server" />
</div>
<br />
<div>
   <asp:GridView ID="gvGrid" runat="server" AutoGenerateColumns="true">
   <Columns>
      <asp:TemplateField>
         <HeaderTemplate>Name</HeaderTemplate>
         <ItemTemplate><%# Eval("Name") %></ItemTemplate>
      </asp:TemplateField>
   </Columns>
   </asp:GridView>
</div>
```

Listing 5:   A simple ASP.NET web form.

Create a project in Visual Studio, and copy and paste this into a new page. Then, go to the code-behind. This code-behind is simplistic with a number of major errors, so please do not think of this as production-worthy code; neither should any of this be run in a production environment. With that said, Listing 6 provides sample C# code to query SQL Server based on an input search string.

```
protected void Page_Load(object sender, EventArgs e)
{
   if (!IsPostBack)
   {
      //Using .NET 4.0 here. If you want to use 2.0/3.5, change to
      //IsNullOrEmpty.
      if (!String.IsNullOrWhiteSpace(Request.QueryString["search"]))
         LoadData(Request.QueryString["search"]);
   }
}
```

```csharp
protected void btnClickMe_Click(object sender, EventArgs e)
{
   LoadData(txtSearch.Text);
}

protected void LoadData(string Filter)
{
   //Using .NET 4.0 here. If you want to use 2.0/3.5, change to IsNullOrEmpty.
   if (String.IsNullOrWhiteSpace(Filter))
   {
      Response.Write("You need a filter here, buddy!");
      gvGrid.Visible = false;
   }
   else
   {
      using (SqlConnection conn = new
               SqlConnection("server=localhost;database=AdventureWorks;
                              trusted_connection=yes"))
      {
         string sql = String.Empty;
         sql = "select Name, ProductSubcategoryID, ProductCategoryID from
               Production.ProductSubcategory where Name like '%" + Filter +
               "%' order by ProductSubcategoryID;";
         using (SqlCommand cmd = new SqlCommand(sql, conn))
         {
            cmd.CommandTimeout = 30;
            conn.Open();
            SqlDataReader dr =
               cmd.ExecuteReader(CommandBehavior.CloseConnection);
            gvGrid.DataSource = dr;
            gvGrid.DataBind();
            gvGrid.Visible = true;
         }
         lblSearchString.Visible = gvGrid.Visible;
         lblSearchString.Text = Filter;
      }
   }
}
```

Listing 6:   Bad C# code to search product subcategories by name.

Using this code, we now have a functional website we can use for SQL injection attacks. This website's flaws offer us two basic means for injection: through the `querystring`, or through a text-box and button. Both of these eventually call the `LoadData` function in the code-behind, which runs a SQL query to pull back a list of product subcategories, given a filter. Fire up a debug session in Visual Studio and start attacking the site through either mechanism.

Before performing an attack, it is typically a good idea to understand normal behavior. Type "bike" into the text box and click the button. You should see a grid with a list of five bike-related subcategories appear, as per Listing 1, previously. Unfortunately, with just a few more characters, we can begin to perform unexpected actions. Now search for the following:

```
'bike' OR 1=1-- '
```

After entering this code snippet into our text-box, we can see the entire list of product subcategories. From there, the world, or at least the database, is our oyster. We can use this page to perform reconnaissance on the SQL Server instance, searching for databases, tables, and even data. For example, the following query will show all of the databases on the instance, as well as their IDs and SQL Server compatibility level:

```
'nada' UNION ALL select name, database_id, compatibility_level
                from sys.databases;-- '
```

The latter two pieces of information are not necessarily important for an attack, but we needed something to ensure that the second half of our UNION ALL statement has a column structure that is compatible with the first half. This particular column structure includes one `varchar` and two `integer` fields, and so we follow along to match the schema and prevent an error from being returned.

Aside from running select statements that match the "expected" query's schema, we can perform other types of queries, simply by typing them into the available text box. For example, it would be possible to enable `xp_cmdshell`, get the server to connect via

FTP to another server and download malicious software, and then use `xp_cmdshell` again to install this malicious software, thereby giving an attacker full control over a database server.

Alternatively, we could use `xp_cmdshell` to open a web browser and navigate to a specific page that attempts to install malicious software on the server using JavaScript or an ActiveX component. Both of these attack mechanisms would have the same effect in terms of potentially compromising a database server. What follows is an example, showing the first step of this attack, turning on `xp_cmdshell` (in case it is not already enabled).

```
'nada'; exec sp_configure 'show advanced options', 1; reconfigure;
        exec sp_configure 'xp_cmdshell', 1; reconfigure; --'
```

After turning on `xp_cmdshell`, it would be possible to execute malicious code through `xp_cmdshell`. This is not as easy as simply having it open an instance of Internet Explorer and navigating to one's malicious site of choice, but it is possible.

Defending Websites

Now that we have an idea of how to attack a website, we can start to formulate ideas for how to defend one. We'll consider three:

- **Blacklists**, and why they cause problems and don't work.

- **Whitelists,** and why they are essential in some cases, but don't work in others.

- **Parameterized Queries**, the best and most effective form of protection from SQL Injection.

Blacklists

The first line of defense that many developers come up with is a blacklist: we know that keywords like "select," "insert," and "drop" are necessary to perform a SQL injection attack, so if we just ban those keywords, everything should be fine, right? Alas, life is not so simple; this leads to a number of problems with blacklists in general, as well as in this particular case.

The second-biggest problem with blacklists is that they could block people from performing legitimate requests. For example, a user at a paint company's website may wish to search for "drop cloths," so a naïve blacklist, outlawing use of the word "drop" in a search would lead to false positives.

The biggest problem is that, unless extreme care is taken, the blacklist will still let through malicious code. One of the big failures with SQL injection blacklists is that there are a number of different white-space characters: hex 0x20 (space), 0x09 (tab), 0x0A, 0x0B, 0x0C, 0x0D, and 0xA0 are all legitimate white-space as far as a SQL Server query is concerned. If the blacklist is looking for "drop table," it is looking for the word "drop," followed by a 0x20 character, followed by the word "table." If we replace the 0x20 with a 0x09, it sails right by the blacklist.

Even if we do guard against these combinations, there is another avenue of attack.

Why blacklists don't work

Simply put, there are too many ways round them. We'll consider two of the main attack vectors that render blacklists impotent.

HTTP Parameter Pollution

HTTP Parameter Pollution (HTTP://TINYURL.COM/HTTPPOL) uses a quirk in HTML query strings to attack websites. A typical query string looks like the following:
http://[website].com/SomePage.aspx?SearchTerm=Elvis&MemorabiliaType=Clock

In this example, we are looking for an Elvis clock. The `SearchTerm` parameter for this example is set to `Elvis`, and the `MemorabiliaType` parameter is set to `Clock`. The web page can read these parameters (in ASP.NET, these are viewed with calls to `Request.QueryString["SearchTerm"]` and `Request.QueryString["MemorabiliaType"]`, respectively) and handle them as necessary.

What happens, though, when somebody modifies the URL to add in a second `SearchTerm` parameter? The resulting behavior differs, depending upon which web platform is handling the URL request. The web platform could convert the different parameters into a list, ignore all but the first instance of a parameter, ignore all but the last instance of a parameter, display an error on the web page, or take any of a number of other actions. ASP.NET puts the different terms into a comma-delimited string. Thus, if we change the above URL to:
http://[website].com/SomePage.aspx?SearchTerm=Elvis&SearchTerm=Evil&MemorabiliaType=Clock

`Request.QueryString["SearchTerm"]` would return `"Elvis,Evil"` instead of just `"Elvis"` or just `"Evil"`.

Armed with this knowledge, an attacker can use HTTP Parameter Pollution in a SQL injection attack to get around basic blacklist filtering. For example, suppose that the website does in fact filter out the word "drop" followed by any of the seven white-space characters, followed by the word "table." In that case, we could still perform a query-string-based attack and drop a table by putting /* and */ around our HTTP query parameters to comment out the commas.

This leaves us with a valid SQL statement:

`SomePage.aspx?SearchTerm=`**`drop`**`/*&SearchTerm=*/`**`table dbo.Users;--`**

There is no white space after the "`drop`" keyword, or before the "`table`" keyword, so this attack gets right around the blacklist rule described above; best of all, because HTTP Parameter Pollution is not well known among developers, they probably have not even thought of this particular behavior, leaving the website exposed while creating a false sense of security.

Queries as binary strings

Even if a developer has created a blacklist that plans around the HTTP Parameter Pollution attack vector, there are yet more methods available. For example, we can convert a SQL statement to binary, and then execute the binary. Suppose that we want to get a list of names, database IDs, and compatibility levels from all databases on the server, but we cannot use the "`select`" keyword at all because of a blacklist. One way around this limitation would be to get a binary representation of the query, which is easy to do in SQL Server Management Studio.

```
SELECT  CAST('select name, database_id, compatibility_level
              from sys.databases;' AS VARBINARY(8000));
```

Listing 7:   Returning a binary representation of a query.

This returns a long hexadecimal string. Copy and paste that string in Listing 8 and you have an attack.

```
DECLARE @i VARCHAR(8000);
SET @i = CAST([long hex string] AS VARCHAR(8000));
EXEC(@i);
```

Listing 8:   Using a binary string form of a query in an injection attack.

This attack, combined with HTTP Parameter Pollution, means that attackers can bypass more blacklists. In this particular case, the result would not be interesting, because this query would run separately from the SQL query that .NET runs, so the results would not be in the same data set and would not appear on our grid. With that said, however, there have been several attacks that used the execution of binary representations of SQL queries to update all textual columns on databases, inserting code into each row that tries to open malicious JavaScript on rogue servers.

Whitelists

Blacklists are an untenable option, so the next thought might be to switch to whitelists. A whitelist is the opposite of a blacklist: instead of expressly prohibiting specified elements, and allowing anything not on the list, a whitelist allows specified elements and prohibits everything else.

In some cases, whitelists are essential. For example, with a radio button list, the server side should check whether the form value returned is valid. If the only possible values are "0," "1," and "2," but the value "monkey" is received back, somebody has, well, monkeyed with the form; from there, the server could either use a default value or throw an exception. Also, if the structure of a text field is known, such as a Social Security number, credit card number, amount of money, or date, a whitelist can accept certain patterns, rejecting all others. This helps detect data entry errors and also protects against SQL injection in these particular form fields, at least until "'; `drop table Users--`" becomes a valid Social Security Number.

This kind of whitelist breaks down for general searches, though. With free-form text fields, there is no necessary pattern, and so we cannot create a regular expression against which to check the data. Thus, a whitelist is not a valid option in all circumstances.

Parameterized queries

Forget about blacklists, and move whitelisting into the world of data validation rather than SQL injection prevention. There is only one effective method for preventing SQL injection through an application: query parameterization.

In our sample code, we used a `SqlCommand` object to execute a SQL statement and return the results in a `SqlDataReader`. This worked but, as we have subsequently learned, it is not a safe way of doing things. The reason is that the `Filter` variable was not parameterized correctly. Instead, our data access code concatenated various strings, including the `Filter` parameter, to create one SQL query. The correct alternative to developer-led concatenation is to build a `SqlParameter`, put the contents of the `Filter` variable into the parameter, and pass that off to SQL Server as a contained parameter rather than simply being part of the text. This change is relatively simple, making our data access code look as shown in Listing 9.

```
using (SqlConnection conn = new SqlConnection("server=localhost;database=AdventureW
orks;
                    trusted_connection=yes"))
{
   string sql = String.Empty;
   sql = "select Name, ProductSubcategoryID, ProductCategoryID
           from Production.ProductSubcategory
           where Name like '%@Filter%' order by ProductSubcategoryID;";
   using (SqlCommand cmd = new SqlCommand(sql, conn))
   {
      //create a parameter for @Filter
      SqlParameter filter = new SqlParameter();
      filter.ParameterName = "@Filter";
      filter.Value = Filter;
      //attach our parameter to the SqlCommand
      cmd.Parameters.Add(filter);
      cmd.CommandTimeout = 30;
      conn.Open();
```

```
        SqlDataReader dr = cmd.ExecuteReader(CommandBehavior.CloseConnection);
        gvGrid.DataSource = dr;
        gvGrid.DataBind();
        gvGrid.Visible = true;
    }
    //Continue along with our code
}
```

Listing 9:   A `SqlParameter` object in C# eliminates our prior SQL injection vulnerability.

With this minor change in data access code, we eliminate the possibility of a SQL injection attack on this particular query. We can try any combination of characters or attack techniques but it will be to no avail: we are unable to get "outside" the parameter.

The way this works is that, when we have a `SqlCommand` object with associated `SqlParameter` objects, the query sent to SQL Server actually changes somewhat. Open up an instance of SQL Server Profiler and start a new trace using the T-SQL template, and then return to the sample web page. This web page simply creates a SQL string and does not parameterize the query. Using our classic "`bike' or 1=1--`" SQL injection code, we can see the end result as follows:

```
select Name, ProductSubcategoryID, ProductCategoryID
  from Production.ProductSubcategory
  where Name like '%bike' or 1=1--%' order by ProductSubcategoryID;
```

This is just as we would expect; the query runs, and the user's unexpected SQL code changes its basic structure. In comparison, on a web page that parameterizes the query correctly, there is quite a different result.

```
exec sp_executesql N'select Name, ProductSubcategoryID, ProductCategoryID
    from Production.ProductSubcategory where Name like ''%@Filter%'' order by
    ProductSubcategoryID;',N'@Filter nvarchar(14)',@Filter=N'bike'' or 1=1--'
```

We now see a call to `sp_executesql`, passing in the `Filter` parameter we used earlier. We can also see that our apostrophe, the character used to escape the confines of the parameter, has been doubled up, thus making it safe. There is absolutely no way to perform a SQL injection attack here; each apostrophe is doubled up and the query will remain safe. Despite that, here are a few more words of wisdom for added protection and perhaps even better system performance.

Be sure to match field sizes to the size of the character data types, wherever possible. For example, suppose there is a column on a table defined as a `varchar(10)`. In that case, the text box should only allow 10 characters of text. Even if the query were still susceptible to SQL injection, there are only a limited number of attacks possible with just 10 characters. You should also use matching field sizes in `SqlParameter` objects, setting a fixed size. As seen above, because we did not use a fixed size for the filter, the `SqlParameter` object's size was set to the length of the string: 14 characters. If somebody else types in 15 characters-worth of text, this creates a new execution plan and both end up in the plan cache. This is potentially a waste of precious plan cache space so, by having one specific size, SQL Server generates one plan in the cache, saving room for the plans of other queries.

Protecting Stored Procedures

At this point, I would like to leave the world of websites and return to the database server proper. We know that parameterized queries are the ultimate solution to SQL injection in our applications, web or otherwise. On the database side, however, we should look at stored procedures.

Fortunately, static stored procedures are, by themselves, invulnerable to SQL injection. For example, consider a stored procedure with the structure shown in Listing 10.

```
CREATE PROCEDURE GetProductSubcategoryByName
    @ProductSubcategoryName NVARCHAR(MAX)
AS
    SELECT  ProductSubcategoryID ,
            ProductCategoryID ,
            Name ,
            rowguid ,
            ModifiedDate
    FROM    Production.ProductSubcategory
    WHERE   Name = @ProductSubcategoryName;
GO
```

Listing 10:   A static `GetProductSubcategoryByName` stored procedure.

All of the attack attempts shown in Listing 11 will fail when run in Management Studio.

```
EXEC GetProductSubcategoryByName N''' OR 1 = 1--';
EXEC GetProductSubcategoryByName N''' UNION ALL select 1, 2, 3, 4, 5--';
EXEC GetProductSubcategoryByName N'''declare @i varchar(8000); set @i =
CAST([binary truncated so you can read this more easily] as varchar(8000));
exec(@i);'
```

Listing 11:   Some failed injection attacks on `GetProductSubcategoryByName`.

There is no way to "break out" of the parameter and so our query is safe from SQL injection. This is not a trivial result; it means that we can replace ad hoc SQL in our data layer with calls to stored procedures. This does not mean that ad hoc SQL is necessarily unsafe. The parameterized query in Listing 9 uses ad hoc SQL, and is immune from SQL injection. For this reason, I would not use the threat of SQL injection as a core reason for supporting stored procedures over ad hoc SQL in a .NET environment.

However, stored procedures do force you to use parameterization, whereas a developer might accidentally forget to parameterize an ad hoc SQL query. Unfortunately, there are ways to abuse stored procedures, such as using a .NET 1.1 `SqlDataAdapter`. This is an old and terrible method for getting data, and yet there is sample code out on the Internet that still uses it. Listing 12 shows an example of a dataset populated by a `SqlDataAdapter`.

```
//HINT: If your code looks like this, you're doing it wrong.
using (SqlConnection conn = new
     SqlConnection("server=.;database=AdventureWorks;trusted_connection=yes"))
{
    DataSet ds = new DataSet();
    SqlDataAdapter sda = new
SqlDataAdapter("Production.GetProductSubcategoryByName '" + Name + "'", conn);
    //Problem #1: running a stored procedure as a regular SQL query.
    //sda.SelectCommand.CommandType = CommandType.StoredProcedure;
    //If you uncomment the line above, at least the query would fail.

    sda.Fill(ds);
    gvGrid.DataSource = ds;
    gvGrid.DataBind();
}
```

Listing 12:   Stored procedures can be vulnerable to SQL injection attacks.

As mentioned in the comments, by not setting the `CommandType` of the `SqlData-Adapter` to that of a stored procedure, the code is susceptible to SQL injection, even when only static stored procedures are used. If we uncomment the line of code that sets the command type, and try to run this same process, we would get an exception and the query would fail, rather than performing potentially malicious actions.

The more interesting case involves stored procedures that use dynamic SQL. When somebody hears that stored procedures are "safe" whereas ad hoc SQL is "unsafe," that person might go around creating stored procedures like the one in Listing 13.

```
CREATE PROCEDURE dbo.ReallyBadAttempt @sql NVARCHAR(MAX)
AS
    EXEC(@sql);
GO
```

Listing 13:   A really bad stored procedure using dynamic SQL.

Code like that is just as susceptible to SQL injection as ad hoc SQL, because this stored procedure is essentially a vessel for executing ad hoc SQL. In fact, it is actually worse, because at least with legitimate ad hoc SQL, we can still parameterize the queries in .NET and turn them into good dynamic SQL calls, whereas with this procedure, we do not even get that benefit.

The stored procedure in Listing 13 is, admittedly, ridiculous, but more complicated stored procedures often make the same basic mistake. Take, for example, a stored procedure that retrieves a set based on some partial search criteria, or a procedure which takes as input a list of values rather than a single item, and returns all elements in that list. Listing 14 shows an example of the former.

```
CREATE PROCEDURE Production.VulnerableSearch @Filter VARCHAR(50)
AS
    DECLARE @sql VARCHAR(250);
    SET @sql = 'select * from Production.ProductSubcategory
                where Name like ''%'
        + @Filter + '%'';';
    EXEC(@sql);
GO
```

Listing 14:   Another bad stored procedure using dynamic SQL.

In general, attacking dynamic SQL is the same as attacking ad hoc SQL through a website: escape out of the current query, perform the attack, and comment out the rest of the expected query. We can perform a similar attack on this procedure through SQL Server Management Studio (or any other client that connects to the database), except this time, we have to double up the apostrophe used to escape out of the parameter, as shown in Listing 15.

```
EXEC Production.VulnerableSearch 'Bike'' OR 1 = 1--';
```

Listing 15:   An injection attack on the `VulnerableSearch` stored procedure.

By using a dynamic stored procedure with @Filter limited to 50 characters, we do gain a little bit of protection because an attacker could not craft a very long string. However, a "drop table" statement isn't that long.

Another form of fundamentally broken dynamic SQL statement is the list search. It is inevitable that a developer will want to create something like an array in SQL, to pass in a list and search for rows that match any value in that list. If they stumble upon Erland Sommerskog's excellent essay on the topic (HTTP://TINYURL.COM/2J4ZFX) then, hopefully, these developers will use one of the proper methods for simulating an array. Unfortunately, there are certain solutions that are more problematic. Listing 16 shows an example of one.

```
CREATE PROCEDURE Production.NotSecure
    @NameList NVARCHAR(MAX)
AS
    DECLARE @sql NVARCHAR(MAX);
    SET @sql = N'select * from Production.ProductSubcategory where Name IN ('
        + @NameList + N');';
    EXEC sp_executesql @sql, N'@NameList nvarchar(max)', @NameList;
GO

--try it out
EXEC Production.NotSecure N'''Mountain Bikes'', ''Road Bikes''';
```

Listing 16:   Bad list search using dynamic SQL and sp_executesql.

This procedure uses sp_executesql, which takes three primary parameters:

- **@statement** – the SQL statement to run

- **@params** – an nvarchar string containing a list of the set of parameters the query will use

- a series of **@param(x)** – a comma-delimited set of the actual parameters used.

The idea is that, by entering the parameters directly into the statement, we allow SQL Server to parameterize these variables correctly, ensuring that users cannot escape out of the query. Going back to correctly parameterized queries through ASP.NET, they all use `sp_executesql` and the variables are all "inside" the SQL query.

Unlike the correctly parameterized queries that ASP.NET generated before, this particular way of using `sp_executesql` is not safe. The reason is that, even though we pass `@NameList` as a query parameter, we actually make use of `@NameList` before `sp_executesql` has a chance to run. The `sp_executesql` procedure will not throw an exception or generate any type of error if a parameter is listed that is not actually used in the SQL query, meaning that developers and DBAs must remain vigilant when it comes to using `sp_executesql` correctly. The consequences are potentially devastating.

```
EXEC Production.NotSecure N''MountainBikes'') OR 1 = 1--';
```

Listing 17: Injection attack on bad list search.

In this case, we can pass in a specially crafted string and get around `sp_executesql`'s built-in SQL injection protection mechanism. On the web form, we would need to double up the apostrophe after "MountainBikes" and add a closed parenthesis before using our "OR 1=1" statement. Getting the correct syntax may take a few tries for an attacker who does not have access to source code, but it is fundamentally no more difficult than the basic examples we have covered already. Once the attacker has the correct syntax, the results are the same, `sp_executesql` or no `sp_executesql`.

The fact that we were able to exploit an SQL injection vulnerability in a dynamic SQL statement that uses `sp_executesql`, however, is certainly not the fault of the system stored procedure; rather, it is the fault of the developer who did not use `sp_executesql` correctly in the first place. The `sp_executesql` system stored procedure translates parameters and makes them safe for use, but we did not actually pass any parameters into the command; instead, we translated the parameters first and passed in a basic string of text to the `sp_executesql` procedure. Listing 18 shows a more appropriate use of `sp_executesql`.

```
CREATE PROCEDURE Production.InvulnerableSearch @Filter VARCHAR(50)
AS
    DECLARE @sql NVARCHAR(250);
    SET @sql = N'select * from Production.ProductSubcategory where Name like ''%@
Filter%'';';
    EXEC sp_executesql @sql, N'@Filter varchar(50)', @Filter;
GO
```

Listing 18:   Good list search using dynamic SQL and `sp_executesql`.

This particular dynamic SQL search, which matches `Production.VulnerableSearch`'s intention and result set, is invulnerable to SQL injection attack. Note that, unlike our previous attempts at using `sp_executesql`, `@Filter` is entirely "within" the `@sql` variable. `sp_executesql` translates the value of `@Filter` and makes it safe from SQL injection *before* executing the dynamic SQL statement, therefore offering the same level of SQL injection protection as a static stored procedure or parameterized ad hoc query.

Other Forms of Defense

At this point, we know how to create code that is invulnerable to SQL injection. We learned that the correct way to handle application-level SQL calls is through parameterized queries. In .NET languages like C# and VB.NET, we have access to easy-to-use classes and methods, some of which we discussed in this chapter. Other web frameworks and programming languages have their own parameterization libraries, so if you're using something other than the Microsoft stack, use whatever equivalent parameterization functionality is available.

In addition to parameterization at the application level, we also learned how to secure stored procedures in SQL Server. Static stored procedures are already safe from SQL injection, and we can protect against SQL injection in dynamic stored procedures through proper use of `sp_executesql`.

Before wrapping up this chapter, I would like to touch upon a few additional areas of interest with regard to SQL injection. It would be easy to write entire chapters on these, but I will have to settle for a few sentences on each topic.

QUOTENAME and REPLACE instead of sp_executesql

Kimberly Tripp has a great set of blog posts on how to protect against SQL injection attacks by making appropriate use of the built-in QUOTENAME and REPLACE functions when calling the exec command. She argues in favor of using these instead of sp_executesql because it can perform significantly better in certain circumstances. By contrast, Aaron Bertrand prefers sp_executesql.

- **Little Bobby Tables, SQL Injection and EXECUTE AS**
   HTTP://TINYURL.COM/PWCKPKZ

- **EXEC and sp_executesql – how are they different?**
   HTTP://TINYURL.COM/ON68EQJ

- **Bad Habits to Kick: Using EXEC() instead of sp_executesql**
   HTTP://TINYURL.COM/P5UJW9X

In this particular debate, I side with Bertrand, which is why I tended to use sp_executesql above instead of exec with QUOTENAME and REPLACE. Although sp_executesql is often slower than simply running exec with appropriate use of QUOTENAME and REPLACE, it is also a lot easier to get everything right. This is especially true for application developers writing stored procedures that use dynamic SQL. In that case, I would not automatically trust them (or even myself!) to get it right and, instead, would focus on the easier safe method, at least until performance simply is not good enough.

Appropriate permissions

Throughout this chapter, I have assumed that the account running these stored procedures and ad hoc SQL statements has some hefty rights, probably db_owner, and maybe even sysadmin. Sadly, this is usually a safe assumption.

If a procedure runs a SELECT statement that only hits three tables in the Adventure-Works database, it does not need permission to insert records, create user accounts, run xp_cmdshell, or view the INFORMATION_SCHEMA or sys schemas! Erland Sommarskog's outstanding essay, *Giving Permissions through Stored Procedures* (HTTP://WWW.SOMMARSKOG.SE/GRANTPERM.HTML), describes in detail various methods available for granting appropriate permissions for stored procedures (see also, the previously referenced Kimberly Tripp blog post on the EXECUTE AS functionality in SQL Server, and how to use that to allow only limited access to SQL stored procedures).

Even if the resources are not available to create appropriate permissions and signed certificates for each stored procedure, at least create limited-functionality accounts and run stored procedures through those accounts. Reader and editor logins that use the sp_datareader and sp_datawriter security roles, respectively, would at least protect against certain shenanigans, such as attempts to drop tables, or to use what a developer intends to be a SELECT statement to insert or delete records.

Automated tools

A number of tools can help discover possible weaknesses in code, and so prevent attacks. One of my favorites is **sqlmap** (HTTP://SQLMAP.ORG/), which allows SQL injection attack attempts against a number of database vendors' products, not just SQL Server. It also lets the user perform advanced SQL injection techniques not covered in this chapter, such as timing-based injection attacks.

In addition to those features, it can tie into Metasploit (HTTP://METASPLOIT.COM), an outstanding penetration-testing suite. Inside Metasploit, there are SQL Server-specific modules such as one that tries to guess a SQL Server instance's **sa** password. If it is successful, the module automatically tries to create a Metasploit shell, giving the attacker full access to the database server. Both tools come with thorough documentation and can be automated for enterprise-level penetration tests.

Web application firewalls

Web application firewalls (WAFs) are a hot topic in the security world at present. Most of them claim to protect against SQL injection attacks, and they often do a reasonable job. Given what we've discussed in this chapter, there are many ways to sneak in injection code, so I would not recommend using a WAF as the only line of defense.

Even if your web application firewall does block all SQL injection attempts perfectly, does it fail open or fail closed? In other words, in the event that somebody targets a denial of service attack on the web application firewall and it ceases to function, will it allow all traffic to go on through, or will it effectively shut down the website by failing closed? If the product fails open, then an attacker could still perform SQL injection, although the attacker would need to be considerably more sophisticated than if there was no WAF.

WAF products are worth investigating, if the price is right, as they can be a valuable addition to a security infrastructure. They are not, however, the best line of defense against SQL injection: good development practices and parameterized queries are.

Additional Resources

Thanks to the prevalence of SQL injection attacks, finding examples of attacks is a simple exercise. As of this chapter's publication, a few recent attacks include:

- Stratfor – HTTP://TINYURL.COM/STRATFORSQLI

- IRC Federal – HTTP://TINYURL.COM/IRCFEDERALSQLI

- Sony – HTTP://TINYURL.COM/SONYSQLI

- Arthur Hicken of Parasoft – a curated list of high-profile SQL injection attacks, located at HTTP://CODECURMUDGEON.COM/WP/SQL-INJECTION-HALL-OF-SHAME/.

In terms of thwarting SQL injection, I recommend the following additional resources:

- **Bobby Tables** – a compendium of ways to parameterize queries in different programming languages, including technologies outside of ASP.Net and SQL Server HTTP://BOBBY-TABLES.COM/

- **Microsoft's best practice guidance on SQL** HTTP://TINYURL.COM/NQHGJ3G

- **Erland Sommarskog's essay on dynamic SQL – includes a primer on SQL injection** HTTP://TINYURL.COM/PXPGC82

Using Database Mail to Email Enable Your SQL Server

John Barnett

The job of a DBA team is, in essence, to maintain a "steady ship," ensuring that the database systems in their care are available, reliable and responsive. When problems do arise, the team must respond quickly and effectively. One of the keys to a fast response time is swift notification of problems as they arise and, for this purpose, we have a solution, Database Mail, built directly into SQL Server.

We can use Database Mail to:

- **send email from T-SQL** containing, for example, the results of a T-SQL statement and including reports and other necessary files as attachments

- **report on the success or failure** of SQL Server agent jobs

- **provide a real-time notification system** for SQL Server alerts.

This chapter describes how to enable, configure and use Database Mail in your applications. I'll also provide advice on troubleshooting Database Mail, and maintaining the `msdb` log table, where SQL Server retains details of email status messages, errors, and so on.

Getting Started with Database Mail

Over the coming sections, I'll walk through the process of enabling and configuring Database Mail, and then provide sample code, demonstrating its use in building an email notification system.

A note of caution before we start...

The examples in this chapter will show how to send automated emails from SQL Server to your staff, customers, and suppliers. This could have legal implications. Refrain from sending near-identical content to large numbers of people, unless absolutely necessary. Even if you only send these emails within your organization, get agreement with staff, and offer opt-outs. Exercise special care if you use Database Mail to send to external recipients. If not handled correctly, the company hosting the server could be blacklisted.

To set up Database Mail, and work through the examples in this chapter, you'll need any version of SQL Server 2005 and later, and any edition except the Express editions.

Database Mail uses SMTP (Simple Mail Transport Protocol), the Internet standard for transmission of email, so you'll need access to an SMTP server, along with its fully qualified DNS name for setting up the Database Mail profile. It will look something like `smtp.example.com`. Depending how security is configured on the SMTP server, the email administrator may also need to:

- supply a username and password for connecting

- grant permissions for connections to come from your SQL Server's IP address.

You can download the code examples as part of the code bundle for this chapter, all tested against SQL Server 2005 and 2008 Developer Editions with the `AdventureWorks` sample database for that version.

All screenshots were taken using SQL Server 2008 Developer SP3 running on Windows 7 Professional; minor changes may exist due to differences in operating system or SQL Server version. Lastly, in the walk-through, I assume the reader has a basic understanding of both SQL Server and email client configuration.

Enabling Database Mail

By default, Database Mail is disabled for security reasons, so we need to enable it before we can use it. Open SQL Server Management Studio (SSMS) and log in as a user with sysadmin rights. Expand the server, open **Management** and right-click on **Database Mail**. Click **Enable Database Mail** (see Figure 1).

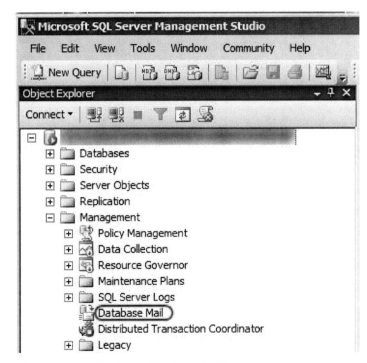

Figure 1:   Enabling Database Mail.

Alternatively, we can enable Database Mail using the SQL Server Surface Area **Configuration** tool from the **Start** menu group, use the `sp_configure` system stored procedure, or enable it through the configuration wizard, as discussed next.

Configuring Database Mail

We can configure the Database Mail subsystem either using the GUI interface, or via T-SQL. From SSMS, expand **Management** then **Database Mail**, right-click and choose **Configure Database Mail** to open the Database Mail Configuration Wizard. Enter a profile name and description, as in Figure 2.

New Profile

Specify the profile name, description, accounts, and failover priority.

Profile name: testprofile

Description: Test Profile for Tribal SQL

A profile may be associated with multiple SMTP accounts. If an account fails while sending an e-mail, the profile uses the next account in the priority list. Specify the accounts associated with the profile, and move the accounts to set the failover priority.

SMTP accounts:

Priority	Account Name	E-mail Address	Add...
			Remove

Figure 2:   Configuring Database Mail – creating a new profile.

Click **Add** to create a database mail account to add to your new profile. You need to provide an account name and description (narrative text for future reference) along with details about the SMTP server, obtained from the email administrator.

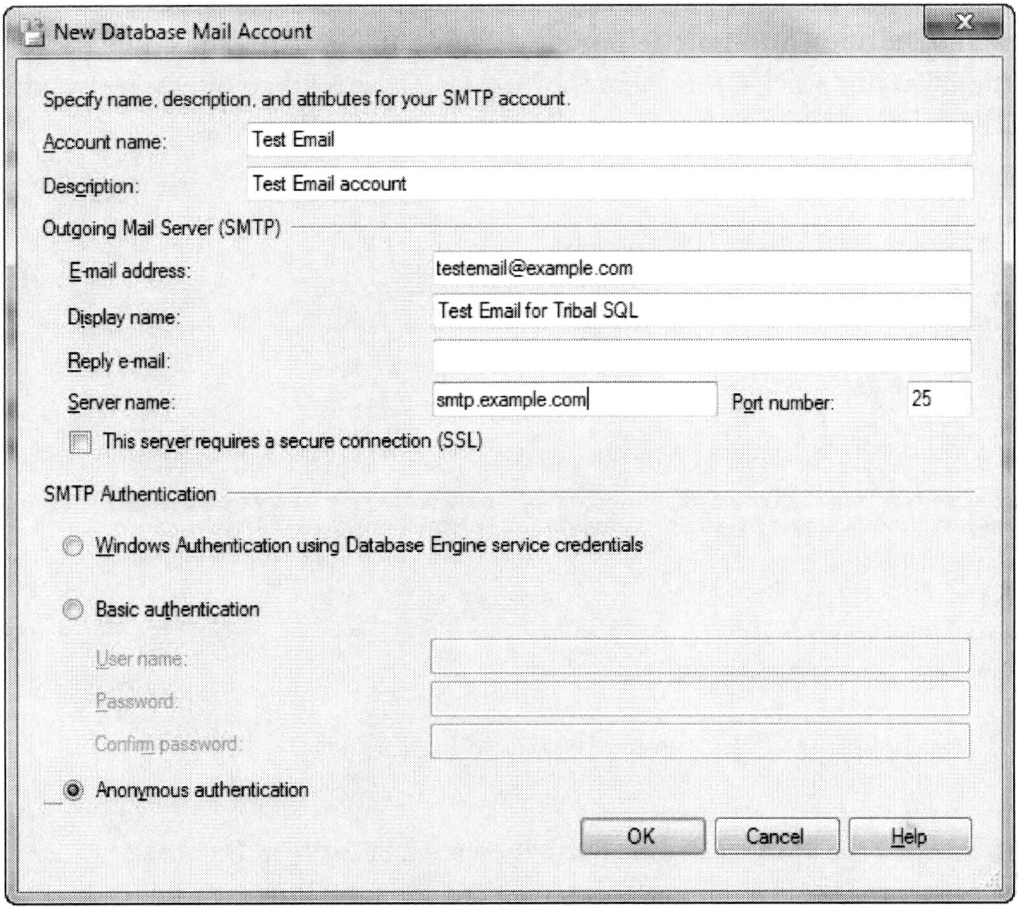

Figure 3: Configuring Database Mail – creating a new Database Mail account.

In the **E-mail address** field, enter the sender (**From:**) address. In the **Display name** field, enter the name for the sender that will appear alongside their address. Optionally, we can provide a **Reply e-mail** to populate the "Reply to" email header.

Test email accounts

If you need some test email addresses, example.com is a safe domain. IANA maintains the site specifically for documentation and training materials (see HTTP://WWW.EXAMPLE.COM *for more information).*

In the **Server name** box, enter the DNS name of the server. For the remaining options, port number, SSL and authentication, accept the defaults, unless instructed otherwise by your email administrator. Click **OK** to close the **New Database Mail** account screen and you will see the newly created email account added to the profile (Figure 4).

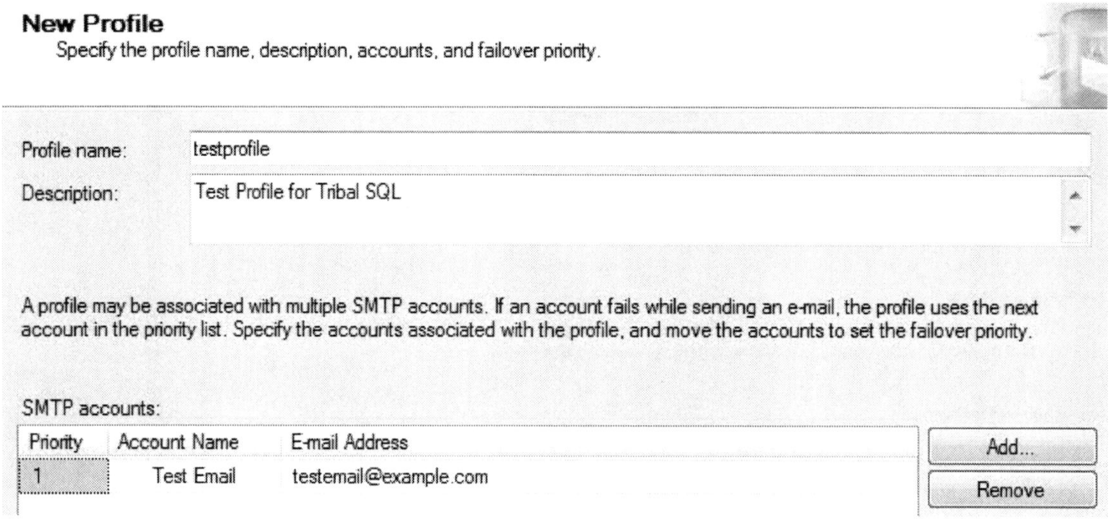

Figure 4:   Configuring Database Mail – an email account added to a profile.

Click **Next** to move to the **Manage Profile Security** screen. Security in Database Mail uses the concept of profiles, and on this screen are two tabs, **Public Profiles** and **Private Profiles**.

Public profiles are accessible by any SQL user with permissions within the msdb database, whereas a private profile is accessible only to specific named users within msdb. Members of the sysadmin role automatically have access to all profiles.

The guest database user has access to a public email profile, which means that any SQL Server Login can access the public profile and send email, without the DBA configuring a database user account for its explicit use. For obvious security reasons, I advise against this; SQL Server is a database server and should only send email to known recipients, not act as an email relay for unauthorized traffic.

Therefore, leave the **Public Profiles** tab untouched and switch to **Private Profiles**, to create our `testprofile` as a private profile. You can use the **User name** drop-down to grant access to the profile to specific users within the `msdb` database.

You can tick the **Access** box on the left-hand side to grant access to specific profiles to users within the `msdb` database. Optionally, you can set the **Default Profile** to **Yes** to designate a maximum of one default profile per user. Setting the default profile option to **Yes** means that if a database user within `msdb` attempts to send an email without specifying the `@profile_name` option, SQL Server will use the default private profile. Setting it to **No**, as in Figure 5, stipulates the use of a specific profile to send a notification.

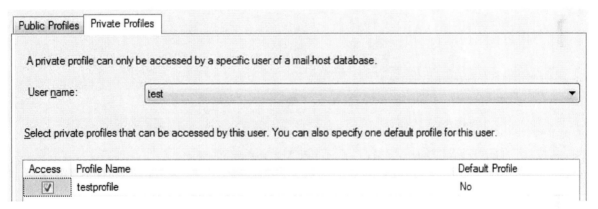

Figure 5:   Configuring Database Mail – granting the `test` user access to `testprofile`.

Click **Next** to advance to the **Configure System Parameters** screen, shown in Figure 6.

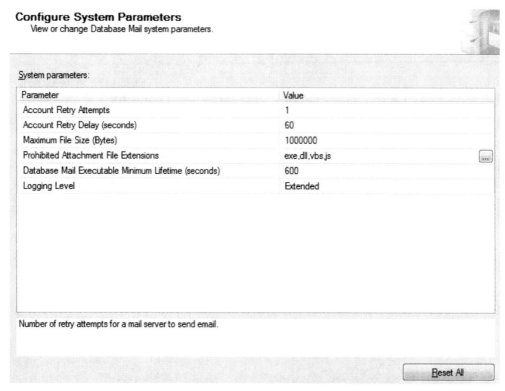

Configure System Parameters
View or change Database Mail system parameters.

System parameters:

Parameter	Value
Account Retry Attempts	1
Account Retry Delay (seconds)	60
Maximum File Size (Bytes)	1000000
Prohibited Attachment File Extensions	exe,dll,vbs,js
Database Mail Executable Minimum Lifetime (seconds)	600
Logging Level	Extended

Number of retry attempts for a mail server to send email.

Reset All

Figure 6: Configuring Database Mail – Database Mail system parameters.

The following system parameters for Database Mail can be configured. Mostly, I use the default options for each of these, but there may be good reasons to change them:

- **Account Retry Attempts** – number of attempts Database Mail will take before recording a message failure. If you have a slow network or a heavily loaded SMTP server, you might consider increasing this value.

- **Account Retry Delay (seconds)** – time Database Mail will wait between send retries.

- **Maximum File Size (Bytes)** – largest file size it will attempt to transmit; increase the default only if you really need to send large files.

- **Prohibited Attachment File Extensions** – list of file extensions it won't send; some secure environments will have tighter restrictions, and you may need to add extensions such as `ps1`, `com` and `bat` to the prohibited list.

- **Database Mail Executable Minimum Lifetime (seconds)** – shortest time the Database Mail process will remain running before closing down.

- **Logging Level** – the amount of information recorded in the logs; you may occasionally need to use a more verbose level when troubleshooting.

Clicking **Reset All** will revert settings to the default.

When you click **Next**, and then **Finish**, SQL Server will configure Database Mail as specified, including security, access rights, and parameters.

Testing Database Mail

To test Database Mail, right-click on the **Database Mail** node, choose **Send Test E-Mail**, enter the destination email address in the **To:** box, a test subject line and message body similar to Figure 7, then click **Send Test E-mail**. A few seconds later, depending on the speed of the email system and network, an email will appear in your inbox.

If the email appears, carry on to the next step. If it doesn't, revisit the earlier steps as something is configured incorrectly for the environment, or refer to the *Troubleshooting Database Mail* section, later in this chapter, for advice.

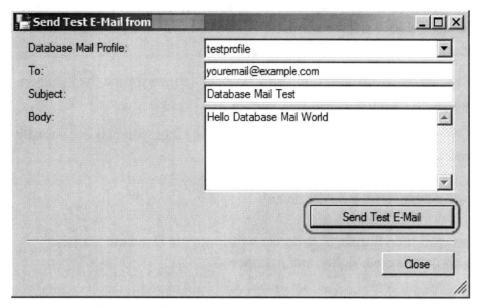

Figure 7:   Testing Database Mail.

Security requirements

Once configured, any user with `sysadmin` privileges can utilize Database Mail. Otherwise, the user must be a member of the `DatabaseMailUserRole` role in the `msdb` database. This grants it access to the `sp_send_dbmail` stored procedure as well as the logs and maintenance stored procedures, all detailed later in the chapter.

To add to the `DatabaseMailUserRole` a user that exists in `msdb`:

- Log in as a user with `sysadmin` rights.

- In SSMS, go to the `msdb` database and select **Security | Roles | Database Roles**.

- Double-click `DatabaseMailUserRole` and use the **Add** button at the bottom to add the database user to the role.

To add to `DatabaseMailUserRole` a user that is not present in `msdb`:

- Log in as a user with `sysadmin` rights.

- In SSMS, go to the `msdb` database, navigate **Security | Users**, right-click and select **New User**.

- On the **General** page, create a new user from a login.

- On the **Membership** page, tick the **DatabaseMailUserRole** box.

Using Database Mail in Your Own Applications

To use Database Mail in your own applications, simply pass the correct set of parameters into the `sp_send_dbmail` system stored procedure, as you would for any other stored procedure call, and let it do its work.

Books Online details the full set of parameters, including sending HTML email, priority flags, sending to multiple recipients simultaneously, and more, at HTTP://MSDN.MICROSOFT.COM/EN-US/LIBRARY/MS190307.ASPX.

The code in Listing 1 calls the `sp_send_dbmail` system stored procedure to send an email from SQL Server, using our new `testprofile` database mail profile. It is the T-SQL equivalent of clicking the **Send Test E-Mail** button in the previous step.

```
EXEC msdb.dbo.sp_send_dbmail @profile_name = 'testprofile',
    @recipients = N'youremail@example.com',
    @subject = N'Test email Message Subject 1', @body = N'Test email Body 1';
```

Listing 1:   Sending a test email from T-SQL.

If successful, the output, "Mail queued" will appear in the results pane, and the message will arrive in your mailbox a few seconds later.

Sending an email with a file attachment

As with all email clients, Database Mail allows us to send attachments with the email. We attach items through its `@file_attachments` parameter, as shown in Listing 2. In this manner, we can send users the results of a pre-generated report.

```
EXEC msdb.dbo.sp_send_dbmail @profile_name = 'testprofile',
    @recipients = N'youremail@example.com',
    @subject = N'Test email Message Subject 2', @body = N'Test email Body 2',
    @file_attachments = N'C:\temp\testfile.txt';
```

Listing 2:   Sending an email with a file attachment.

To send multiple file attachments, simply separate the file paths with a semicolon.

```
EXEC msdb.dbo.sp_send_dbmail @profile_name = 'testprofile',
    @recipients = N'youremail@example.com',
    @subject = N'Test email Message Subject 3', @body = N'Test email Body 3',
    @file_attachments = N'C:\temp\testfile.txt;C:\temp\testfile2.doc';
```

Listing 3:   Sending an email with multiple file attachments.

Obviously, each file must exist at the specified location. In addition, ensure that there are no leading or trailing spaces between the end of one path, the semicolon and the start of the next as, otherwise, SQL Server tries to interpret it as part of the pathname for the relevant file and you will get "Attachment file invalid" error messages.

There are a few other caveats to this:

- Database Mail uses impersonation to determine if the Windows network account of the connected user is able to access the files specified. Therefore, users authenticated to SQL server using SQL logins won't be able to use the `@file_attachments` option.

This also ensures that Windows authenticated logins can only send files that they have permission to read using normal permissions.

- As discussed earlier, in relation to Database Mail system parameters, we can configure Database Mail to:

  - prohibit file attachments with specific extensions; files must not have an extension that is on this blocked list

  - prohibit file attachments over a maximum file size; files must be this size or smaller.

In addition, it is worth noting that email client configurations may impose further restrictions on access to file attachments, on the receiving end. This normally relates to files that could contain executable code or scripts and pose a risk to your computer's security.

Sending an email with the results of a T-SQL statement

Database Mail allows the sending of the results of an SQL statement either as a message body or as an attachment to another email. This is handy when we need to check that an overnight procedure ran correctly. For example, we can return the last run execution date from a table that the procedure updates at the end of execution, or return data with error statuses that may indicate further action is required.

Listing 4 shows how to send the results of an SQL statement in a message body. Note that there is no `@body` parameter and the addition of the `@attach_query_result_as_file` parameter is set to 0.

```
EXEC msdb.dbo.sp_send_dbmail @profile_name = 'testprofile',
    @recipients = N'youremail@example.com',
    @subject = N'Test Email message Subject 4',
    @query = 'select FirstName, LastName from AdventureWorks.Person.Contact
            where ContactID = 1',
    @attach_query_result_as_file = 0;
```

Listing 4:   Sending an email with a message body containing the results of executing
                a T-SQL statement.

Alternatively, Listing 5 sends the results as an attachment, referenced in
the message body.

```
EXEC msdb.dbo.sp_send_dbmail @profile_name = 'testprofile',
    @recipients = N'youremail@example.com',
    @subject = N'Test Email message Subject 5',
    @query = 'select FirstName, LastName from AdventureWorks.Person.Contact
            where ContactID = 1',
    @body = 'Please see attached file for query results',
    @attach_query_result_as_file = 1;
```

Listing 5:   Sending an email with a file containing the results of executing a T-SQL statement.

In both cases, you will notice that the results look untidy when viewed using a variable
width font (where different characters take up different widths of the page, for example,
the letter "I" takes less space than the letter "W"). While this may be acceptable for a
quick process completion spot check, sent to IT staff, it won't be acceptable for emails to
end-users or customers.

To get around this, we can use HTML email with a layout using CSS or tables, or build up
the result set for the recipient using text concatenation, then set the message body to the
result set. Both techniques are complex, but shortly I'll demonstrate the use of the latter
to send customized email alerts.

Sending an email to multiple recipients

It is very easy to adapt any of the previous examples to send the emails to multiple addresses. We simply use a semicolon-separated list of email addresses, as shown in Listing 6.

```
EXEC msdb.dbo.sp_send_dbmail @profile_name = 'testprofile',
    @recipients = N'youremail@example.com;youremail2@example.com',
    @subject = N'Test Email message Subject 5',
    @query = 'select FirstName, LastName from AdventureWorks.Person.Contact
            where ContactID = 1',
    @attach_query_result_as_file = 0;
```

Listing 6:   Sending an email to multiple recipients.

Of course, all recipients get the same email. In some cases, we need to customize our emails depending on the recipient. In the next section, I show how to do that. An alternative to this is to send to a distribution list.

Producing customized email alerts

The stored procedure in Listing 7 produces customized email alerts for managers, requesting timesheets for their team members.

This example uses nested loops rather than being set-based or a single stored procedure call – one loop for each user, then one loop for each row for that user. The outer loop retrieves a distinct list of recipients, whereas the inner loop handles the content for that recipient.

```
USE AdventureWorks
GO

CREATE PROCEDURE [dbo].[email_alerts]
AS
    SET NOCOUNT ON

/* Declare variables */
    DECLARE @empid INT                      -- Current employee ID
    DECLARE @message NVARCHAR(MAX)          -- Message body text

    DECLARE @manager_id INT                 -- Loop of Manager's ID
    DECLARE @manager_name VARCHAR(50)       -- Manager's name
    DECLARE @manager_email VARCHAR(50)      -- Manager's e-mail address

/* Initialise employee ID, manager ID and message content - can be replaced with
DECLARE and initialise above if running under SQL Server 2008 or newer */

    SELECT  @empid = 0
    SELECT  @manager_id = 0
    SELECT  @message = ''

    WHILE ( @manager_id IS NOT NULL )
        BEGIN
            -- reset message content for each manager
            SELECT  @message = ''

            -- get first manager ID
            SELECT  @manager_id = MIN(managerID)
            FROM    HumanResources.Employee
            WHERE   managerid > @manager_id

             -- Pull in manager's details for customising email header
            SELECT  @manager_name = p.FirstName + ' ' + p.LastName ,
                    @manager_email = p.EmailAddress
            FROM    Person.Contact p
            WHERE   ContactID = @manager_id

            -- Initialise custom message
            SELECT  @message = 'Dear ' + @manager_name + ',' + CHAR(13)
                    + CHAR(10) + CHAR(13) + CHAR(10)
                    + 'Kindly note that we are expecting from you staff timesheets
                        from the previous month, for the following staff.'
                    + CHAR(13) + CHAR(10)
```

```
        -- Reset employee loop for list
        SELECT  @empid = 0

        WHILE ( @empid IS NOT NULL )
            BEGIN
                SELECT  @empid = MIN(EmployeeID)
                FROM    HumanResources.Employee
                WHERE   ManagerID = @manager_id
                        AND EmployeeID > @empid
                -- Get employee details
                SELECT  @message = @message + ''
                        + Person.Contact.FirstName + ' '
                        + Person.Contact.LastName + CHAR(13) + CHAR(10)
                FROM    Person.Contact
                WHERE   Person.Contact.ContactID = @empid
            END
    -- Complete the message.
    SELECT  @message = @message + CHAR(13) + CHAR(10)
            + 'Please submit them to HR by the end of next week.'
            + CHAR(13) + CHAR(10)
    SELECT  @message = @message + 'Kind Regards,'
                            + CHAR(13) + CHAR(10)
            + CHAR(13) + CHAR(10)
    SELECT  @message = @message + 'HR Director.'
    -- Send the email
    /* Put your Database Mail profile name here */
    EXEC msdb.dbo.sp_send_dbmail @profile_name = 'testprofile',
        /* normally you would use @manager_email here */
        @recipients = N'testemail@example.com',
        @subject = N'Signed timesheets required from your staff',
        @body = @message
    END
GO
```

Listing 7:   Customized emails.

If run with the default data, 48 "Mail queued" messages will be the result, and 48 emails turn up in your inbox.

You can run this stored procedure on a recurring basis from a SQL Server Agent job step, but you should add functionality to ensure that it doesn't run over public holidays, and you should offer staff the facility to opt out of receiving these email alerts.

Why use this technique rather than a more conventional report writer (such as SSRS) with an email recipient? Many of the software companies that provide such tools charge license fees by the number of report recipients; this method removes this expense.

Reporting On Success or Failure of SQL Server Agent Jobs

Database Mail can automatically email a nominated SQL Server operator when any SQL Server Agent job runs, or on success or failure of specific Agent jobs.

Before we can implement this functionality, we must enable notification of SQL Server Agent jobs, configure it to use Database Mail and use a specific named profile for notification of jobs. We must also set job steps to report success or failure, as appropriate.

Enable a database mail profile for alert notification

In SSMS, right-click on **SQL Server Agent** and choose **Properties** and select the **Alert System** page. Configure the screen as appropriate but at a minimum, you must enable the alert system, choose **Database Mail** as the mail system, and select the **Mail profile**.

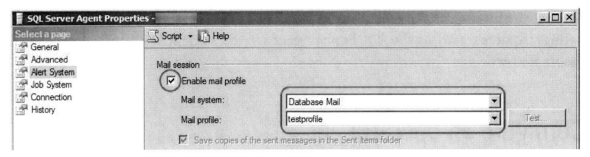

Figure 8:   Enabling our `testprofile` database mail profile for SQL Server Agent.

Leave the rest of the screen as is. We can ignore the section relating to Pager notification.

....

Why no Test... option?

The **Test...** *button next to the* **Mail Profile** *box (at least up to SQL Server 2008) is disabled when Database Mail is selected as the mail system. According to Books Online, this feature is only available if using SQL Mail (the older, deprecated email functionality in SQL Server).*

....

Designate a Fail-safe operator

At the bottom of the **Alert System** page, you'll see an option to set a **Fail-safe operator**. This is the operator and method of communication that Database Mail will use in the event that SQL Server Agent cannot access the `msdb` database to get the operator details, or if attempts to send to the designated operator fail, or if the designated operator is offline (due to day and time restrictions on pager-type notification).

You can enable the Fail-safe operator check box to designate a Fail-safe operator. Once configured, you cannot clear this designation, only transfer it to another operator, so think carefully about this. It is a good idea to set up one Fail-safe operator per instance of SQL Server, which never changes, even if it shares the same email address as other operators.

When you're finished on the **Alert System** page, click **OK**. Changing the notification settings requires restarting the SQL Server Agent service, so right-click on it, then choose **Restart**.

Configure an operator

The next step is to configure an operator (the recipient of the email notifications). Navigate **SQL Server Agent | Operators**, right-click and choose **New**, then add a description for the operator, their email address and tick the **Enabled** flag as per Figure 9. Using a distribution list tends to work better than a comma-separated list of operators, if multiple recipients need to receive the message.

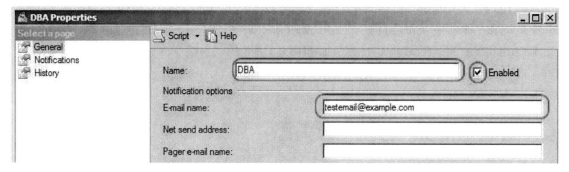

Figure 9:   Creating a SQL Server Agent operator.

MSDN articles and Books Online indicate that the **Net send** and **Pager** notification types have been deprecated from SQL Server 2008, so I would advise against using them (reference: HTTP://MSDN.MICROSOFT.COM/EN-US/LIBRARY/MS179336.ASPX).

We can ignore the rest of the screen, relating to specifics for pager notification setup.

Configuring notifications for Agent jobs

The next task is to apply notifications for each SQL Server Agent job, as required. Navigate **SQL Server Agent | Jobs**, right-click on the required job and choose **Properties**. Go to the **Notifications** page, tick **E-mail** and choose whether to receive an email on success, failure or every time the job runs, then click **OK**.

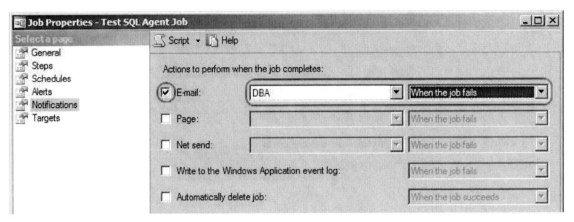

Figure 10:   Configuring notifications for a SQL Server Agent job.

Provide a Real-time Notification System for SQL Server Alerts

In addition to notifying on success or failure of Agent jobs, Database Mail can also provide real-time monitoring of SQL Server alert conditions. Such conditions can give advance warning of possible hardware issues on the server, enabling preventative action. However, be very careful that the frequency of alerts is not such that you deluge recipients with messages.

In SSMS, expand **SQL Server Agent | Alerts**, select **New Alert** and configure alerts, as recommended by Microsoft, for error severities 18, 19, 20, 21, 22, 23, 24 and 25, as shown in Figure 11.

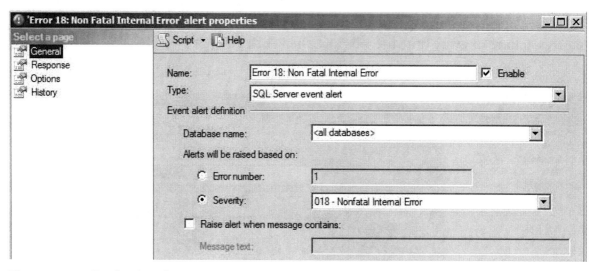

Figure 11:   Configuring alerts.

Microsoft provides further guidance on Error Message Severity levels. The article dates back to SQL Server 2000 but the principles apply equally well to newer versions. (HTTP://TINYURL.COM/PYQGYMT)

To avoid recipients receiving an email every time the same error occurs until it is resolved, go to the **Options** tab and set an appropriate delay between responses. You can also include extra information in the message text. Figure 12 shows the settings to send an email notification once an hour, rather than every time the alert fires.

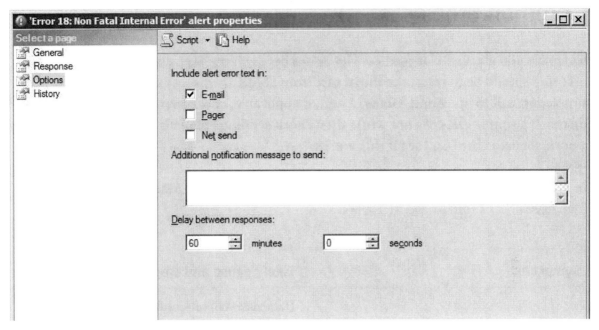

Figure 12:   Sending email notifications once an hour.

It is just a matter of tweaking the minutes and seconds delays for each alert property to suit your requirements.

Next, set up the operators, exactly as described in the previous section, *Reporting on success or failure of SQL Server Agent jobs*.

Troubleshooting Database Mail

Sometimes Database Mail doesn't work as expected. In this section, I recommend some simple checks that will often reveal the root cause. If you need to look deeper, you can use the Database Mail-related system views.

Common problems

bleUnless you are aware of connectivity issues between the SQL and SMTP servers, the first step should be to rerun the initial test from SSMS. If this test still works, perform a simple test call to `sp_send_dbmail` and, if applicable, check permissions for file attachments. If a simple call does not work, then check sending email via the SMTP server using a normal email client and see if that works.

In my experience, the vast majority of problems with Database Mail resolve into one of four reasons, as summarized in Table 1.

Symptom	Likely cause and troubleshooting steps
Initial test from Management Studio fails. SMTP email to the same server from other applications works properly.	Database Mail misconfiguration or restrictions in place on SMTP server for what can connect to it. Check settings and contact SMTP server administrator for further assistance. Check that the **From:** address is valid – in some secure environments a non-existent `noreply`-type address would not be accepted as a sender. Check that the user issuing the request is a member of the `DatabaseMailUserRole` role in the `msdb` database or a `sysadmin` on the server.
Sending single emails works fine, sending large numbers fails (or a single email to large numbers of recipients fails).	SMTP restrictions on number of recipients or sending large numbers of emails over a short period as an antispam measure. Contact your SMTP server administrator.

Sending emails without attachments works fine, sending emails with attachments fails.	User calling the function is logged in using SQL rather than Windows authentication, or the user is trying to access files that they can't access using normal means. If attaching multiple files, check that there are no spaces between the end of one path and the start of the next semicolon separator.
Large numbers of emails within a batch work fine, one or two fail.	Check to ensure that the correct email addresses are in the source data for the recipients that are failing.

Table 1: Troubleshooting steps for common Database Mail problems.

Interrogating the Database Mail system views

As part of the sending process, Database Mail writes logs to the `sysmail_mailitems` table within the `msdb` system database. Five views in the `msdb` database provide access to that data, or useful subsets of it, for troubleshooting purposes.

View name	Contains	Useful for
`sysmail_allitems`	All items, regardless of sending status.	Record of what was processed.
`sysmail_attachments`	File attachments sent with emails.	Record of what was attached. Note that these are BLOBs – the table size can increase quickly if you use this feature a lot.

sysmail_faileditems	All items that failed.	Quickly identifying those that had problems.
sysmail_sentitems	All items that have been successfully sent.	Identifying those that have been successfully sent, including a copy of the message body.
sysmail_unsentitems	Messages waiting to be sent.	Waiting to see what is in the queue.

Table 2:   Database Mail system views.

The stored procedure in Listing 8 uses the sysmail_faileditems view and Database Mail to email a list of emails with "failed" status to a nominated mailbox, for administrator action.

We can schedule this procedure to run every day, through a SQL Server Agent job step, to get a list of failed notifications from the previous day.

```
CREATE PROCEDURE [dbo].[email_dbmail_errors]
AS
    SET NOCOUNT ON

    DECLARE @tempsubj VARCHAR(80)
    DECLARE @tempdate DATETIME
    DECLARE @tempsql VARCHAR(300)

    -- calculate todays date with 0:00 time component
    SELECT  @tempdate = DATEADD(d, DATEDIFF(d, 0, GETDATE()), 0)
     -- subtract 1 day for yesterday
    SELECT  @tempdate = DATEADD(dd, -1, @tempdate)

    -- build subject line
    SELECT  @tempsubj = 'Database Mail failed errors '
            + CONVERT (VARCHAR, @tempdate, 106)
```

```
        -- build SQL query to run
        SELECT  @tempsql = 'select mailitem_id, recipients, [subject], body,
                        file_attachments, send_request_user
                        from msdb.dbo.sysmail_faileditems
                    where DATEADD(d,DATEDIFF(d,-1,send_request_date),0)= '''
            + CONVERT (VARCHAR, @tempdate, 120) + ''''

        -- send email
        EXEC msdb.dbo.sp_send_dbmail @profile_name = 'testprofile',
            @recipients = 'testemail@example.com',
            @subject = @tempsubj, @query = @tempsql,
            @attach_query_result_as_file = 0;
GO
```

Listing 8:   A stored procedure to send notifications of failed notifications.

Maintaining the Database Mail log table

If you use Database Mails heavily, Database Mail will write many log records to the `sysmail_mailitems` log table, and it will expand rapidly in size, especially if using the file attachments feature. Microsoft provides a stored procedure named **msdb.dbo. sysmail_delete_mailitems_sp** to remove records from the Database Mail table, with parameters to control deletion based on sent status and date. Listing 9 shows a few examples.

```
--Example 1: Remove all failed messages regardless of date
EXEC msdb.dbo.sysmail_delete_mailitems_sp @sent_before = NULL,
    @sent_status = 'failed';


--Example 2: Remove all sent messages over 6 months old regardless of status
DECLARE @tempdate DATETIME
SELECT  @tempdate = DATEADD(m, -6, GETDATE())
EXEC msdb.dbo.sysmail_delete_mailitems_sp @sent_before = @tempdate,
    @sent_status = NULL;
```

```
--Example 3: Remove all sent messages over 1 year old
DECLARE @tempdate DATETIME
SELECT  @tempdate = DATEADD(yy, -1, GETDATE())

EXEC msdb.dbo.sysmail_delete_mailitems_sp @sent_before = @tempdate,
    @sent_status = 'sent';
```

Listing 9:   Cleaning up the Database Mail log.

To call `sysmail_delete_mailitems_sp` the user must be logged in as a `sysadmin` or be a member of the `DatabaseMailUserRole` in the `msdb` database.

Depending on your requirements for email retention, you may wish to schedule regular cleanups, or use the `@query` parameter to email a list of failed items to an administrator on a daily basis.

In some industries or jurisdictions, there are legal requirements relating to customer correspondence or communications. Appropriate advice from a qualified professional should be sought if there are any questions about the legalities of keeping or removing this data.

The SSMS Database Mail log

In addition to the `sysmail_mailitems` log table, which stores details at a message level, we can also view the Database Mail log in SSMS (at the server level, navigate **Management | Database Mail**, then right-click and select **View Database Mail log**). This records the log messages as well as high-level process startup and shutdown, and use of the cleanup procedure, `msdb.dbo.sysmail_delete_mailitems_sp`. We can also read this data through the view `msdb.dbo.sysmail_event_log`.

Summary

I hope that this chapter has provided everything you need to get started with Database Mail and shown you how to use it to send a single email, develop a multi-user custom email notification system for applications, or as a notification system for monitoring and troubleshooting error conditions on your SQL Servers.

I've used Database Mail for tasks ranging from email notification of overnight data transfers between servers to sanity checking overnight jobs, to batch sending email alerts for a commercial costing and accounting system. With careful use, taking care not to deluge people with mail, you can build on the foundation I've provided here to create a very effective means to receive swift notification of any issues with the SQL Server instances in your care.

Taming Transactional Replication

Chuck Lathrope

SQL Server Replication is a set of technologies that allows us to copy our data and database objects from one database to another, and then keep these databases in sync by replicating any data changes from one to the other. We can replicate the changes in near real-time, bi-directionally, if required, while always maintaining transactional consistency in each database. In a typical case, we might offload a reporting workload from our primary server (the Publisher, which produces the data) to one or more dedicated reporting servers (Subscribers). After the initial synchronization, we can replicate the data in near real-time; in the best cases, replication can offer a transit latency of just a few seconds. In another case, we might want to replicate schema changes from one database to one or more databases on another server, including partially offline SQL instances.

SQL Server offers several flavors of replication to support these and many other tasks, depending on your exact requirements. Fortunately, by far the most common, *transactional replication with read-only Subscribers*, is also the easiest type of replication to understand, and is the focus of this chapter; and many of the definitions, concepts, and performance tuning tips in this chapter apply to all types of replication.

SQL Server Replication has a reputation with some DBAs for being "difficult" to set up and maintain, and prone to "issues." However, having implemented and supported replication environments in very large enterprise deployments, I've come to view it as a remarkably fault-tolerant and versatile technology. My goal in this chapter is to offer not only a solid overview of transactional replication and how it works, but also to impart some tribal knowledge that only real-world experience provides, covering topics such as:

- **Good use cases for replication** – and, equally important, when not to use it.

- **Requirements** – and a practical example of how to set up transactional replication.

- **Monitoring replication** – using ReplMon and custom email alert alternatives.

- **Performance tuning** – server and replication-specific tuning for optimal performance.

- **Troubleshooting replication** – common issues I've encountered and how to trouble-shoot them.

Having read the chapter, I hope you'll be able to put the technology to good use in your environment, while avoiding common issues related to poor configuration, unrealistic requirements, or plain misuse.

Transactional Replication Architecture

The components in replication are defined using a publishing industry metaphor: a **Publisher**, a SQL Server instance, produces one or more **publications** (from one database). Each publication contains one or more **articles**, with each article representing a database object such as a table, view or stored procedure. A **Distributor**, typically a separate SQL Server Instance, distributes articles to any **Subscriber** (one or more SQL Server instances) that has a **Subscription** to the publication articles.

Figure 1 highlights the main components of transactional replication, which we'll be discussing in more detail over the coming sections.

Various **Replication Agents**, run by SQL Server Agent jobs, control each part of the process of moving the articles from Publisher to Distributor to Subscriber.

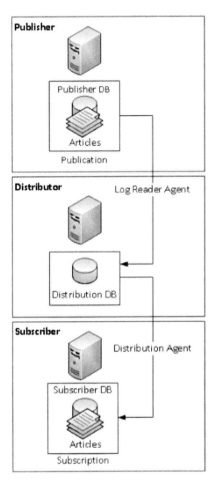

Figure 1:   Core transactional replication components.

A **Snapshot Agent** (not shown in Figure 1), running on the Distributor, copies the initial data and schema objects from the publication database to a snapshot folder that is accessible to all Subscribers. Once all Subscribers receive the snapshot, the transactional replication process begins, with a **Log Reader Agent** reading every row of the transaction log of the publication database to detect any INSERT, UPDATE, and DELETE statements, or other modifications made to the data in transactions that have been marked for replication.

The Log Reader Agent will transfer these modifications, in batches, to the distribution database, marking the point it reached in the transaction log with a checkpoint entry. The Log Reader Agent runs continuously by default, which means the Subscribers should "lag" behind the Publisher by only a short period (referred to as the latency). Alternatively, we can run it on a set schedule, such as hourly, so the Subscribers have data from the time of the last execution of the log reader job.

Continuous replication performs better, as big batches are difficult for replication to process. It requires careful monitoring of log file growth on the publication database, as the presence in the log file of commands awaiting replication (not yet committed to the distribution database) could delay the log file truncation, and cause it to grow rapidly.

A **Distribution Agent** applies the transactions stored in the distribution database to the log of the subscription databases and, consequently, the destination tables. The Distribution Agent can run on the Distributor, pushing the changes to Subscribers (called **push subscriptions**) or on the Subscriber, pulling the changes from the distribution database (called **pull subscriptions**). The Distribution Agent runs continuously, by default, or we can set the schedule to run on a periodic basis, to delay data delivery to the Subscribers. As for the Log Reader Agent, continuous delivery to Subscribers tends to perform better there. This is because big batches are more difficult to push through and you need to monitor database file growth on the distribution database and possibly the Subscriber, depending on the Subscriber's database recovery mode. It is fine to use a delay, but make sure to closely monitor file sizes for a period after implementation.

The typical replication method used is **transactional read-only** (though other methods are available, which we'll cover briefly later). This means the Subscribers are read-only with respect to replication. No changes will ever make it back to the Publisher, even though nothing prevents users from updating the Subscribers. However, doing so can destabilize the replication environment and this is a common mistake made by those new to transactional replication. I'll cover how to fix such issues later, in the *Troubleshooting Replication* section, but the way to avoid them is to secure object permissions to the replicated tables on the destination Subscriber database such that only replication has the permission to make changes.

We will discuss all of the replication components in in more detail later, but I hope this paints the high-level picture of how transactional replication works. Let's now move on to consider some good use cases for the technology, take a brief look at other types of replication, and then consider a few situations where replication may not be the best fit.

Transactional Replication Use Cases

At its heart, transactional replication offers us a quick and robust method to distribute data on a single server, to many other SQL Server instances. Transactional replication is available to any SQL Server edition (SQL Express can only be a Subscriber), and can be connected by LAN, WAN, or Internet.

Common use case ideas for replication (not limited to transactional replication) include:

- Improving scalability and availability (by offloading work onto Subscribers).

- Replicating data to data warehousing and reporting servers.

- Integrating data from multiple sites.

- Integrating heterogeneous data (such as Oracle and SQL Server data).
  Note: Microsoft is deprecating heterogeneous replication, Oracle publishing, and updatable transactional publications in SQL Server 2012, in favor of Change Data Capture and SSIS. See HTTP://MSDN.MICROSOFT.COM/EN-US/LIBRARY/MSI43323.ASPX for more information.

The most common use case for transactional replication is to offload a read-only query workload from the application's primary "source of record" server, which may be overwhelmed, to another server, or to several remote servers. Scaling by distributing workload to many Subscribers is a **scale-out** deployment, as opposed to scale up, which is just purchasing a bigger and faster server (*a.k.a.* throwing money at the problem to make it go away).

Typically, my goal when implementing replication has been to reduce the workload on the Publisher, scaling out by offloading, to Subscribers, time-consuming or complex processes. For example, in one case, I used transactional replication to offload authentication responsibilities (encrypted passwords) to many Subscribers, so that our publication server didn't have to deal with the workload of tens of thousands of queries that utilize native SQL Server encryption. In another, I replicated data, using a dedicated remote Distributor, from one publication to fifteen Subscribers, spread across four datacenters, to provide data to a near real-time application that gets an aggregate of one billion hits a day. Try doing that with some other technology as easily as you can with replication!

Another common use case is consolidating data, or sending data to a data warehouse or reporting server. In such cases, we can tune the Subscriber differently than the Publisher. For example, on the Subscriber we can "over index," change up the security, create a dedicated batch processing system, and utilize many other optimization techniques for fast processing of the Subscriber data, as appropriate for a data warehouse or business intelligence scenario.

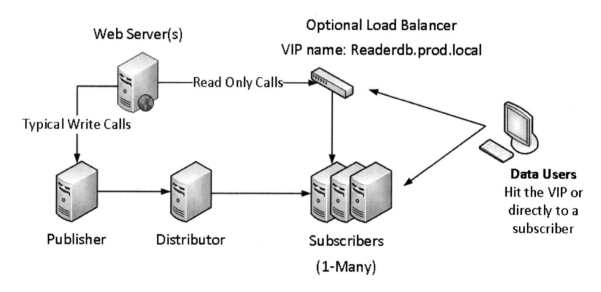

Figure 2:   A scale-out replication topology for a medium-to-large deployment (simplified).

As depicted in Figure 2, the Publisher accepts writes from webservers or other SQL Servers, and publishes out through the Distributor to one or more Subscribers that are optionally part of a load-balanced set. The advantage to using a load balancer, such as Microsoft load balancing or a network hardware-based load balancer such as BigIP or Netscaler, is to provide, to your application or users, a single VIP name, that is a highly available data repository, and offload from the Publisher as much of the read-only query workload as possible. It also enables easy maintenance opportunities with the Subscribers.

Other Types of Replication

Transactional replication is the focus of this chapter, but one of the other replication options may be a better fit for you, for example if data changes need to go in multiple directions.

Snapshot replication

We discussed earlier how the process of transactional replication starts with capturing a snapshot of the data and objects. Snapshot replication is simply a version of replication that does this on a scheduled basis. We create a new, full snapshot of the publication on a periodic basis, typically nightly, and apply it to a Subscriber (typically, a data warehouse). This form of replication works well if the Publisher can handle the workload and the maintenance window can accommodate the time required to perform a nightly, full snapshot of the data, and replicate it to a data warehouse. It must also be acceptable that the Subscriber data will be stale (for example, out of date by one day).

If for some reason we need to modify the Subscriber data, after applying the snapshot, we can do so without worrying about breaking replication.

Merge replication

This is a two-way change replication process, appropriate for use with offline Subscribers, which synchronize when a network connection is available. It tracks changes with triggers and only needs to synchronize the last state of the data, instead of every change, as with transaction replication. We can also filter data so the Subscribers receive different partitions of data.

Transactional replication with updating subscriptions

This form of transactional replication is like merge replication, but much simpler in its design and use case, which is a small number of Subscribers, and very few updates to the Subscribers. Microsoft has deprecated it in SQL Server 2012, but I believe that you can still implement it with stored procedures, just not the wizards.

Peer-to-peer transactional replication

This is a SQL Server Enterprise Edition-only feature that improves scalability and availability of transactional replication where minimal latency is required, data is un-partitioned, and conflicts (updates to the same data rows) typically don't occur. There are many caveats to using it, so check Books Online for more details.

When Not to Use Replication

For all its utility, there are times when I've seen transactional replication used to provide a sort of "poor man's" disaster recovery (DR) solution. I don't recommend this; in my opinion, Microsoft offers far better DR and high availability solutions than replication, including clustering, mirroring, log shipping, or the SQL Server 2012+ AlwaysOn technology.

In addition, there are a few other cases when you would not want to use replication:

- **You want synchronous writes to your Subscribers** – if so, use database mirroring, AlwaysOn, or Service Broker instead.

- **You don't need synchronous writes, but require almost instantaneous updates to Subscribers** – you may just have to continue to perform such operations on your Publisher. Replication has latency in seconds, but this can extend to minutes or hours, if the system in overloaded or something fails.

- **Your organization lacks the appropriate DBA skills** – replication requires careful design and does run into issues occasionally. Developers typically have very different skill sets.

Deeper into Transactional Replication

It's time to delve deeper into the particular brand of replication that is our focus, transactional replication. Over the coming sections, we'll discuss all of the components that we need and how they work. Having done that, we'll move onto implementation requirements, and then a full walk-through for setting up a simple transactional replication environment.

Publishers, publications and articles

Once we enable transactional replication on an instance of SQL Server, it becomes a Publisher. We must enable each database to participate in replication and we create **publications** from these databases. Under the covers, SQL Server creates in these databases all the necessary replication-related objects (you can view their definitions to see what they do, but we don't typically interact with them).

We can have multiple publications for each database. The publications in turn comprise the set of articles we wish to publish. In transactional replication only, we can replicate the same articles in different publications.

The article objects available to publish are quite extensive and include:

- tables, including partitioned tables

- stored procedures (CLR included, and their definition and execution)

- functions (CLR included)

- user-defined types (CLR included)

- views

- indexed views

- indexed views as tables

- alias data types

- full text indexes

- schema objects (constraints, indexes, user DML triggers, extended properties, and collation).

In each publication, we group together the relevant set of articles, and apply to the publication the appropriate properties and custom settings, such as filters, indexing, and security (covered later in *Transactional Replication Walk-through*).

The Distributor

In many ways, the **Distributor** is the beating heart of transactional replication. Its role is to store metadata, history data and, in the case of transactional replication, it holds temporarily the transactions we wish to replicate to the Subscribers. The Distributor will hold the data in a system database, by default called `Distribution`, and it will run the Log Reader Agents (discussed in more detail later) that read the log files from your publications.

We assign a Publisher (SQL Server instance) to one Distributor, so we can't have different databases on a single Publisher using different Distributors. However, we can have multiple distribution databases, although only the very largest replication environments, the 0.1% minority, will need this.

Given that most of the replication agents responsible for the various data transfer processes run on the Distributor and access the distribution database, the location and configuration of the Distributor instance, and the distribution database, are key factors in determining transactional replication performance.

If the Distributor is local to your publications, it is a Local Distributor; otherwise it is a Remote Distributor. When implementing transactional replication on a busy Publisher, and especially if you have many Publishers on different SQL Server instances, I recommend using a dedicated remote Distributor (SQL Server instance on its own hardware), rather than a local Distributor. If your replication is small-scale, and going to stay small, it is fine to have the Publisher and Distributor on the same SQL instance.

You can even use SQL Server Standard edition on your Distributor, with the Publisher using Enterprise, but with the proviso that, at minimum, the *major version* of SQL Server on the Distributor must match what you use on the Publisher. For example, let's say you have a Publisher running SQL Server 2008 R2 SP2; 10.50.4000 is the full build number and 10 is the major version. In this case, your Distributor must run SQL Server version 10 (SQL Server 2008) or higher.

Keeping track of SQL Server builds

HTTP://SQLSERVERBUILDS.BLOGSPOT.COM *is my go-to site for build numbers.*

The Subscribers

A **Subscriber** is any SQL Server instance that subscribes to, *i.e.* has a subscription to, a publication, and so receives the articles from the publication. A SQL Server instance can be a Subscriber, Publisher, and Distributor at the same time, although this is typical only of development or small production environments. As replication environments get larger, we would install each component on a separate SQL Server instance.

Subscribers can subscribe to many publications, making sure not to overlap data, which is great for consolidating data to a reporting server when there are many sources of data. They are not limited to use of one Distributor, like the Publisher.

Some DBAs forget that we can tune the subscription database on the Subscriber differently from the publication database, adding indexes and so on, as appropriate for the workload for the Subscriber. We can also republish some of the data from the Subscriber, for example using an intermediate server to denormalize the data and turn complex queries into simple ones, without affecting the main replication process. We'll discuss this in more detail later, in the *Tuning Query Performance on the Subscriber* section.

The Replication Agents

SQL Server Agent controls the execution of separate external applications that comprise the replication feature of SQL Server. Each agent controls a part of the process of moving data between the various replication components. In other words, SQL Server Agent jobs run replication, not the SQL Engine.

Snapshot Agent

In all forms of replication, the **Snapshot Agent** (`snapshot.exe`), executed on the Distributor, is responsible for producing the initial snapshot of the Subscriber's schema and data. It produces bulk copy and schema files, stored in the **Snapshot Folder** defined by the Distributor and consumed by the distribution agent (discussed later). Typically, the snapshot folder will live on a Windows file share, so that all Subscribers can access it and pull data. Alternatively, in cases where most, or all, of the tables are included in the publication, we can use a backup and restore process to initialize replication on the Subscriber, but we have to script this part as there is no wizard (for more information, see HTTP://MSDN.MICROSOFT.COM/EN-US/LIBRARY/MS147834%28SQL.90%29.ASPX).

SQL Agent cleanup jobs, on the Distributor, will purge the snapshot folder periodically, based on a defined **retention period** (72 hours, by default), or when, according to metadata stored in the distribution database, no Subscriber still requires the snapshot.

Log Reader Agent

In transactional replication, one of the most important replication agents is the **Log Reader Agent** (`logread.exe`), which runs on the Distributor. It reads every log record in the publication database's transaction log file, in order, looking for transactions marked for replication, and sending them in batches to the distribution database.

Once the batches are committed in the distribution database, the log reader calls `sp_repldone` to mark where it go to in the publication log file. Finally, the agent marks the rows in the transaction log that are ready to be truncated. By default, the Log Reader Agent checks the log file every 10 seconds, called the **polling interval**. If you increase this value, be aware of the fact that the log file is likely to grow quickly, since a large portion of the log file will remain active, so SQL Server cannot truncate it, until the Log Reader Agent applies to all Subscribers the changes described by those log records.

Distribution Agent

The **Distribution Agent** (`distrib.exe`) moves the snapshot (for transactional and snapshot replication) and the transactions held in the distribution database (for transactional replication) to the destination database at the Subscribers. By default, the distribution agent polls the distribution database every 60 seconds for data to replicate.

The distribution agent will reside on the Subscriber, for pull subscriptions, and on the Distributor, for push subscriptions.

Other Agents

Several other replication agents exist that we won't touch on further in this chapter. For example:

- **Merge Agent** (`ReplMer.exe`) – used only in merge replication to send snapshot data on initialization and for sending changes to Subscribers.

- **Queue Reader Agent** (`QrDrSvc.exe`) – used to read messages stored in a SQL Server queue or Microsoft Message Queue and apply those messages to the Publisher. It can be used with transactional and snapshot replication.

Transactional Replication Requirements

Transactional replication has the fewest limitations and restrictions of any of the replication technologies:

- Tables in the publication must have primary keys.

- The Distributor's SQL Server version must be at least as high as the major version of the Publisher.

- All editions of SQL Server can participate in replication to some extent, but some editions are limited – see Table 1 for an edition capability map.

- Sysadmin privileges are needed to set up replication.

- If you have remote Subscribers with pull subscriptions, you will need to share out the replication snapshot folder, so the Subscriber's distribution agent can get the data over a UNC path.

- The account used for replication on the Distribution server will need db_owner rights on the publication database.

Feature	Express	Express Advanced	Workgroup	Standard	Enterprise	Web	Evaluation	Developer
Merge Replication	Subscriber only	Subscriber only	<= 25 subscribers	Y	Y	Subscriber only	Y	Y
Transactional / Snapshot Replication	Subscriber only	Subscriber only	<= 5 subscribers	Y	Y	Subscriber only	Y	Y
P-P Transactional Replication	N	N	N	N	Y	N	Y	Y
Oracle Publishing	N	N	N	N	Y	N	Y	Y

Table 1:   SQL 2008 Edition capability map.

Transactional Replication Walk-through

We'll walk through how to set up transaction replication on a stand-alone server (Publisher, Distributor and Subscribers all on the same SQL Server instance).

I'm going to set up transactional replication for the `AdventureWorksDW2012` database, though any version of an `AdventureWorks` database will be fine. I will show how to publish a table and, along the way, I'll describe the important dialog windows in the wizards and highlight some best practices. Of course, we could equally well script out the replication, either manually, or using the Wizard to produce the script.

Configuring the Distributor

The setup process requires membership of the `sysadmin` server role. Assuming you have these rights, the first step in setting up replication is to elect and configure the Distributor. In SQL Server Management Studio (SSMS), connect to the test SQL Server instance, right-click on **Replication,** and select **Configure Distribution**, as depicted in Figure 3 (notice the lack of a distribution database under the **System Databases** section – an easy way to tell that this isn't yet a Distributor).

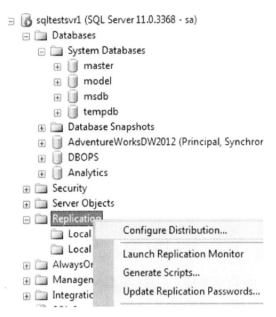

Figure 3:   Configure Distribution context menu in SSMS.

If you did not install the replication components when you set up SQL Server, you will see the error message in Figure 4.

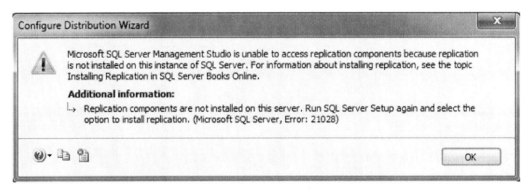

Figure 4:   Warning error message (SQL 2008 and later) if you didn't install replication components.

To solve this error, you just need to install the replication components with the SQL Server setup tool, as shown in Figure 5.

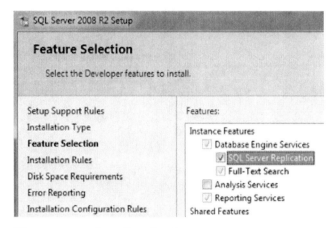

Figure 5:   Install replication components.

Assuming you've installed replication, after selecting **Configure Distribution** from the context menu, the Configure Distribution Wizard starts. As shown in Figure 6, select the current server as the Distributor and click the **Next** button.

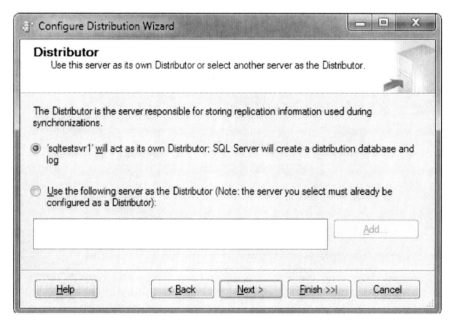

Figure 6:   Configure Distribution Wizard – select or create a Distributor.

Click **Next**, and you'll reach the dialog where you can set up the Snapshot folder. By default, this is located next to your SQL Server Logs folder, in a folder called **ReplData**. However, if you have remote Subscribers, it's best to pre-create a windows share called **Snapshot** (for example, \\sqltestsvr1.prod.local\snapshot). For a multi-domain environment, you will want to fully-qualify the server name.

The next step is to name the **distribution** database and specify a location for its data and log files. By default, it's called Distribution, and I recommend you don't change the name, as it can be confusing and make custom coding more difficult. Furthermore, validate the file locations, and do remember that the Distribution database, like any other user database, will adopt the size and growth characteristics of the model database. You may need to alter them for optimum efficiency. A general guideline for a medium-to-large replication environment is to size the distribution database between 5–10 GB for the data file and 500 MB for the log file, with growth rates of 2 GB and 800 MB respectively. Be sure to back it up and monitor the file sizes.

Finally, we enable which Publishers (SQL Server instances) can use this Distributor. The current SQL Server instance is all we need for this simple setup.

Configuring the Publisher and publication

Having configured our Distributor and enabled the same SQL Server instance to be a Publisher, our next job is to replication-enable the AdventureWorksDW2012 database, create the publication, define the articles that we wish to publish within this publication and then configure the Snapshot Agent to capture the initial snapshot.

Enabling replication

We need to enable the replication feature in our database before we can create the publication. In Figure 7, we select **Publisher Properties** from the replication context menu of the Publisher (notice, in the figure, our new distribution system database).

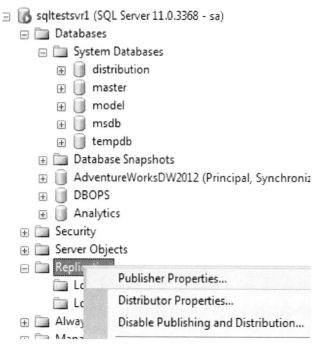

Figure 7:   Publisher Properties context menu in SSMS.

Check the **Transactional** box next to AdventureWorksDW2012 to enable this database to use transactional replication, as shown in Figure 8.

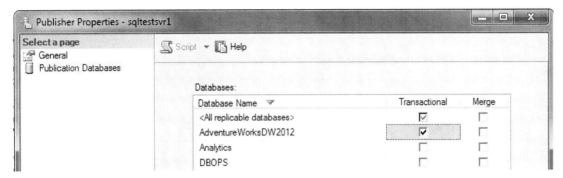

Figure 8:   Publisher Properties – enable replication on a database.

Now that it is enabled for replication, we can create a new publication using the New Publication Wizard by selecting **Replication | Local Publications – New Publication**. Over the next two screens, select `AdventureWorksDW2012` as the database from which we wish to publish, and choose **Transactional publication**.

Selecting articles

Next, we select the articles to publish, in this case the `FactInternetSales` table, as depicted in Figure 9. For optimal performance, don't select all the columns; be precise about what data you want on the Subscribers and only publish the columns these Subscribers really need.

As an aside, take care when modifying the schema of a published table on your Publisher. When you add the column, use the ALTER TABLE...ADD COLUMN T-SQL syntax, and if you use a tool to add the column (such as a schema comparison tool), make sure it does the same thing, rather than re-create it and then drop the original table. If you append a column to the end of a published table, replication will add the column without intervention on your part, which is a nice feature.

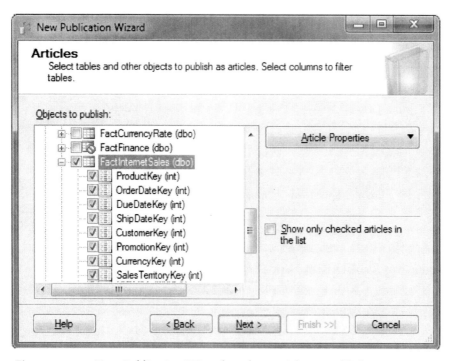

Figure 9:   New Publication Wizard – select articles to publish.

However, if you want to add a previously unpublished column in the middle of a published table, you will need to re-initialize the whole publication. A re-initialization marks the publication as needing a new snapshot and, once generated, on the Subscriber it will drop *all* the published tables in the publication and then start bulk copying the data. One trick I learned to get around this is to remove the table from the publication, add the required column, add the table back to the publication and run the Snapshot Agent. Doing it this way will just snapshot the table and not the whole publication. Always remember that the applications using the Subscribers rely on the table and the data, and when you reinitialize, you will be dropping the tables and causing a service interruption to your application.

Article properties

Next, we want to set the properties of our published articles, as shown in Figure 12, which determines exactly what data we replicate to our Subscribers.

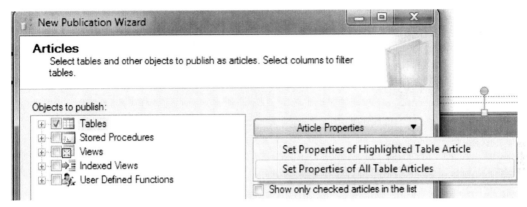

Figure 10:   New Publication Wizard – set properties for all articles or individual articles.

This is a confusing interface, but we can use it to set the properties of all articles of a given type (such as tables), or to set the properties of each individual article. Figure 11 shows all the configurable article properties in SQL 2008 R2 and SQL 2012.

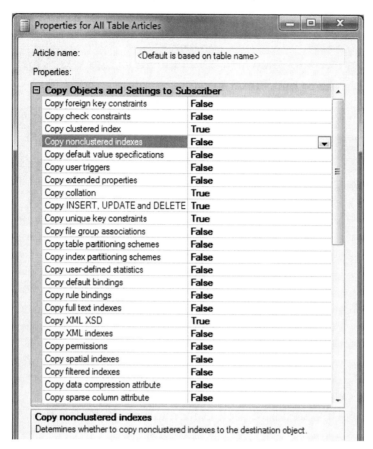

Figure 11:   New Publication Wizard – article properties.

By default, replication copies over the clustered index only, not the nonclustered indexes. We can simply set the **Copy nonclustered indexes** property to **True** if our Subscribers need all of the indexes. We can also use the post-snapshot script option (available on the publication's properties dialog, post-creation) to create a custom indexing strategy for the Subscriber, which we'll discuss in more detail later, in the *Tuning Query Performance on the Subscriber* section.

Filters

Next, we can add filters to our publication tables, as depicted in Figure 12. For example, we might want to limit rows of data to certain status values such as WHERE OrderStatus IN (5,6,7). My advice is to keep filters simple, or don't filter at all, as SQL Server evaluates every row in the table to find those that meet the filter criteria.

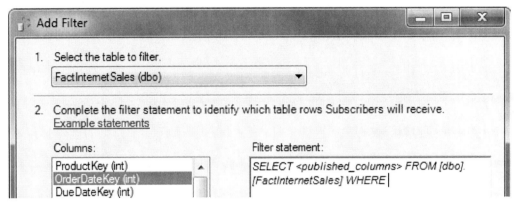

Figure 12:   New Publication Wizard – set data filters.

Configuring the Snapshot Agent

On the first of the **Snapshot Agent** dialogs, shown in Figure 13, we specify when to create the snapshot and for how long to keep the snapshot available to future Subscribers.

The first option, "create a snapshot immediately and keep it available to initialize subscriptions," dictates whether we enable the immediate_sync property of the publication.

If we don't check this box, then the Distribution Agent Cleanup will remove a snapshot as soon as all Subscribers have it, or when the retention period has elapsed (72 hours, by default), whichever is sooner.

When enabled, SQL Server will always retain the snapshot files and distributed transactions in the `Distribution` database for the retention period, so that any Subscribers we add or reinitialize within that period can use them. Check this box if you plan to add new Subscribers soon, or for easy re-initialization of a Subscriber. However, be aware that it may cause performance issues, as we'll discuss later, in the *Performance Tuning* section. If it does cause problems, we can simply switch it off again.

Since we are using transaction replication, we only need to run the snapshot agent on demand when we need to initialize the Subscriber, so we don't need to schedule it, therefore leave the second box unchecked.

Figure 13:   New Publication Wizard – configure the Snapshot Agent.

Next, we select the security accounts for both the **Snapshot Agent**, and the **Log Reader Agent**. I've never found a reason to use different accounts, so I have always used the same account.

We need to specify the **process account** that the Snapshot Agent process runs under. You can use a dedicated Windows account to run the Snapshot Agent process, or select the SQL Server Agent service account, as depicted in Figure 14. Since this is a simple, stand-alone install, I chose to use the SQL Server Agent service account. The account needs to be a member of the `db_owner` database role on the distribution database, which SQL Server Agent will have, in our example, so I am not breaking any best practices. However, in multi-server replication environments, running these agents under a separate account from the SQL Server Agent will grant the least privilege access and be the most secure configuration.

We also specify the account used to connect to the Publisher. Again, this Windows or SQL Server account must be a member of the `db_owner` fixed database role in the publication database and, again, I've chosen to make the connection under the SQL Server Agent service account.

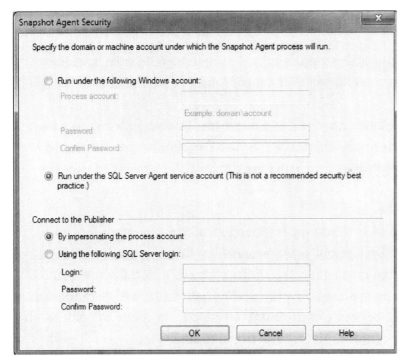

Figure 14:   New Publication Wizard – Snapshot Agent Security.

In the final window, give your new publication a name, I chose `Sales`. That's it for publication setup! Now we just need to set up some Subscribers to our new Publication.

Configuring the Subscriber

We now need to create a subscription, which will define that server as a Subscriber. In our example, our subscription database will be an empty database called `Analytics`, on the SQL Server instance that is also the Publisher and Distributor.

Start the New Subscription Wizard (**Replication | Local Subscriptions – New Subscriptions...**). Select the `Sales` publication that we created in the previous section as the target of the subscription, and click **Next**.

Choosing pull versus push subscriptions

Next, we specify whether this is a pull or a push subscription which, in turn, specifies whether the Distribution Agent runs on the Distributor (push) or on the Subscriber (pull).

Subscribers can actively pull articles from the Distributor (**pull subscriptions**), in which case the Distribution Agent runs on the Subscriber, or the Distributor can push articles to the Subscribers (**push subscriptions**), in which case the Distribution Agent runs on the Distributor.

The default, as shown in Figure 15, is to use push subscriptions, but in larger replication environments, the use of pull subscriptions is more scalable, since it spreads the work across the Subscribers rather than on a single Distributor. This is especially relevant on WAN connections, as when using push subscriptions, the Distributor will need to wait for a Subscriber to receive the data before continuing to process its queue of commands (*i.e.* the log records, containing details of the transactions) to replicate.

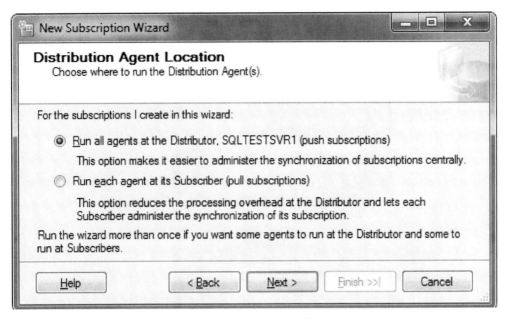

Figure 15:   New Subscription Wizard – push or pull.

The general advice is to use push subscriptions if you have fewer than ten Subscribers, all located in same local datacenter, or pull subscriptions otherwise. You can mix and match push and pull subscriptions to meet your needs.

Since we have fewer than ten Subscribers and all in same local datacenter, we'll stick with the default and create a push subscription.

Local versus remote Subscribers

Next, we check the box for the local server, since we want to create a local subscription. To create a remote Subscriber, click **Add Subscriber** and connect to the remote SQL Server instance(s). Then choose the database in which the subscription will reside, Analytics in this case, as shown in Figure 16.

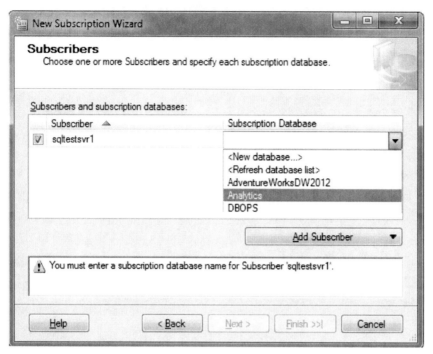

Figure 16:   New Subscription Wizard – Subscriber selection.

Distribution Agent Security

The next task is to set up the process account to run the Distribution Agent and accounts to connect to the Distributor and Subscriber. To do this, click the ellipses button (....), as depicted in Figure 17.

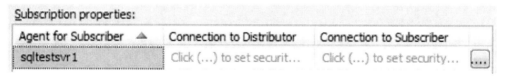

Figure 17:   New Subscription Wizard – subscription properties.

This brings up the Distribution Agent Security windows, where we can establish the accounts to use. For this example, on a single, stand-alone SQL instance, I chose to use the SQL Server Agent service account for synchronizing the subscription. In larger environments, you may want to review the TechNet article, which describes in more detail the account(s) requirements for push or pull subscriptions: HTTP://TECHNET.MICROSOFT.COM/EN-US/LIBRARY/MS189691.ASPX.

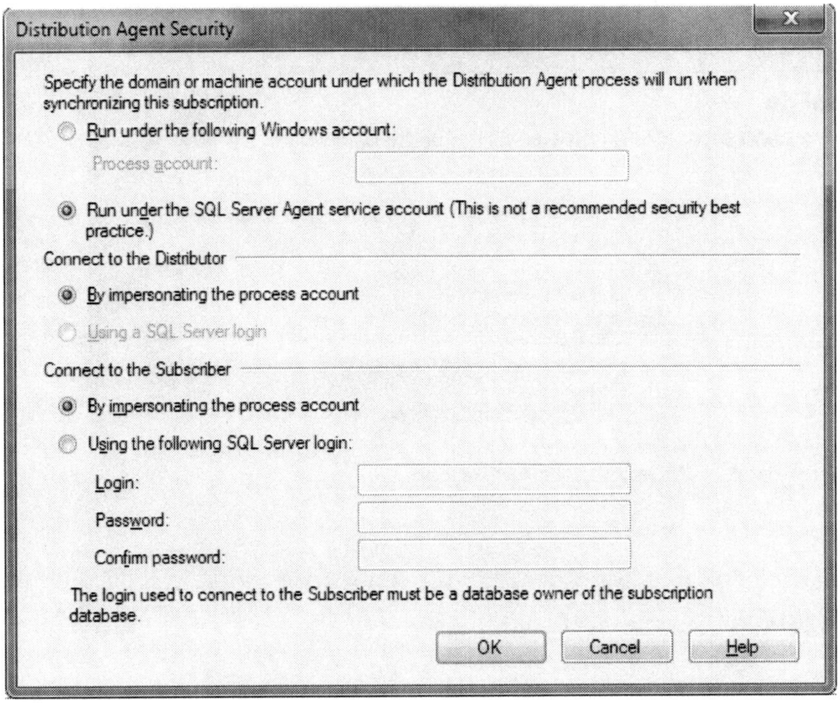

Figure 18: New Subscription Wizard – Distribution Agent Security.

Synchronization and initialization

Next up is the **Synchronization Schedule** dialog, where I recommend, for performance reasons as discussed earlier, that you select **Run continuous**.

We then reach the **Initialize Subscriptions** screen, where I recommend you choose to initialize immediately, as shown in in Figure 19. The Snapshot Agent will immediately generate a snapshot and the Distribution Agent will start immediately, in order to apply the snapshot to the Subscriber. The Distribution Agent job will report an error until the snapshot is complete, so you may need to disable it in the meantime, if the snapshot is large.

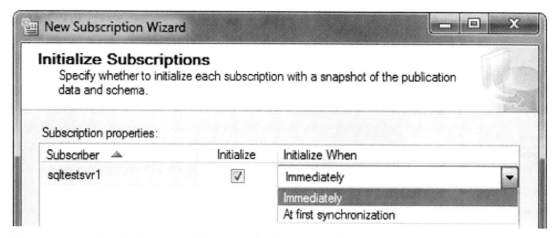

Figure 19: New Subscription Wizard – initializing the Subscribers.

That's the last major step. Once you exit the Wizard, your replication node in SSMS should look as shown in Figure 20.

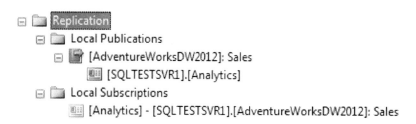

Figure 20: SSMS replication node.

Tuning Query Performance on the Subscriber

The Subscriber will often be subject to a very different workload than the Publisher (for example, a reporting rather than OLTP workload), and we can tune the subscription database differently from the publication database, in order to optimize processing of the Subscriber data.

Via the GUI, we can add one post-snapshot script to each publication, which will run immediately after the Snapshot Agent applies a snapshot to the Subscriber (see HTTP://TECHNET.MICROSOFT.COM/EN-US/LIBRARY/MS152525.ASPX for further details). We can also run a pre-snapshot script, though I've only rarely needed to do this. If you require more than one customization script, use the `sp_addscriptexec` built-in stored procedure.

As we discussed earlier, during the walk-through, when defining our publication articles, we copy across from the Publisher the clustered index for a table and optionally, the non-clustered indexes. However, a completely different set of non-clustered indexes might be appropriate for the Subscriber. We can use the Dynamic Management Views to find potentially useful missing indexes for the Subscriber workload and run the post-snapshot script to create them (checking for existence first) on the Subscriber.

We can also republish Subscriber data in a denormalized form, in order to improve performance of a specific Subscriber query. In one case, for example, a common reporting query against the reporting server (Subscriber) was taking minutes to complete, as it required a complex eight-way table join. On a separate server, I subscribed to the data, created an Indexed View based on his data, to do the complex joins, and republished this data to Subscribers, as a dedicated publication consisting of just the indexed view. It reduced the query response time to seconds!

Monitoring Replication with ReplMon

SQL Server has a nice built-in tool called Replication Monitor (*a.k.a.* ReplMon). It is a program, called `sqlmoniter.exe`, and you can run it from anywhere you have the SQL client components installed. To open it from SSMS, expand any server, right-click **Replication** and select **Launch Replication Monitor**.

ReplMon displays replication metadata and metrics for your entire replication environment. We can also use it to initiate replication processes, such as starting the Snapshot Agent (very handy). We can add and group servers just like in the SSMS interface.

Before we start, note that Replication Monitor can be a performance hindrance to the Distributor, although it does cache all the metadata to help mitigate this. However, if you have a large number of publications or subscriptions, consider setting a less frequent automatic refresh schedule for the user interface (under the **Action** Menu). I have seen cases where so many people were using ReplMon, that it caused performance issues.

Subscription Watch List

Typically, when monitoring the environment for potential issues, I will look at the **Subscription Watch List** to look for error icons and latency values (Publisher to Subscriber times), as shown in Figure 21. The data displayed depends on the context. Typically, you will want to have the **publication** selected in the left navigation window.

Figure 21:   Replication Monitor Subscription Watch List tab example.

Double-click the subscription, in Figure 21, to see details of its history, as shown in Figure 22. For our newly created subscription, we specified immediate snapshot creation and ReplMon shows the history of the snapshot being applied, and the actions it performed.

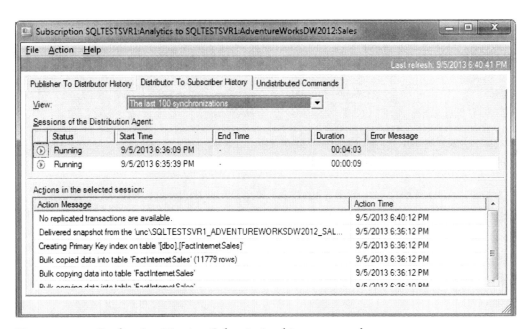

Figure 22:   Replication Monitor Subscription history example.

Replication latency and tracer tokens

One of the cool features of Replication Monitor is the ability to see near-current latency values and to use tracer tokens to get current latency broken down by latency values (the speed to Distributor and speed to Subscriber, from the Distributor).

Tracer tokens will help you to pinpoint the part of your infrastructure causing bottle-necks when troubleshooting replication. Find the **Tracer Tokens** tab in ReplMon and click the **Insert Tracer** icon, as shown in Figure 23.

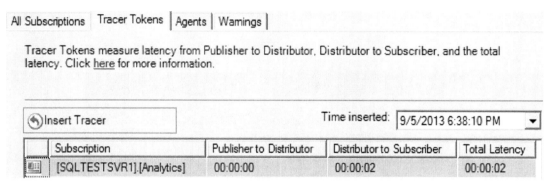

Figure 23:   Replication Monitor Tracer Tokens view of Sales Publication.

We can script tracer tokens, but I typically just use ReplMon to create and view them. They add an entry mark into the log file, watch each point in the replication path, and show the time it takes to get there. You always want to see seconds in all three fields. If you have an issue, typically one will be waiting on a response and have a much larger number than the other, and the latency data will give you a starting point for your troubleshooting.

Alternatively, we can look at the Distributor to Subscriber latency in the **Undistributed Commands** tab, as shown in Figure 24. I watch this tab after I have noticed a latency problem, as the estimated time to apply remaining replicated transactions is quite accurate if you refresh the page (**F5**).

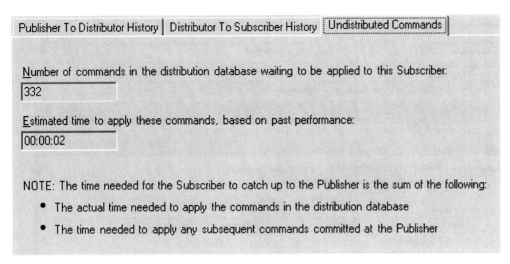

Figure 24: Replication Monitor Undistributed Commands tab example.

Getting details of errors

A word of warning – appearances can be deceptive! Figure 25 shows two windows, the Subscription Watch List, with all the subscriptions, and the details of a Subscriber's subscription, which I brought up by just double-clicking the row in the Subscription Watch List.

In this figure, it looks like there are no issues, as the icons are all green. In reality, not all is well. Replication has failed and is in retry mode (because I deleted a row on the Subscriber and then updated on the same row on the Publisher). Look harder and you will see that latency is low on our test publication and ReplMon reports an error in the subscription history details. ReplMon will flip to error mode, then out of it when it retries, making errors easy to miss. You need alerting configured to catch these, which we will talk about in the next section, *Configuring Alerts*.

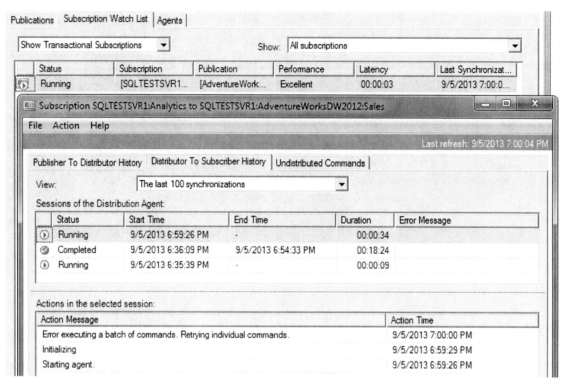

Figure 25:   ReplMon limitation with Subscriber errors – in retry mode and all is green.

Figure 26 shows the error after the first set of retries and provides some useful information. Firstly, the **Action Message** area reveals that the distribution agent found a missing row at the Subscriber, and then tried to break the batch down into smaller batches, but it still failed. Finally, the error details section shows the **Transaction sequence number**, and we will discuss how to use this to find out which row it failed on and what it was attempting to do, in the later section, *Troubleshooting Replication*.

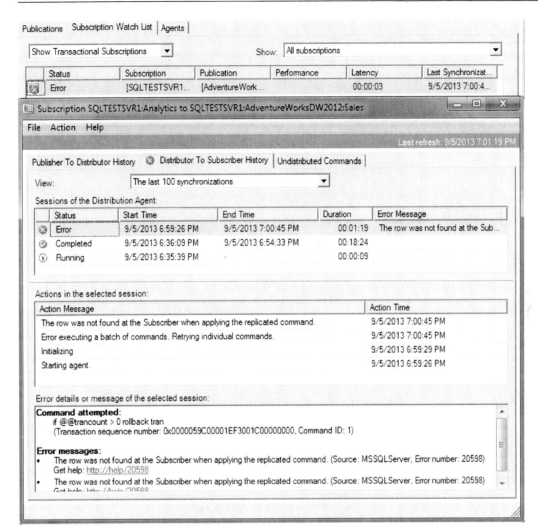

Figure 26: Replication Monitor – what a Subscriber error looks like.

Then it retries and we are seeing green status icons (retry is always green).

Figure 27 depicts the Distribution Agent history, as it goes through its retry process (see the **Agents** tab in Figure 25). We can click on previous rows in the history to see their details, or query the distribution database errors table, as we will discuss in the *Troubleshooting Replication* section.

Sessions of the Distribution Agent:

	Status	Start Time	End Time	Duration	Error Message	
⊙	Running	9/5/2013 7:01:46 PM	-	00:00:05		
⊗	Error	9/5/2013 6:59:26 PM	9/5/2013 7:00:45 PM	00:01:19	The row was not found at the Su...	
⊘	Completed	9/5/2013 6:36:09 PM	9/5/2013 6:54:33 PM	00:18:24		
⊙	Running	9/5/2013 6:35:39 PM	-	00:00:09		

Figure 27: Replication Monitor history of Distribution Agent after errors.

Configuring Alerts

To avoid having to watch ReplMon all day long, we need to configure some replication alerts, to receive automatic warnings of any problems. Out of the box, SQL Server offers many SQL Agent alerts, which we can configure with the **SQL Agent Alerts** dialog in SSMS. Alternatively, we can configure replication alerts within ReplMon, by selecting **Configure Replication Alerts** from the **Action** Menu.

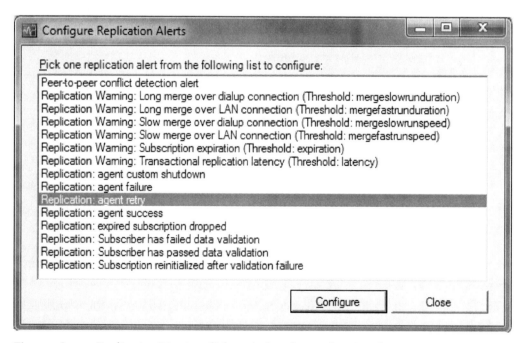

Figure 28: Replication Monitor dialog window for configuring alerts.

Select the alert and click the **Configure** button, to bring up the standard SQL Agent Alert dialog window. The alert will be disabled by default, so check the Enable check box.

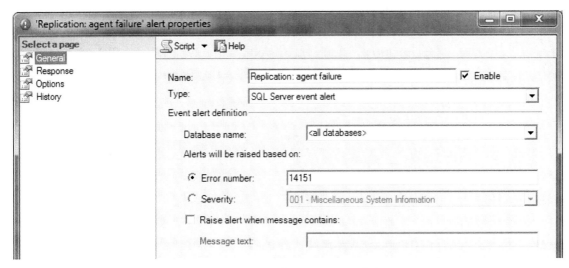

Figure 29: SQL Agent Alert configure for Replication: agent failure.

Configure the remaining pages of the alert with the desired method to alert, taking note that you may want to set the delay between responses to be higher than the typical retry interval of three minutes, unless you like spam alerts. Following is the alert text generated when I deleted the row at the Subscriber.

```
SQL Server Alert System: 'Replication: agent failure' occurred on \\SQLTESTSVR1
DATE/TIME:     9/5/2013 7:12:28 PM

DESCRIPTION:  Replication-Replication Distribution Subsystem: agent SQLTESTSVR1-
AdventureWorksDW2012-Sales-SQLTESTSVR1-1 failed. The row was not found at the
Subscriber when applying the replicated command.

COMMENT:      (None)

JOB RUN:      (None)
```

To fix the problem, I decided to reinitialize my subscription, which is a right-click option on the subscription status in ReplMon (alternatively, we can use SSMS, or a system stored procedure – see the *Reinitializing Subscribers* section, later).

A dialog window will ask to use a new snapshot, and you may not be able to check the box for **generate new snapshot now**, which means you will have to kick off the job manually, or from the Agents tab in ReplMon, right-click the **Snapshot Agent Job** and select **Start Agent**.

Alerts can overwhelm users with emails, so I created a couple of custom error emails; one of which is strictly for replication errors, while the other is for very latent Subscribers. These are available on my site at HTTP://TINYURL.COM/YZ4TLNS; as part of the code download for this chapter; and at HTTP://TINYURL.COM/YKK74ZM.

Figure 30 shows a sample of my custom replication error email that shows all errors in the past hour.

Hourly Replication Errors Reported on Jun 4 2010 6:00PM by server BLV31WDB03\INS2

PublisherDB-Subscriber	subscriber_db	StatusDesc	LastSynchronized	Comments	Query to get more info
BLV31WDB01-Auctions-BLV31WDB02-	Reports	Failure	2010-06-04T17:59:17.157	Cannot DROP TABLE 'dbo.TransferOrderDetail' because it is being referenced by object 'VWTransferDenorm'.	select * from distribution.dbo.msrepl_errors (nolock) where id = 237119

Last Hours Logged Replication Errors

Cannot DROP TABLE 'dbo.TransferOrderDetail' because it is being referenced by object 'VWTransferDenorm'.
Communication link failure
Source: mscorlib Target Site: Void WinIOError(Int32, System.String) Message: Access to the path
'D:\SQLDATA\MSSQL10.INS2\MSSQL\ReplData\unc\BLV31WDB01_AUCTIONS\20100604170007\' is de
Source: mscorlib Target Site: Void WinIOError(Int32, System.String) Message: Access to the path
'D:\SQLDATA\MSSQL10.INS2\MSSQL\ReplData\unc\BLV31WDB01_AUCTIONS\20100604171559\' is de
Source: mscorlib Target Site: Void WinIOError(Int32, System.String) Message: Access to the path
'D:\SQLDATA\MSSQL10.INS2\MSSQL\ReplData\unc\BLV31WDB01_AUCTIONS\20100604171828\' is de
TCP Provider: An existing connection was forcibly closed by the remote host.
The process could not execute 'sp_replcmds' on 'BLV31WDB01'.
The subscription(s) have been marked inactive and must be reinitialized. NoSync subscriptions will need to be dropped and recreated.

Figure 30:   Custom email on replication errors.

In my custom email, I provide a lot more information than the built-in alerts. I display a T-SQL query to use to see the errors with the ID of the error, which is very handy and about which we will talk more in the *Troubleshooting Replication* section. After that is the summary of the first hundred characters of the recent error messages since the last email, as I typically run it every 30 to 60 minutes.

The replication latency customer email alert (Figure 31) shows the status of the distribution agent job and current latency.

From: VDB3\INS2 [mailto:dbprocesses@.com]
Sent: Friday, June 04, 2010 12:00 PM
To: IT Database Operations
Subject: Hourly Replication Status Jun 4 2010 12:00PM VDB3\INS2

Hourly Replication Status Jun 4 2010 12:00PM VDB3\INS2

Status Code	Last Synchronized	PublisherDB-Subscriber	Undelivered Cmds	Subscriber DB	Subscription Type
InProgress	Jun 4 2010 11:59AM	Auctions-Reports-VDB4	584	Denorm	Pull
InProgress	Jun 4 2010 11:59AM	Auctions-Reports-SJL01WREAD08	584	Reports	Pull
InProgress	Jun 4 2010 11:59AM	Auctions-Reports-SJL01WREAD09	584	Reports	Pull
Fail	Jun 4 2010 10:50AM	MailSettings-MailSettings-SJL01WVAS01	16622	MailDB	Pull
InProgress	Jun 4 2010 11:59AM	Auctions-Reports-SJL01WREAD07	584	Reports	Pull
InProgress	Jun 4 2010 12:00PM	Auctions-Reports-SJL01WREAD10	584	Reports	Pull
Fail	Jun 4 2010 10:50AM	Auctions-SJL01WVASDB01	31766	MailDB	Pull

Figure 31:   Custom replication status email.

Performance Tuning

Since this is a chapter on replication, we're mostly concerned with specific tips for tuning the performance of the replication process. However, certain broader server configuration issues will also affect its performance so let's start there.

Server and database file configuration and tuning

Although a robust feature, replication can suffer the same performance problems as any database application if we make poor choices for server and database settings, use bad coding practices, or design the architecture poorly.

If you are using replication to offload work from a busy server, but there is an underlying architectural problem on your Publisher, then adding the overhead of replication will only exacerbate it. This is why it's doubly important in a replication environment to ensure that the storage I/O architecture is correct and optimized, as you will be adding more workload to reading and writing to database files. Here are a few tips for any SQL instance:

- Use a dedicated distribution server for large replication environments, as this helps to remove overhead from the Publisher.

- On Windows 2003 Server and below, make sure the disks are partition aligned: HTTP://MSDN.MICROSOFT.COM/EN-US/LIBRARY/DD758814(V=SQL.100).ASPX.

- If a SAN engineer agrees, format disks with 64 KB allocation unit size (cluster size). Default is 4 KB.

- Use RAID 10 if the budget allows.

- The transaction log file for the publication database needs to be on fast disks, so avoid RAID 5 and go with RAID 10 or equivalent.

- The SQL Server Service account should have the `Perform Volume Maintenance Tasks` Local Security Policy right.

- Pre-grow all your databases to the size you expect they will become in the near future with optimized growth settings. Default of 1 MB growth will hurt performance.

- Watch for high VLF counts (>200) on replicated databases – a fragmented log can degrade the I/O performance for any process that needs to read the log file, such as the log reader agent. This can be a hidden performance killer – Kimberly Tripp has the best advice on the subject at HTTP://TINYURL.COM/O49P5MV.

- Keep the snapshot folder on a separate array (4 KB cluster format) from the database files.

- Set limits of how much RAM SQL Server can use so that Windows doesn't page to disk. A good starting point for this is to be found at HTTP://TINYURL.COM/OFHD9RF.

Tuning replication

If we set up replication with all its default settings, it will work fine for small implementations that don't require high transactional volume. Microsoft designed the defaults for typical low-volume use cases. However, once we start to scale up to many Subscribers, some Subscribers residing miles away over the WAN, and to high transactional volumes, we need to think about our overall replication architecture, and about changing some of the default values. All the replication components in the full end-to-end path have to be in peak shape. Here are a few tips (some of which we've discussed along the way):

- If there are >10 Subscribers, use pull subscriptions, as discussed earlier.

- Minimize the use and complexity of publication filters.

- Run distribution agents continuously instead of infrequently, if data changes all day long. It is better to spread the load out evenly than having big pushes at the end of the day.

- Consider using the **SubscriptionStreams** option on the distribution agent, which uses multiple threads to write to the Subscriber. There are a few drawbacks when using **SubscriptionStreams**, so read BOL carefully on the subject.

- Evaluate any triggers on the publication database, and decide whether they need to run on Subscribers. Use the NOT FOR REPLICATION clause to exclude them.

Custom Replication Agent profiles

Each Replication Agent (Snapshot, Log Reader, Distribution and so on) has default properties, and other properties for which no value is defined, that we can use to help with performance or error conditions. I recommend creating custom agent profiles to control the behavior of the various agents. The default settings of each agent work for a majority of use cases but, again, for high transaction volumes and many Subscribers, I recommend creating custom agent profiles. From the default agent profiles provided, create multiple profiles, tailored to your infrastructure.

Start with the Distribution Agent, since it has settings that affect the Subscriber and Publisher, 4 so this is where tailor-made setting will reap the most benefit. Figure 32 shows the settings for the custom Distribution Agent profile that I use in a WAN environment.

Parameter ▲	Default Value	Value
-BcpBatchSize	0	2147473647
-CommitBatchSize	100	1000
-CommitBatchThreshold	1000	2000
-FileTransferType	0	
-HistoryVerboseLevel	2	1
-KeepAliveMessageInterval	300	300
-LoginTimeout	15	15
-MaxBcpThreads	1	4
-MaxDeliveredTransactions	0	0
-MessageInterval	3600	
-OledbStreamThreshold	32768	
-Output		
-OutputVerboseLevel	0	
-PacketSize	4096	8192
-PollingInterval	5	5
-QueryTimeout	1800	3600
-QuotedIdentifier		
-SkipErrors		
-TransactionsPerHistory	100	300
-UseOledbStreaming		

☐ Show only parameters used in this profile

Figure 32: A custom Distribution Agent profile, viewed in Replication Monitor.

To create a new Replication Agent profile in Replication Monitor, right-click a Subscriber and select **Agent Profile**, copy the default one and modify it; uncheck the **Show only parameters used in this profile** check box and tweak the values, as appropriate, then monitor replication to test the impact each time (did it help performance, or make it worse?).

Following are my suggestions for agent properties you might want to tune, for high volume environments (with the proviso, of course, that you test them in your environment):

- BCPBatchSize (2147473647) – Maximum size of the bulk copy batch of commands (log records to be replicated) in a transaction. Only change this if a large transaction on the Publisher has effectively halted replication in your system, waiting to push it through. It will break the transaction into parts with the size you specify. This adds overhead, so use it only if you frequently make large data changes.

- CommitBatchSize (1000) – number of transactions issued to the Subscriber before issuing a COMMIT.

- CommitBatchThreshhold (2000) – approximate max total commands for all batches.

- HistoryVerboseLevel (1) – BOL has a definition of all four possible values, but if no errors are occurring, limit verbosity, possibly even choosing 0 (no history) for even greater gains in performance.

- MaxBCPThreads (4) – used only when a snapshot is created or applied, so that it won't be single threaded. Warning: if you set this number too high, it could degrade the server's performance, so don't exceed the number of processors on the Distributor, Subscriber or Publisher.

- PacketSize (8192) – this is on a good network. Adjust it up or down in 4096 increments until SQL Agent Job doesn't crash – pre-SQL 2005 SP3 there is a bug with large packet sizes. Windows 2008+ network stack is greatly improved, so this really only helps lower versions of Windows Server.

- `QueryTimeout` (4000) – to ensure it has enough time for a large batch.

- `TransactionsPerHistory` (1000) – limits the frequency of history updates you see in ReplMon; adjust to your preference with higher numbers providing better performance.

Replicating stored procedure calls

Another great performance tip is to replicate out stored procedure calls, rather than all the data they would change, as documented here: HTTP://TINYURL.COM/PR3QEXP.

This means that for a stored procedure that updates a million rows we send one row to the Subscriber, instead of a million DML statements. This only works if the Subscriber has all the data in the same state as the Publisher (filters may cause issues). The default replication property setting is to replicate only the stored procedure definition. Figure 33 shows where to find this dialog box, nested in the **Publication Properties**, **Articles Properties**, **Replicate** drop-down under **Destination Object** grouping.

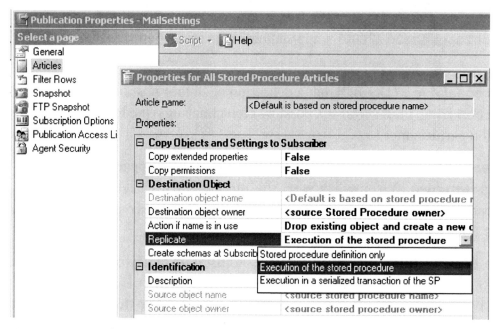

Figure 33: Dialog window for changing replicating execution of stored procedures.

immediate_sync subscriptions

As discussed during the walk-through, when configuring the Snapshot Agent (Figure 13), we may want to enable the `immediate_sync` property of publications for the convenience it offers when setting up future Subscribers or re-initializing existing Subscribers without the need to generate another snapshot. However, it is a hidden performance killer in bigger replication environments.

When enabled, instead of removing data as soon as all the Subscribers have it, SQL Server preserves all the replicated data for the default retention period (72 hours). For example, if we move ten million rows a day, we would store at least 30 million rows in the distribution database, and this could cause issues with very large `Distribution` database file sizes, and with frequent failures of the Distribution Agent Cleanup job, since it has to look through so much data to find commands it can delete.

With `immediate_sync` enabled, we also can't simply add a table to a publication and create a snapshot for the table; instead, we need to generate a full snapshot for the Subscribers.

ReplTalk MSDN blog post has a lot of good information on how `immediate_sync` works: HTTP://TINYURL.COM/OBGT7V2.

Listing 1 shows how to check for use of `immediate_sync` and disable it.

```
--Find if publication has immediate_sync property enabled
EXEC sp_helppublication @publication = 'your_publication_name'

--Disabling immediate_sync property
EXEC sp_changepublication @publication = 'your_publication_name',
    @property = 'immediate_sync',
    @value = 'false'
```

Listing 1:   Checking for `immediate_sync` property and changing its setting.

Troubleshooting Replication

In my experience, SQL Server Replication is quite a resilient feature. For example, replication in SQL Server 2005 and later is resilient to SQL Server restarts; replication will just come back online and restart where it left off.

As noted earlier, though, this resilience can make troubleshooting harder. If a replication process fails to complete, SQL Server will just retry until the subscription expires and in the meantime, as discussed earlier, when viewing ReplMon, it's easy to miss the fact that anything is wrong (use alerting to combat this).

The coming sections describe some common issues I've encountered in my replication environments, along with troubleshooting steps and resolution. Remember, the distribution database stores the replication metadata, SQL Agent jobs control the replication process, so examining them is key to finding issues and error messages.

Finding more details on an error

In an earlier section, *Getting details of errors*, I deliberately deleted a row at the Subscriber to demonstrate that ReplMon can provide good information about the error. However, to find details on the actual row that caused the error, we can run the code in Listing 2, on the Distributor.

```
--This is my go to table for finding errors.
SELECT TOP 300 *
FROM    distribution.dbo.MSrepl_errors (NOLOCK)
WHERE   time > GETDATE() - .05
ORDER BY time DESC
```

Listing 2:   Querying `MSrepl_errors` for latest replication errors.

The error row will provide the Transaction Sequence Number and the Command ID that caused the failure. Listing 3 shows you how to use the `sp_browsereplcmds` replication stored procedure to browse all the commands pending distribution for that transaction batch; find the row with a value of 1 for the `command_id` column, as defined in our error example in Figure 26.

```
--Paste in the seqno into both variables in this command
EXEC sp_browsereplcmds @xact_seqno_start = '0x0000059C00001EF3001C',
    @xact_seqno_end = '0x0000059C00001EF3001C'
```

Listing 3:   Using `sp_browsereplcmds` to view a specific batch of commands.

These steps will reveal the primary key of the missing row that caused the replication command to fail, and then we can manually insert the row into the Subscriber, or use a third-party data sync tool, such as Red Gate's SQL Data Compare.

Another option, to get past an error, is to skip the latest transaction batch and restart the Distribution Agent job. I like to use this technique in response to the error, "Row already exists at Subscriber." I learned this from a prominent CSS support engineer blog post: HTTP://TINYURL.COM/N94DXM. The other option is to remove the row from the Subscriber manually, but you could have issues with the entire replication batch and spend a long time finding the rows with `sp_browsereplcmds` to delete.

Using verbose error output

If you are unsure what is causing an error on any Replication Agent, change the verbose settings of the Distribution Agent job to send output to a file, as described in HTTP://SUPPORT.MICROSOFT.COM/KB/Q312292, which describes how to append the required parameters to the replication "Run agent" job step. Stop and start the job to see the output, but don't forget to set back to normal!

Finding large batches

Often the root cause of replication issues is a large batch of data changes. You may see in ReplMon the warning "no activity in the last 10 minutes." Often, a chat with the developers will reveal the culprit and you can request, politely, that they use smaller batch changes with delays between them, so that replication has a chance to breathe.

The queries in Listing 4 help locate large batches as a source of latency, or allow you to count them out as the cause of the latency.

```
--Locate large batches
SELECT   COUNT(*) ,
         xact_seqno
FROM     MSrepl_commands (NOLOCK)
--where xact_seqno > 0x0017B2C50003BDF40008000000000000
GROUP BY xact_seqno
--ORDER BY xact_seqno
HAVING   COUNT(*) > 1000
ORDER BY COUNT(*) DESC


--Total by batch and article
SELECT   cm.xact_seqno ,
         ma.article ,
         s.publisher_database_id ,
         COUNT(*) AS CommandCount
FROM     msrepl_commands cm ( NOLOCK )
         JOIN dbo.MSsubscriptions s ( NOLOCK )
           ON cm.publisher_database_id = s.publisher_database_id
              AND cm.article_id = s.article_id
         JOIN MSpublisher_databases d ( NOLOCK )
           ON d.id = s.publisher_database_id
         JOIN msarticles ma ON ma.article_id = s.article_id
--and subscriber_db = 'analytics'
--and d.publisher_db = 'AdventureWorksDW2012'
GROUP BY cm.xact_seqno ,
         ma.article ,
         s.publisher_database_id
ORDER BY xact_seqno
```

```
--Total by table
SELECT  ma.article ,
        s.article_id ,
        COUNT(*) AS CommandCount
FROM    msrepl_commands cm ( NOLOCK )
        JOIN dbo.MSsubscriptions s ( NOLOCK )
         ON cm.publisher_database_id = s.publisher_database_id
            AND cm.article_id = s.article_id
        JOIN MSpublisher_databases d ( NOLOCK )
         ON d.id = s.publisher_database_id
        JOIN msarticles ma ON ma.article_id = s.article_id
--and subscriber_db = 'analytics'
--and d.publisher_db = 'AdventureWorksDW2012'
GROUP BY ma.article ,
        s.article_id
ORDER BY COUNT(*) DESC
```

Listing 4:   Useful scripts to find large batches of commands.

Restoring accidentally dropped replication objects

If you accidentally dropped some of the replication stored procedures, use
sp_scriptpublicationcustomprocs to regenerate them. One possible
cause of this is using schema comparison tools to generate change scripts between
environments when the other environment didn't have replication setup. I highly
recommend you duplicate replication in your development and staging environments.
In addition, remember to script out your environment, in case of disaster.

Reinitializing Subscribers

There are a few reasons why you might want to re-initialize a Subscriber, a process of
resetting the Subscriber with a new snapshot of data. Usually, it's in response to latency
issues. We discussed earlier the use of tracer tokens to help identify the cause of latency

issues, but sometimes the issue is so bad that it's easier to "give up" and start over. Similarly, you might need to push out to your publication a massive update, knowing it will cause latency issues the business can't handle. In such a case, it's often better to perform the update and then re-initialize the Subscribers. Finally, you might occasionally meet a situation, due perhaps to very high latency or failure on the Distributor, where a snapshot is removed, because the retention period, 72 hours by default, is exceeded before a Subscriber receives it. When this happens, the Distribution Agent will mark the subscription as expired and you must **reinitialize** the Subscribers.

To reinitialize a Subscriber through SSMS, right click on the Subscriber in SSMS Replication node and select **Re-initialize**. Alternatively, we can use a system procedure `sp_reinitsubscription` as shown in Listing 5.

```
EXEC sp_reinitsubscription @publication = N'Sales', @subscriber = N'all'
```

Listing 5:   Reinitializing all Subscribers for a publication.

After that, we need to manually kick off a new snapshot.

Summary

You made it to the end of what I know was a long chapter, but I hope you learned enough about replication to give it a try, or to improve your existing replication infrastructure.

Once you understand how transactional replication works, you realize that tuning it is just like tuning any new application running on SQL Server that uses SQL Agent jobs. Small implementations will generally work fine out of the box, but sometimes we need replication to scale very high, even to the billions of rows mark. If you run into issues as you scale up, break open this chapter again, and use it alongside the same tools you use to monitor for general SQL Server performance issues such as profiler, extended events, and DMV queries. After all, transactional replication reads and writes data with stored procedures, with SQL Agent jobs running a couple of executables (Log Reader and Distribution Agent) to move around that data.

If you are stuck, search the web and ask questions in forums; there are usually many people who like to help. Here are a few links I've found consistently useful when trying to solve replication-related issues:

- The Microsoft SQL Server Replication Support Team's blog
  HTTP://BLOGS.MSDN.COM/B/REPLTALK

- Microsoft replication forums
  HTTP://TINYURL.COM/PHUS929

- Brandon Williams's blog
  HTTP://WWW.SQLREPL.COM

- A community Q&A forum for SQL Server Replication
  HTTP://WWW.REPLICATIONANSWERS.COM

Building Better Reports

Stephanie Locke

A great report is one that, firstly, presents accurate information, and secondly, strikes the perfect balance between satisfying user requirements and implementing best design practices. Without correct information in a readily understood layout, reports are at best a hindrance and at worst a disaster. There are numerous examples of how bad information and bad report design have had a huge impact on companies and government organizations. If you don't believe me, read through a few of the horror stories the *European Spreadsheet Risks Interest Group* website (HTTP://BIT.LY/QWRSZE).

In my experience, three key factors influence the overall success and quality of your reports:

- **Your overall skills as a report developer** – not just report-building skills, but communication skills, knowledge of the business and versatility.

- **Report design** – good design turns data into information that business can use to make decisions.

- **Report platform and tools** – understanding the right tool for the task, and a willingness to fit the tool to the report user, rather than vice-versa.

In this chapter, I'll explore all three areas. You won't find in here technical tips for how to make specific styles and types of report look good, but what you will find are the skills I believe you need to make sound report development decisions, based on well-understood user requirements, and then produce clean, easily understood reports.

Key Report Development Skills

Given the importance of getting reports right, report builders have a very real and significant responsibility that extends far beyond the writing of the actual report to ensure it is accurate.

We have a responsibility to allow the report consumers to make the required decisions. Generally, users do not see the underlying system from which we, as report builders, extract our data, and nor do they care about our reporting platforms. To the majority of users, the report *is* the data, and as long as that data is correct and the reports presented in a way they like and find intuitive, then they will accept them. Too many report developers get lost in the mechanics of collecting and returning the required data, and fail, ultimately to give the end-user the report they really need.

We have a responsibility to ensure that the reports are available when required. Behind a report are the source OLTP (Online Transaction Processing) system, the ETL (Extract, Transform, Load) system, the data warehouse, the network, and the reporting platform. In short, a reporting system has one of the longest lists of dependencies of any piece of software in the company. Many things can go wrong. Coupled with this, our reporting system is also one of the most visible systems in a company; the proverbial "canary" that provides the first warning of the presence of one or more of these many possible underlying problems.

Along with sys admins and DBAs, report developers are the often-underappreciated masses keeping chaos from reigning supreme. To fight the good fight, our strongest weapons, alongside our report-building skills, are our people and communication skills, our knowledge of the business and our versatility.

Communication

Over the course of developing and maintaining reports, and dealing with the various problems that can derail them, you will need to communicate with people right across the company. You cannot sit in a cubicle, safely isolated from "the business" and expect to do a good job. The following sections cover just some of the people with whom a report developer should communicate regularly.

Business owners and managers

Report developers need to know the ins and outs of every business process on which they report, and to communicate regularly with the team leaders and managers who own these processes. Getting to know the competent and key non-managerial staff will also give you a much more accurate insight into the processes, since they are the ones who often perform them and know how they actually work.

Without this sort of communication, incorrect assumptions arise and the reports produced will fail to bring business benefit. When this happens, the business will start to rely on gut feeling instead of solid information.

IT department

Strong working relationships within the IT department are a necessity. Each person in IT contributes in one way or another to the quality of our reports. Project managers and Business Analysts may gather requirements or make promises on our behalf; developers will build and maintain the systems on which we need to report; DBAs look after the databases and ensure they run well; system administrators maintain the hardware and networks that ensure the availability and performance of the reports.

You may be one, many or all of these people within your organization, but there is still value in keeping the roles divided, if only to provide an easier way of determining impacts when making changes.

Developers

Every time a developer changes a system, it will likely affect the data feeding into the data warehouse. Ensuring reports are adapted to accommodate such change is the responsibility of the report writer, and developers have other priorities than thinking about what happens to reports after they've delivered their changes, so keep a close eye on what they're doing, to ensure that necessary report amendments get picked up sooner rather than later.

Working closely with developers has the added benefit that the development team's work will benefit from the report developer's knowledge of the business process that needs to be automated or amended. In this respect, the report developer provides a useful "halfway house" between technical and business knowledge.

Network/infrastructure admins

The performance and availability of reports rely on many different systems, but report writers, unless we also happen to be the DBA or system administrator, are unlikely to be on the email distribution lists that receive news of system problems, like running out of disk space on the OLTP server.

By regularly popping down to chat with the network admins and DBAs, it's possible to gain forewarning of issues that may affect report performance, or mean that users can't reach the front-end via IP for a certain period, and so on.

In addition, the report writer might be the person on the receiving end of an angry phone call because reports aren't loading, or due to some other issue, which is actually an early warning that the whole network is about to crumble. Knowing who to go to, and having a good relationship with them, could mean the difference between the issue being fixed before it affects other systems, or the whole company network falling over.

Project managers and business analysts

For every new project, it's imperative to work with project managers and analysts, both to gather the new reporting requirements and to assess the impact of the project on the existing report suite. The people who write reports for different areas of the business have an excellent understanding of how the systems interact, and become a huge source of information on how a change could affect other areas of IT and the business as a whole. They can play a vital role in ensuring the projects don't waste time and in preventing nasty pitfalls and surprises later on down the line.

End-users

Finally, of course, we need to work closely with the consumers of our reports. A report is just a vehicle for transferring information, and the most important thing is ensuring that it succeeds in helping the user do what they need to, as quickly as possible. In order to do that, understanding exactly what they need, and when, comes in very handy. I'll cover requirements gathering a little later, but here are a few general tips for smooth relations with your users:

- Avoid detailing how something was achieved unless asked; success is what matters, not how hard you worked (also, any difficulties or complexities that would delay delivery should already have been raised).

- When explaining concepts and the work required, use the simplest terms and examples that can be used.

- Understand a person's overall objectives and how their request fits into them.

- Frame conversations in terms of how their objectives will be met.

- Always be willing to help with computer woes as it builds a good relationship and it is a great opportunity to educate people.

- Try to discuss topics in person at their desk or over the phone.

- Remain honest about deadline feasibility. It is much worse to be told at the deadline that something won't be delivered than it is if you know a few days in advance.

- Be tactful and nice if they screw up – not only does it prevent you from burning bridges but often a lot of value can be derived from preventing similar mistakes in future.

- Keep things documented – send confirmation emails of discussions with actions and key agreements.

One thing we report writers quickly come to dread is the phone call or support ticket that starts with *"Your report is wrong/broken"* (sometimes, that's practically *all* the support ticket says). It can lead to frustration because we tend to hear the dreaded phrase for users regardless of whether there really is a problem with the report, or the data. More often, the problem will be with the underlying servers or source systems, or email, or the report user's typing (GIGO, as developers say) but, still, at the moment the report stops working, it transitions from being their report, to being your report, and they will expect you to be able to help.

It is worth remembering in times of frustration that the user came to you for help. They may be stressed, under pressure, or simply not know how best to help you help them, but they do need your help. Take as many deep breaths as required to let the stress go, and then talk to the user sensibly and calmly.

Technical skills and versatility

Jack of all trades...master of one!

Our primary job is not to write SQL to collect the required data, marshal it into some form of report, and deliver that report to the users that need it. Our ability to write intricate reporting queries may be unimpeachable, but this is only part of what it takes to build good reports.

The job also requires us to be able to triage report requests, communicate with the business, investigate a myriad of network, source data and desktop issues, design and test reports, move data around environments and any number of other tasks.

As noted earlier, as soon as there is a problem with a report, the user will call the person who made the report. As such, we frequently need to tackle an issue outside of the "main scope" of our role. Being able to converse intelligently on a broad range of topics and technologies really helps because it means the user gets a smooth, seamless resolution, handled, or at least coordinated, by us. This can breed reliance but that is the price of competence, and it builds significant respect amongst the team.

Table 1 lists the topics on which I would expect a report developer to be able to converse intelligently, and the minimum level of understanding I feel they should work to attain. It isn't exhaustive, and I'm sure many of you would debate its contents (see the end of the chapter for my contact details!).

Area	Topic	Level
Coding	Client-side (HTML, CSS)	Fair
Coding	MVC	Basic
Coding	Object-orientated programming	Basic

Area	Topic	Level
Coding	Standard computing theory	Strong
Database	Administration	Fair
Database	Data modeling	Strong
Database	ETL	Strong
Database	OLAP	Fair
Database	SQL	Strong
Database	XML	Basic
General	Business Process Management	Basic
General	General design theory	Fair
General	Report design and visualization	Strong
General	Statistics	Fair
Microsoft	Office	Strong
Microsoft	SharePoint	Fair
Microsoft	SQL Server	Fair
Microsoft	Visio	Fair
Networks	Architecture	Basic
Networks	Authentication and security	Basic
Networks	Server management	Fair
Networks	Virtualization	Fair

Table 1: Range of technical knowledge for report developers.

Ultimately, mastering all of these technologies is a means to an end, and that end is to excel at **conveying information**. Having a broad skill-base and an open mind makes it much easier to acquire any extra technical and practical knowledge needed, in order to deliver consistently reports that convey information, in a form the company can understand and on which it can reliably base business decisions.

Report writer, Business Intelligence (BI) specialist or data scientist?

From the range of skills presented in Table 1, it becomes clear that the term "report developer" embraces a broad spectrum of skills. Correspondingly, you'll find many different paths into and through a career as a report developer. Personally, I started out from a non-technical, analytical background. Many others migrated from being DBAs or developers, other still from mathematics and science backgrounds. Quite often, having made the sideways move into reporting, previous expertise lingers and there's a tendency to specialize in that area, and job titles can vary accordingly. For example:

- Visualization and specialist reporting – Infographics Designer.

- Database (and cube) design and development – BI Developer.

- The back-end architecture and platform – BI Architect.

- Integration with other systems – Developer.

- Analysis of data and implementing conclusions – Data Scientist.

The latter title, Data Scientist, seems to spring up everywhere right now, and I'm reluctant to jump on the bandwagon. Nevertheless, it seems to me a laudable goal for a good report developer, with skills in ETL and data warehousing, to attempt to broaden their skills in analyzing data and extracting from it realizable and meaningful conclusions.

Irrespective of specialism, our "generalist" skills, along with a solid foundation in computing, strong communication skills, and solid design principals will always provide benefit.

What it takes to be a data professional

I recommend the link list compiled by Buck Woody on all the possible facets of being a "data professional" and the required skills: HTTP://BIT.LY/16EP6U6.

The Fundamentals of Good Report Design

A good report presents necessary information in a style that is easy to assimilate. This is not something that we can achieve in one fell swoop. We start with two vital, initial stages in the iterative processes: requirements gathering and initial visualization. Spare effort here and you could end up with a poor report, even after subsequent hard work designing and building it.

Requirements gathering

Requirements are rather like Prometheus' liver. It's painful to expose them to the light of day and they are always growing. We cannot expect to capture all requirements in a single conversation with our users. We can do our best to get a good set of starting requirements, but more often than not reports are iterative and the first draft is usually a prototype that we will throw away entirely.

Requirements gathering meetings, done in the typical "big design up front" style, can be interminable, stodgy affairs. Avoiding them is reason enough for some teams to adopt a more iterative approach, often termed "Agile." While not convinced entirely by Agile (see *Dilbert on Agile*, HTTP://BIT.LY/NKK5MV), I do think prototyping, constant communication with users, and rapid turnaround, are good ideas. Certainly, while requirement gathering, I avoid formal meetings in favor of informal chats that don't take up too much time and don't result in reams of paper. Try to meet at the user's desk or a set of sofas nearby, to ensure that it's quick and easy for them to show an example or scribble a diagram.

Some users shun all meetings, formal or otherwise. We can either say, "so be it," or we can try to counter the behavior by "just popping down" or "just calling" to ask a quick question. Not every request needs a meeting, particularly if a user is more conversant with reporting and it's a simple change, but a quick phone call can give the personal touch that keeps the relationship strong and ensures reports are more likely to be correct first time.

There's no hard and fast set of rules when requirement gathering for reports, but we need to ask intelligent questions and, most importantly, listen to the user. Distil their responses and repeat them, asking the user to confirm that you've understood what he or she really needs.

The five Ws are a very good foundation for solid requirements gathering:

- **Who** – the report audience.

- **What** – the criteria and content of the report.

- **Where** – the format in which the report needs to look at its best.

- **When** – data update frequency, availability, delivery.

- **Why** – what questions does the report need to help answer? Which business decisions will it inform?

The most important question is "Why." Asking questions that tease out of the user the reasons for a request, and give them a chance to explain what it is they really need. It also gives us the chance to listen to the actual business requirement and evaluate the best solution.

Most users find it hard to articulate their requirements and, often, they won't have thought them through very thoroughly. These informal conversations are your best chance to get them thinking about what they really want, and provide an opportunity to discuss any potential changes to systems or processes it might engender.

Initial visualization

Once I understand the requirements fully, it's time to start prototyping. I'll write some quick and dirty SQL to gather the sort of data I think I'll need and mock up a basic report in Excel. Once I've finished prototyping I typically throw away my report query and start from scratch, to ensure that it runs as quickly as possible.

I use Excel for all prototyping. Firstly, it's usually a very quick process to grab the data and apply the necessary pivot tables, and secondly because it's a familiar environment for most users, and they can often make their own amendments, or add notes.

While we're not overly concerned with table and graph design formalities at this stage, it's easy to use Table styles (at least in Excel 2007 and later) to produce good-looking reports in Excel and apply a few basic formatting principles (see, for example, *15 Spreadsheet Formatting Tips*, HTTP://BIT.LY/163QJJ). If even your prototypes look good, it will help ensure you get early, high-quality feedback from the users.

My design process starts with an initial raw data table, and from there I spawn further graphs and summary tables based on the requirements, both the originally received ones, and new ones arising from the user being able to see the data, until I've captured everything needed for the user to achieve their aim.

I also take the time at this early stage to check for any trends or issues, knowledge of which might add value, even if it extends a little beyond the stated scope of the report, or that might cause unexpected political repercussions. For example, if your report exposes the fact that call center agents are "dodging calls," then we need to be prepared for impact of that revelation.

Designing tables and graphs

Regardless of our specific reporting platform and tools (covered later), we need to apply some sound design principles to ensure that our tables and graphs present their information with visual clarity and precision.

Fortunately, there are a few giants on whose shoulders we can stand. All report developers and, in fact, anyone involved with the display of information, should read the following books:

- *Don't Make Me Think!* by Steve Krug
  HTTP://WWW.SENSIBLE.COM/DMMT.HTML

- *Show Me the Numbers* by Stephen Few
  HTTP://TINYURL.COM/YF39LV8

Show Me the Numbers, for example, offers rare insight into the concepts that underpin great report design, and provides many examples. In the following sections, I'll offer some tips on how to present your graphs and tables, but the most important thing is to experiment. You probably know of some particularly bad spreadsheets in your company. Take a copy and give it a facelift, consider showing it to key users and discuss whether making the changes to the real report would be of benefit. Since all change has a cost, if only just the time needed to learn a new layout, it may be that the shiny new report doesn't add enough benefit to be put live, but that makes it a perfect opportunity to practice those requirements-gathering skills.

Tables

> [A perfect table] is achieved, not when there is nothing more to add, but when there is nothing left to take away – Antoine de Saint-Exupéry

The only good way to demonstrate good design principles is with examples, so I'll show two examples of bad table design, explain why they are bad, though some of the reasons are obvious, and then how to rehabilitate them.

Example 1 – A jumbled mess

Table 2 shows a report of the last three years' profit. It lands on your desk with a bunch of questions from a user who can't work out what it all means:

- Is profit pre- or post-taxes?

- Why is 2011 so different to 2010 and 2012?

You've never seen the report before and know even less than the poor confused person asking for help. Since nobody wants to hear the words "not my problem," you consider how you might rework the table to remove any confusion.

		Profits 2010	Profits 2011	Profits 2012 (£000's)	Profits -->
Country	America (North)	£345	1,900	£250	2495
	South America	£346	1,901	£251	2498
	Europe	£348	1,902	£252	2502
	Asia	£348	1,903	£253	2504
	Africa	£321	1,904	£254	2479

Table 2:   A badly designed yearly profits table.

I'm sure you can tell that it's a bad design, and spot most of the flaws, even without having read any design theory. Table 3 lists the problems I see with this table and how to resolve them.

Area	Problem	Resolution
Don't Repeat Yourself (DRY)	The word 'Profits' is unnecessarily repeated in every header	An umbrella heading
Labels	1) Row labels aren't consistently named 2) Incorrect vertical umbrella header 3) Confusing last column label	1) Rename rows 2) Amend or remove header 3) Clarify label
White space	Spacing is uneven and not properly used to aid legibility	Standardize the spacing
Order	With only five rows the situation isn't dire but rows should have an obvious order	Order rows by name or the column considered most important by the users
Alignment	Consistent alignment is not used for column headers or contents	Make numbers and headers right aligned
Formatting	1) Inconsistent borders 2) Unnecessary colors 3) Inconsistent number formats	1) Borders should be kept to a bare minimum 2) Use colors sparingly 3) Standardize formats
Footnotes	Missing important information about calculation methods and anomalies	Add footnotes where useful, but don't overburden the report

Table 3:   Issues with the yearly profits table.

Having corrected all these issues we have a much simpler and more legible table.

	Profit after tax (£000's)			
	2010	**2011***	**2012**	**Total**
Africa	£321	£1,904	£254	**£2,479**
America (North)	£345	£1,900	£250	**£2,495**
America (South)	£346	£1,901	£251	**£2,498**
Asia	£348	£1,903	£253	**£2,504**
Europe	£348	£1,902	£252	**£2,502**
Worldwide	**£1,708**	**£9,510**	**£1,260**	**£12,478**

* Company released provisions held for regulatory reasons causing bumper profits

Table 4:   A well-designed Yearly Profits table.

Example 2 – A big heap

A user has asked for a report showing recent profits and trends in ice cream sales. The report developer produced Table 5 in a mighty rush before going on holiday. You pick up the "Help me!" ticket raised by the confused user.

	Units Sold	User rating	Cost per unit	Revenue	% defects	Profits	Volume trend
Vanilla Ice Cream (5l)	50000	2.5	10.5	75000	2.50%	69750	Up
Vanilla Ice Cream (2l)	45000	3	11.2	45000	2%	39960	Steady
Vanilla Ice Cream (10l)	1501	4.2	60.9	6004	1.80%	5089.891	Decreasing
Chocolate Ice Cream (5l)	100000	3.4	10.5	150000	2.50%	139500	Up
Chocolate Ice Cream (2l)	150000	4.9	11.2	150000	2%	133200	Increasing
Chocolate Ice Cream (10l)	20000	3.8	60.9	80000	1.80%	67820	Increasing
Coffee Ice Cream (5l)	10000	2.4	10.5	15000	2.50%	13950	Decreasing
Coffee Ice Cream (2l)	200000	4.8	11.2	200000	2%	177600	Steady
Coffee Ice Cream (10l)	1000	1.1	60.9	4000	1.80%	3391	Decreasing
Strawberry Ice Cream (5l)	99999	4.6	10.5	149998.5	2.50%	139498.6	Up
Strawberry Ice Cream (2l)	66666	4.6	11.2	66666	2%	59199.41	Steady
Strawberry Ice Cream (10l)	45000	4.4	60.9	180000	1.80%	152595	Steady

Table 5:   A heap of unwieldy ice cream sales data.

You need to find out why the user is struggling with the report, so you arrange a time to chat and go through the requirements. It turns out that the user needs the report to show the last month's Key Performance Indicators (volume and profit) in order to make operational decisions on what flavors to produce next month and in what volumes. The user also needs to decide which recipes or processes require improvement.

The current report does provide the data the user requested (and not a jot more), but doesn't present it in a way that gives the user the information needed to make these operational decisions.

You decide to retain all the data from the previous report, but to structure it in a different way. The key figures will be visible, with the extra data structured in a format easier for any initial analysis.

Area	Problem	Resolution
DRY	1) We get it – the report is about ice cream! 2) Cost per unit (and consequentially revenue) and the defect rate are repeated data that relates to the product size	1) Split out the word and use it as a higher level header 2) Split out this information away from the product level data
Labels	No units specified for columns	Add units in brackets
White space	A lot of tightly packed rows and columns	Remove excess columns to allow for more room
Order	1) What sort of order is V, Ch, Co, S and 5, 2, 10? 2) Columns aren't in any pertinent order	1) Split rows out into pot size and order alphabetically 2) Move tub-level data into its own table and reorder remaining items

Area	Problem	Resolution
Alignment	No standard alignments and headers are not matching the data	Maintain default alignments but with an indent
Formatting	No formatting is better than too much formatting, but only just!	Add formatting to improve legibility
Size	It's a big quantity of information which is very difficult to scan	Split out the rows into categories to aid decision making
Keep It Simple, Stupid! (KISS)	How much of the data could actually be called information?	Split into logical groupings and make the levels of detail meet the user's requirements

Table 6:   A heap of issues with the ice cream sales report.

Most of the work here is a kind of pseudo-data-modeling. You're normalizing the data by moving repeating elements into their own table and you're looking for the most useful grouping of the residual data. A perfect example of how knowledge in another area can really help! Knowing that the report might be useful to overseas divisions of the company, you even try to ensure that the currency units are clear.

Apply these simple design principles to all your new report tables, and you'll start to avoid the need for the sort of refactoring necessary to correct confusion and misunderstanding.

	Units Sold (000's)	Profits (£000's)	Units Sold trend*	User rating
2l ice cream tubs	**462**	**£410**	▲	
Chocolate	150	£133	▲	▁▂▃
Coffee	200	£178	▭	▁▂▃▄
Strawberry	67	£59	▭	▁▂▃▄
Vanilla	45	£40	▭	▁▂▃▄
5l ice cream tubs	**260**	**£363**	▽	
Chocolate	100	£140	▭	▁▂▃▄
Coffee	10	£14	▽	▁▂▃
Strawberry	100	£139	▽	▁▂▃▄
Vanilla	50	£70	▽	▁▂▃▄
10l ice cream tubs	**68**	**£229**	▭	
Chocolate	20	£68	▲	▁▂▃▄
Coffee	1	£3	▽	▁▂
Strawberry	45	£153	▭	▁▂▃▄
Vanilla	2	£5	▽	▁▂▃▄

* Month on month units sold trend

Size (l=litres)	Cost per unit (p=penny)	Retail price	Defect Rate
2l	11.2p	£1.00	2.0%
5l	10.5p	£1.50	2.5%
10l	60.9p	£4.00	1.8%

Table 7: An improved version of the ice cream sales report.

Graphs and charts

We can apply to graphs and charts many of the same design principles as for tables. However, there's a huge variety of available charts and picking one can be daunting. In fact, most of the issues with graphs and charts stem from a poor initial choice of graph/chart type.

Basic chart types

For the majority of datasets, we can satisfy the visualization requirements with one of the five basic chart types:

- Column
- Stacked column
- Line
- Bar
- Pie

Many people advise against use of pie charts, for the very good reason that humans find it difficult to gauge the real value of pie segments and perform accurate comparisons. Pragmatically, it's hard to avoid them entirely, though I will try the other basic chart types first.

Beware the siren call of every "must have" new chart type that appears in the latest release of your reporting tool. Two recent examples are treemaps and bubble charts. Treemaps make comparative volumes into areas within a square or rectangle. These are easier to compare than circular segments but they make the reader look hard to understand the comparisons. Bubble charts are quite good at mapping a third series onto a chart, but comparing the sizes of the bubbles is visually difficult. In many cases, the humble bar chart will do a better job than the treemap or bubble chart.

Most users will benefit from simplicity and familiarity. If the requirements really do justify elaborate visualization techniques, then let your mind run unfettered by the humdrum report and pick a chart that is perfect for the dataset.

In his book, *Advanced Presentations by Design*, Dr. Andrew Abela condenses into a single diagram the various chart types and when to use each type, (see HTTP://BIT.LY/HRO4UU, reproduced here with his permission). I also recommend the Chart Chooser supplied by Juice Analytics (HTTP://BIT.LY/MFREXD), which helps you pick the relevant chart and provides you with Excel and PowerPoint downloads of the charts.

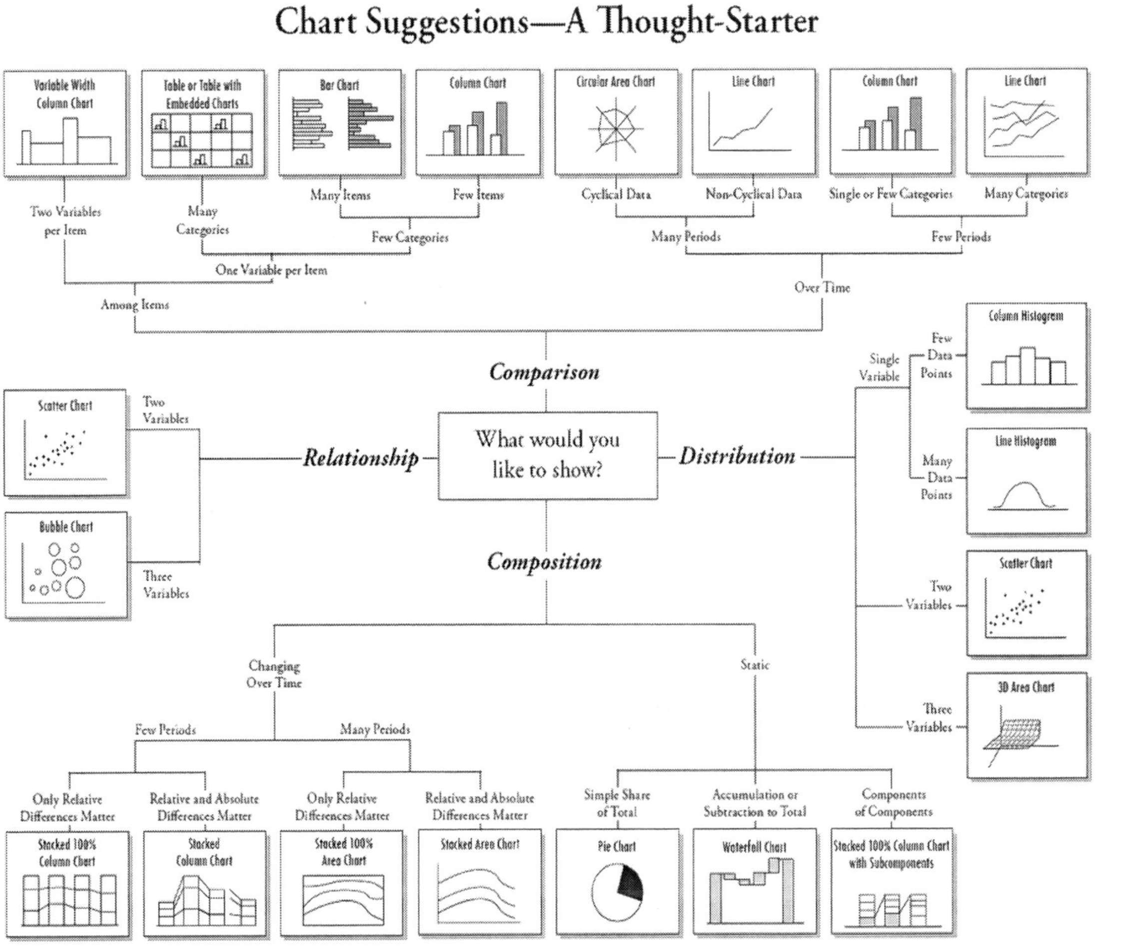

Figure 1: How to choose chart types.

Again, the best way to demonstrate good design principles for charts is by way of an example.

Example – an overelaborate radar chart

At some point, a report developer decided to try a new and exotic way to show predicted annual review (Performance Development Review) grades for the year, using a radar chart. The report user is unsure what to make of it, and turns to you for help.

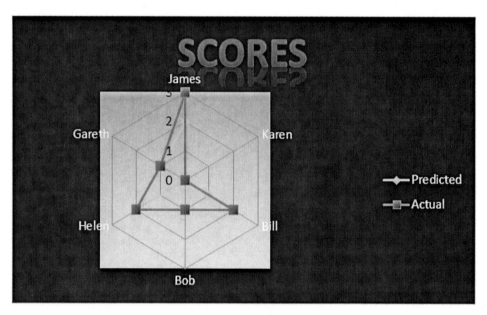

Figure 2:   A bad radar chart.

It looks like the developer, perhaps aware that the results weren't exactly jumping off the page, simply kept adding in extra bits to make it look more important.

Area	Problem	Resolution
Labels	The title is quite vague, although the series labels do help	Make title clearer
Order	No specific order has been used	Adjust to order by either alphabetical or actual score
Alignment	Chart elements are scattered about the page	A central alignment is usually used for charts
Formatting	The WordArt is silly, the sheer quantity of colors makes this chart overwhelming	Return to a white background, remove gradients, standardize fonts
Size	The important bit of the chart takes up too little room	Increase the proportion of the area f or the chart
Keep It Simple, Stupid! (KISS)	Does this really need to be a radar chart?	Change to a bar chart with the predicted values marked as either points or a line

Table 8: The problems with the radar chart.

Changing from a radar to a simple bar chart, reducing graphical complexity, and making the title more informative, allow the user to extract much more information from the chart.

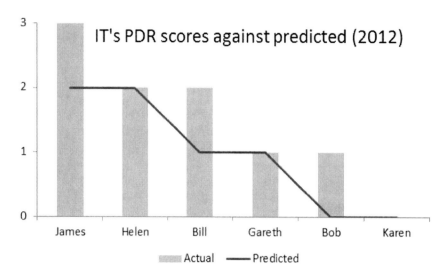

Figure 3:   A simple bar chart succeeds where a complex radar chart failed.

Universal report elements

Certain elements should feature on all reports, to ensure that users are in no doubt as to their intent and can read them with confidence:

- **Title** – avoid shorthand names like *SalesYear2008* in favor of user-friendly ones like *Retail Sales for 2008*.

- **Strapline** – expanding on the title and detailing any key exclusions. For example, a good strapline for the Retail Sales for 2008 report might be *Volumes for completed sales made by the retail channel for the calendar year 2008.*

- **Provenance** – providing details such as major source, who executed the report, and the date you produced it. This enables people to evaluate if the report is now stale or if there were issues at the time of production.

- **Definitions and calculations** – via a page on the report or a link, provide information on criteria, plain-English field definitions, notes about acknowledged flaws or data quality issues and so on.

Choosing the Right Reporting Tools

When you only have a hammer, everything looks like a nail

No single tool is versatile enough for every reporting job. Most organizations should have one centralized tool, and a few other tools that are good for other business needs like ad hoc analysis, exporting to different file formats or rendering on different devices and self-service reporting.

Determining what tools to have and to use is tough, given the investment in time and money that can be required to learn and implement a new tool. Most organizations should have one centralized tool, for reports of any reasonable complexity, or reports that they need to distribute company-wide, over SharePoint. However, for simpler, single table reports, most companies can allow a little flexibility.

Ultimately, your report is simply a vehicle for getting information to the user and, as far as you can, you want to match the reporting tool to the requirements, not the other way round. Users always have a set of "must-haves." If a user has his or her heart set on a great big pie chart filled with 20 shades of green then you should probably try to dissuade them, by demonstrating a better approach during your requirements gathering and prototyping. However, if they really need the data in Excel then you should probably try, if it's a relatively simple report, to put it in Excel, rather than force them to use a reporting mechanism that is more convenient to you.

Most organizations will also need one or two other tools to cover non-standard requirements. New reporting tools appear regularly. If one catches your eye, I recommend trialing it to see how much it helps you, as the report developer, and how much it improves your ability to convey information to the user. It's hard to migrate away from a reporting solution once it is in place, so you will probably need to demonstrate significant benefits over your existing systems. However, analysis of the business benefits encourages you to think about reports as a function, not an end in themselves.

Reporting in the Microsoft stack

Of the "core" reporting tools, I imagine that the vast majority of the readers of a book like this will be using tools within the Microsoft stack, perhaps primarily SQL Server Reporting Services (**SSRS**).

SSRS is the central reporting suite that can cost nothing (if you use SQL Server Express Editions). It is reasonably intuitive, so most people could build a chart or a table in it, either straight away or with some of the myriad tutorials, particularly via Report Builder.

However, SSRS lacks polish. Its strength is creating informative reports, not creating good-looking reports, and where they have incorporated tools from software houses like Dundas they have left relic properties all over the place, so it can be really fiddly to get the look of a report right if you want something a bit unusual.

In addition, of course, we have **Excel**. It is the tool almost *everyone* will have used, at some point, to build reports (I've even seen people use Excel for word-processing). Excel is simple, reliable, powerful and easily updated, so almost all users feel comfortable with it. In short, it's here to stay; I spend a lot of my report-writing time in Excel and provide many reports in this format. Excel spreadsheets can pull data from SSRS, so you can provide reports in a format users like, and ensure that they remain up to date.

For all its advantages, Excel is a risky platform as it's so easy to make mistakes; I would strongly recommend that you read up on developing in Excel to ensure that you minimize the likelihood of errors. One great article I recommend for tips on developing in Excel is found at HTTP://BIT.LY/1MPONQ.

People who move into BI from a business, as opposed to a technical, background tend to do so because they became Excel-addicted. Excel is the software equivalent of a gateway drug, and I can tell you from experience that it creates a powerful hankering for data!

On top of all this, new bits of kit for elaborate and powerful self-service reporting are gaining prominence. Two such tools, are **PowerPivot** and **Power View**, both features of Excel, as well as being tightly integrated with SharePoint. (If Excel is where all reports originate, SharePoint is where many reports end up.)

Predicting the future

It is important to ascertain what the business needs are now and what they are likely to be in the near future. For example, at the time of writing this chapter, Microsoft has, for five years, been moving away from developing their centralized reporting platform, SSRS, and towards delivery in Excel, and embedding Excel in applications, whether SharePoint or their Cloud-based service, Office 365. Microsoft has made significant recent advancements in delivering previously Enterprise-level BI features from SQL Server into Excel, like Power View and Power Pivot.

What this boils down to is a significant shift in strategy and behavior within the business world, which Microsoft believes it must support. Following this vision of the future will mean ensuring sufficient levels of Excel knowledge among your end-users, a risk appetite for Cloud services, and a willingness to invest time and effort in changing feature-sets.

Outside the Microsoft stack

Competing with Excel within the "self-service" area of reporting, are tools such as Tableau and QlikView, which are able to connect to a variety of data sources and produce reports. It isn't necessary to revert to a non-Microsoft product if you need to perform analysis on data from outside SQL Server, but the ease of Tableau, in particular, for the tech-savvy users in a business, can deliver some substantial benefit for self-service reporting.

Recent years have also seen an explosion in the number of open-source or "freemium" excellent-quality applications for analysis, self-service reporting and delivery to tablets and mobile devices. For instance, R is a statistical programming language that is open-source developed and can perform an impressive array of different types of analysis. With the development of packages like Shiny for web delivery, on top of existing integration with ASP.NET and PHP, R can output to lots of different file formats.

These tools don't necessarily come with software assurance and a big support center that we can call upon for a fix if something goes wrong, but they're able to bring capabilities that solve many businesses' problems, without a lot of expenditure. Significant learning will be involved in picking up these tools, and considerations about the risk of using software from smaller (or even non-existent) companies is also a requirement when deciding which tools to use.

Who decides and, most importantly, who pays?

A key issue when discussing the strategy for reporting is who makes the final decision. Every area of the business uses reports, which makes everyone into stakeholders. Some users will be anti-change, others will always want new and shinier reports, and there will be still others who want the latter, in theory, but don't want to spend money.

Given the range of opinions, a wide consultation is unlikely to result in a decision, but implementing a new reporting system without understanding the needs of the business, is likely to end in failure.

My recommendation, therefore, is to avoid company-wide projects as much as possible. Reporting is not a one-size-fits-all area, so there is no point trying to force it to be so. As long as you have gathered user requirements from across the business such that a general strategy can be determined, then you can tackle at the department or team level the need for changes or improvements to the platforms and tools. This sort of implementation allows you to deliver a company-wide platform, if feasible, or at least a tailored, but well-thought-out, set of platforms.

In terms of costs, if you already have SQL Server and Office, you can mitigate a significant proportion of the initial outlay for a Microsoft-based solution by using the existing resources, and then choosing to either upgrade existing hardware or purchase new hardware when the load on the servers increases to a point where performance is becoming inadequate.

In all cases, particularly where costs are unavoidable, it is sensible to work on the strategy collaboratively with the people who'll be most impacted by the new capabilities, as they can really help you frame it in terms of departmental and business benefits. This can make a compelling case that can persuade heads of department to spend out of their own budget or to secure IT budget, where previously it would have been an internal IT debate.

A personal story

When I started with my current employer, reporting tools had a very heavy open-source emphasis, plus a strong reliance on Excel. This meant that reports either conformed to a single table layout on a custom PHP front-end, or were coded individually along with VBA, for regular refreshing of data. As a result, it took a long time to turn around reports.

Many people wanted information that we could not deliver with the existing platform because our report front-end could not connect to it or because they often needed the information with a rapid turnaround and we simply could not code it quickly enough. Where we couldn't deliver, some people would get angry but, worse still, others would stop asking for reports and simply made do with extensive workarounds.

Working with different departments over the past few years, we've implemented a number of solutions:

- A streamlined automated Excel and simple PDF system.

- Excel 2010 installation with training and support for producing their own reports.

- Statistical reports using R.

- Real-time dashboards on big screens using SSRS.

- Complex formatting and calculations in reports using SSRS.

Over time we trialed a number of solutions with different departments that didn't quite work out, like Report Builder 3.0 or refreshable PowerPoint slides.

Not everything has worked, and we're still learning, but crucially we're still making progress and improving, thanks not just to the new reporting tools, but also to a vastly improved approach to education, both for our report writers and our report users.

We produced a decision tree as guidance to our report writers so we consistently produced reports in the "right" tool. It was also incredibly helpful for us when it came to framing discussions amongst ourselves and with others in the business. Internally, we are able to quantify the burden of each system in relation to the proportion and value of the reports utilizing it, and we can discuss replacements for focused scenarios instead of having opinionated discussions about a very large area. Within the business, it also helps us to explain how we are using resources, and why we are delivering improvements in certain areas, on top of being able to identify new scenarios which might need to be taken into account, and homing in on what tool is great for that scenario.

More importantly still, we started educating users on what they can do with existing tools, teaching them good visualization principles, and slowly introducing them to the way the various IT systems interact. In short, we embarked on an education process like the one espoused in this chapter. As a result, there has been an increase in well-thought-out tickets, improved relationships, and decisions becoming more fact-based.

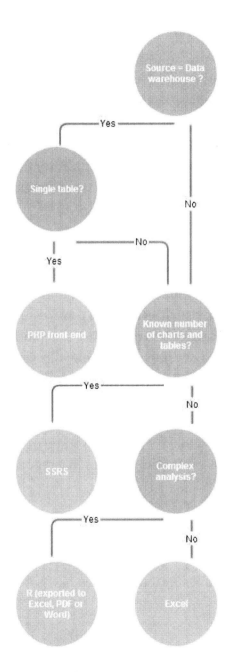

Figure 4:   Flow diagram of report implementation decisions.

Summary

In this chapter, I've tried to provide a whistle-stop tour of what I believe you need to know, and how you need to work, to be a good report developer. Report-writing skills is only one part of your skill set. You need excellent communication skills to find out what the business really needs from a given report. You need broad-ranging technical knowledge to help ensure the performance and availability of your reports, and to help end-users as issues arise. You need a solid understanding of visualization theory and the ability to apply it to produce clear and concise reports that help the user understand key trends and make the right decisions.

I may have scared you, or I may be preaching to the converted, but all components take time to implement fully in any business, and the job is never done. Even if you're not a report developer, think about how well you and your team perform in the three key areas covered in this chapter (communication skills, visualization, and tools/technology). How do you, as a DBA, communicate with relevant parties to make sure they understand why their applications run slowly? How do you, as a developer, evaluate your website designs? Upon what information do you, as an IT manager, base technology decisions. How strong is the link back to clear business benefits?

What gets measured, gets done, so evaluate and make a plan with some metrics and targets on how to improve in these areas. Track your metrics in a report and email it to me!

I'd be happy to receive feedback about this chapter, or to discuss/clarify any of the contents with you, so feel free to email me on STEPHANIE.G.LOCKE@GMAIL.COM or get in touch via Twitter (**@SteffLocke**).

Communication Isn't Soft

Matt Velic

"No one knows what I do."

This may be the Number Two complaint of database administrators and data professionals everywhere, the number one being, "I'm the **D**efault **B**lame **A**cceptor." It doesn't feel great having repeatedly to explain what you do, to coworkers and family, or even to your manager. We've all heard stories about the friend who, despite technical chops, is passed over for promotion, or who can't land a new job, or even the friend who has been fired, not because of poor work, but because no one was quite certain what he or she did on a day-to-day basis.

Any one of us could face these dangerous situations if we fail to communicate properly. There are several kinds of communication: written, spoken, visual. If we're not firing on all three cylinders, it can cause us problems.

Sadly, I think that IT professionals have a branding problem. By popular belief, most of us are "introverted" and "aren't good communicators." Why else would we choose to work with machines and code rather than other human beings? Nevertheless, even the most introverted individual can overcome this image problem. Think for a moment about someone, IT pro or otherwise, whose communication skills you admire, who makes speaking and writing look *easy*. This person has a little secret: *practice*.

No amount of reading, preparation, or mental gymnastics will reward you with massive improvements in your communication skills; purposeful practice will. As such, this chapter is not so much about how to write better, or how to give killer presentations, but how to stop reading about it and start doing it.

The Written Word

Between work email, project updates, Facebook, Twitter and text messages, most IT professionals deal with a lot of written communication in their everyday life, and yet most feel that their writing skills are lacking. Of course, we've all sent vague text messages or poorly worded emails that were too long and grammatically confused, for example using "your" (ownership) instead of "you're" (you are).

Practice won't eradicate this entirely, but it will help you achieve brevity and clarity, as well as improving your longer form writing for reports, documentation, articles and so on.

Read more to write better

It may seem odd, but reading is the prime activity that can improve your writing ability. What you choose to read doesn't matter, though I would suggest a mix of books you enjoy, perhaps fiction or history, and books that challenge you, such as technical volumes and professional books.

The logic behind this tip is that by reading more, by consuming more information, you're opening yourself to new ideas. On a more molecular level, you are studying words and sentence structure, and learning how other writers share their ideas. Reading can help ease that "I-don't-know-how-to-start" feeling when you face the dreaded blank page.

Write right now

You can read any number of articles and books advising how to write better, but the only trick that has a one-hundred-percent success rate is putting pen to page, or fingers to keyboard, and writing.

No amount of mental work or preparation is an adequate substitute for what you will learn by *actually writing*. The rest of this section will offer fun ways to practice.

Start small with Twitter

Most people find it challenging to express their ideas clearly and concisely. Most of us, given free rein, tend to write too much, deploying lengthy paragraphs where a few well-chosen words would suffice.

Twitter is an interesting medium in this regard, precisely because it is *limiting*. Limits force us to think in new ways and to forge workarounds for problems. With Twitter, we have only 140 characters in which to express our thought, question, idea or answer. To do so well, rather than just resorting to strangulated "txt spk," requires us to write more consistently and more concisely.

Signing up for Twitter is simple. I highly recommend Brent Ozar's *Simple Twitter Book* (HTTP://WWW.BRENTOZAR.COM/TWITTER/BOOK/) to learn more about the service in general, and as a guide to begin using it to interact with others. That's another great feature of Twitter: the service is all about interaction.

Using Twitter to talk about your lunch isn't the kind of communication you ought to practice. One simple way to practice is by starting a conversation. Ask questions. Give full answers. Maximize the character limit, and be sure to complete your thought *without* having to resort to a follow-up tweet.

A fantastic way to practice *and* give back to the SQL Server community is to answer questions on the **#SQLHelp** hash tag. Granted, most issues need an email or blog post to resolve, but there are many that, with a little thought, you can answer in a single tweet. Challenge yourself to give a complete, clear reply, and perhaps share a link for additional research, all within 140 characters.

Twitter by example

The following are three tweets that help show the differences between good and poor communication techniques while using the service.

Say, can anyone help me with this problem I'm facing with my log files? I cannot remember for the life of me if I should only have one log file or if SQL Server can utilize multiple log files. Thanks! #SQLHelp

While this first example is friendly, it's too long at 210 characters.

any 1 no if sql use more than 1 log? #sqlhelp

This second tweet is short enough, using only 45 characters, but the question is difficult to understand because of the "txt spk."

Should SQL Server use only one log file? Or can it utilize multiple logs for better performance? #SQLHelp

Finally, a tweet that is both concise (at 105 characters) and clear. This is the balance one should strive for when using Twitter.

Blog to find your inner editor

If you are serious about improving your written communication, you will soon want to move beyond 140 characters. Some great ideas need more than a sentence or two (although don't let Hemingway fans overhear you saying that). Authoring a blog is a great way to practice writing more in-depth articles and, as a bonus, your blog provides an online home for your personal "brand."

Starting a blog is simple, and there are two routes to take: sign up for a service, such as WordPress, or host your own on a domain. There are pros and cons to each, but I recommend hosting your own if you are planning to write often.

Whereas Twitter is an interesting exercise in the art of short-form writing, there are no such limits with a blog post. It can be as long or as short as it needs to be. However, the secret of the beautiful blog is *balance*: finding the proper length; honing the overall feel of a piece; ensuring it has a set-up, strong exposition, and a solid conclusion. You will achieve this balance not in the writing, but in the *editing*. That's the secret of many great writers: the greatness is forged in editing.

By practicing editing, you'll learn to look with a critical eye on what you've produced, and you'll learn to ask questions of yourself. Are these sentences repetitive? Can I find a more succinct way to state this idea? This sentence sounds odd when read aloud, how can I tune it to sound more natural?

Articles are great practice for the editing process, because the best ones tend to achieve optimal balance. If you want to review some examples of balanced blog writing, you could check out pieces by Thomas LaRock, Kendra Little, and Nate Silver. Each of these writers has wonderful balance and style in their articles. Learning to spot unbalanced sections in your own writing is a part of growing as a writer and editor.

NaNoWriMo: find your voice

One of the best experiences I have ever had as a writer, in fact, the event that turned me into a writer, was National Novel Writing Month (commonly referred to as NaNoWriMo, see HTTP://WWW.NANOWRIMO.ORG/). The challenge to participants is to write a 50,000-word novel during the month of November. To keep pace, each author must write 1,667 words per day at a minimum (yes, including Thanksgiving Day!).

If writing a good blog means finding your inner editor, and achieving the right balance, writing a book in a month means shutting up that inner editor for a little while. In NaNoWriMo, there is no time to think of the best word, or the best sentence, or even the best opening paragraph; there is only time to write. Consequently, of course, your first novel will likely be dreadful. What I guarantee however, is that successful participation in NaNoWriMo will help you achieve two valuable goals.

Firstly, it will establish writing as a daily habit. Remember the first rule of writing: the *only* way to practice writing is by writing. Most people, when attempting to get start writing, fire up Word, fiddle with the fonts, set the margins just right, but the page remains blank and it mocks them with its blankness. During NaNoWriMo, there is no time to consider the blank page; it forces you into the habit of *starting*.

Secondly, it will help you find your own voice. At the beginning, your writing will feel forced and, when you read it back, it won't sound like you. As the days turn into weeks, you'll find your rhythm, the words that you like and those that you don't, and when you read those pages back, they'll feel as though they've come from you. I need no further convincing of how much I grew as a writer during that month than to compare what I wrote at the start to what I was writing by the end.

If you think that NaNoWriMo won't fit into your schedule, or if you don't want to wait for November, you can easily apply this tip to other writing activities. It's about keeping a schedule and keeping to it honestly. You could easily start a blog and promise to publish once every other week, or start writing a daily journal. Find the option that you can fit into your life, and stick to it.

The Spoken Word

If there is a broader stereotype than the awkwardly spoken geek, I can't name it. Many people, given the choice between facing down a hungry tiger or a live audience would gladly throw their lot in with the tiger. Sure, there are people who live for the limelight, but for everyone else the only way to remove this fear is to become a better speaker, and the only way to do that is to, you guessed it, practice.

A different kind of audience

One of the challenges to practicing public speaking is finding an audience. Writing requires us to find the appropriate way share articles with our readership, but the timing between publishing and reading is asynchronous. Speaking requires an audience in the literal sense, or does it?

Thanks to cheapening technology and the popularity of YouTube and Vimeo, video cameras have become ubiquitous. You can buy a basic camcorder for about $100. Phones have the ability to shoot video, as do most tablets, iPads, and laptops. All this technology creates a new kind of opportunity to practice speaking *without* an immediate audience. Simply record yourself, play it back, and take critical notes, not only about how you speak but also about your body language.

You may find you have verbal ticks of which you were unaware. The ubiquitous one is use of the word "Um" between every thought, but other common ticks include saying "and," "ah" and "like" too much. I once had one professor who had an unconscious tendency to say "Dontcha know" between sentences. In one class, she deployed her famous catch-phrase over a hundred and thirty times.

Equally, you may learn that you need to improve your *visual* communication skills. For example, you may notice that you have poor posture, that you move around too much and seem fidgety, or that you don't move around enough and appear lifeless. Similar to editing, the purpose of the video is to turn a critical eye towards your performance, attempt to identify and correct poor habits, and to bolster positive ones. It creates a way to edit how you present yourself.

Overall, videos are a great way to get started for anyone wishing to improve their verbal and visual communication skills. You can practice the script, shoot as many takes as necessary, edit out the rough parts, and add a fancy music track. You can publish your best videos on YouTube, let people know about them through Twitter and start to interact with your audience through comments, user requests, and follow-up videos.

However, if you have ambitions beyond this, for example to speak at conferences, you need to start to learn how to handle the anxiety that often accompanies a live audience.

Lunch-and-learn

Even seasoned speakers get nervous in front of an audience but, with practice, they learn to turn that nervousness into an energy that fuels a presentation rather than bogging it down.

Lunch-and-learn events are one of the best ways to start practicing. All it takes to get started is one coworker asking you, "How does that work?" and all you need to do it is a conference room at your office, a projector and some food.

Why are lunch-and-learn events so valuable? First, they are not meetings. Most people hate meetings, because the majority of them are a waste of time. Second, there's food. Lunch is a great way to kick back, forget about that production issue for half an hour, and bond with your coworkers. Third, because of all this good will, it's disarming. It's a relaxed environment to present ideas. When the projector won't start, you can shrug it off with a smile; when Management Studio goes boom you can all laugh at it together.

Even better, if you have ambitions to take your presentations beyond the office, to the conference, you'll start to gain an understanding of what works and what doesn't work. Your coworkers can help identify topics that are the most interesting, questions that the audience are likely to ask in the future, and trim areas that are too slow, complicated or awkward.

You can even bring along your camcorder to video the session for later review, which can be an easier solution than trying to scribble down notes. Of course, you could also turn it into a bloopers reel for the upcoming holiday party.

User groups, SQL Saturday and beyond

Having honed a presentation through private practice and testing in a lunch-and-learn environment, you may wish to take that next step and present it publicly, at a local, regional or even international event.

Local tech user groups are great because they combine want and need. User group leaders tend to *need* new speakers to present topics and ideas to their membership, and the people attending the meetings *want* that knowledge. It creates an ideal situation where you can begin to test your ideas in a supportive environment.

The next step from user groups is a full-fledged regional event, such as a SQL Saturday or the SQL Rally. Most of these events attract submissions nationally, as well as from the local region, so you'll be competing for a slot with some experienced speakers. However, this is where your practice will pay off, since it will help you to step up your performance level and deliver a thought-provoking session that receives good feedback, and so will aid your cause the next time you submit.

Getting your sessions accepted

The point of this chapter is to provide fun activities to practice, and not focus on how to compete to gain acceptance into curated community events. However, if you are looking for advice to help improve your chances, check out these resources on the Brent Ozar Unlimited blog: HTTP://WWW.BRENTOZAR.COM/ARCHIVE/2012/04/WRITING-BETTER-CONFERENCE-ABSTRACTS-PRESENTATIONS/.

Finally, there are international events such as the PASS Summit and SQLBits in the UK, where competition is fiercer still. However, if can attain this level, you can be certain that your practice has paid off. You've become a known entity, a thought leader; but keep practicing!

Practice Pays Off

How can tweeting, blogging or giving lunch-and-learn presentations help you at work? How can you use these skills to grow your career? Good communication is a skill that is always in demand, and once you acquire it, it will help you in many and varied ways.

Self-belief

When I first received the crown of "Accidental DBA," I had no confidence in my skills. In fact, I had no skills. I could barely write a query, let alone protect production data. Instead of being overwhelmed and doing nothing, I read, studied, and practiced. When critical needs arose, I knew how to handle them and had the confidence to do so because of the practice.

It's the same with communication. The experience that allows you to act calmly and decisively when the production environment goes down is the same that keeps you rooted when your laptop dies mid-presentation.

Communicating expertise

The point of practice is gaining confidence in your abilities. Having gained this confidence and belief, you will find that you are much more effective at communicating your expertise.

Having mastered the art of precise communication, through Twitter, these same skills will help you improve your résumé. Just like Twitter, a résumé is a word-restrictive communication medium; you have only a page or two at most to present yourself in the best manner possible. It means choosing the words with the most impact, words that have the greatest meaning. Treat each bullet point item, each nugget of information about your skills and experience, as a finely honed tweet.

Likewise, having found your inner editor and voice through writing blogs and articles, you can use these same skills to perfect your cover letters. Set out why the company ought to hire you, build support for your argument, and close out strongly. Article writing can also help you write cleaner documentation for your products or support, or to edit concisely technical emails to your business users.

As for speaking, confidence in your ability goes a long way in any venue. It will help you handle interviews confidently, both with your manager, during annual reviews, and with prospective new employers. You'll also communicate more effectively with non-technical users, finding yourself better able to explain issues simply, and through the use of analogies.

Practice Makes Perfect

When a person writes or speaks with ease, you can be certain that it is because he or she has put in hours of time and effort beforehand. If we all made a similar effort, we could dismantle the stereotypical image of the IT professional as "introverted geek."

Poor communication skills are a barrier to our successes in life and career, and one we should strive to overcome. I've provided a number of fun ways to practice communication; activities that can help the practice feel natural, all while working towards the goal of bettering your skills. You don't necessarily need to take the route of becoming a public speaker, or community blogger, and there are many more activities that can help you practice that might make more sense for your situation. For example, if you enjoy trying new restaurants, you could strive to write reviews of your experiences on review websites, such as Yelp. If you are involved in your local church, you could practice your public presentation skills by taking up readings. Always feel free to experiment and test different waters, because while planning and practice make perfect, the confidence you gain will help you succeed when life places an unexpected obstacle in your path.

Finally, always remember that communication is two-way. Whether you're writing, speaking, or taking photographs, always encourage interaction and feedback. Ask if you are communicating your message or if there's anything, you can change to make that message clearer. Always be open to constructive criticism and you will continue to grow as a professional and as a professional communicator.

Guerrilla Project Management for DBAs

David Tate

This chapter won't contain any hot T-SQL code or cool execution plans. In fact, the project management tools and advice it contains will not improve your coolness factor at all, although perhaps your choice to become a DBA sealed your fate, in that regard.

Deep in your heart, though, you know that your job as a Database Administrator comes with a lot more responsibility than just speeding up queries and fixing broken servers. Managers expect database administrators to be shape-shifters. We need crazy-deep knowledge of the technology (did you know that SQL Server 7.0's favorite color is black?), communication skills like one of those people on TV with the talking and the podium and stuff (I didn't say I had these skills), and the organizational skills of a retired drill sergeant with OCD.

For DBAs, project management skills, of which organization and communication form a core part, are both our weapon and our shield. With them, we can fight off the causes of long hours and stress, defend against the subjective politics of our employers, and protect our right to do high quality work. Learn them and you need never feel overworked and undervalued again.

A DBA's Crazy Workload

Most people imagine that DBAs typically spend the majority of their time sitting in a dusty cubicle that smells of stale coffee and heated electronics, tapping away at some impenetrable PowerShell script or intricate ETL (Extract-Transform-Load) task. Indeed, they do, for it is the DBA's job to organize, code, schedule and execute a wide variety of administrative tasks. These tasks alone require considerable time-management and organizational skills, as well as quite a bit of sitting in a cubicle in front of a monitor.

However, in addition to these everyday tasks, many DBAs, especially more senior ones, will have multiple other projects going on that they have to schedule and track, and for which they are expected to provide updates. For example:

- **Unplanned support work**
  "Hey – hypothetical question. If I ran an `alter table` statement on the `Customer` table in production rather than in development, that's cool, right? Oh, and I just heard from a customer that the system is down. Can you look into these two totally unrelated things?"

- **Consulting on development projects**
  "Hey, can you help me debug this cursor inside a trigger that I wrote to update my Twitter feed?"

- **Maintenance projects**
  "Why does your status report always include the item *Make Peace Offering to the Replication God?*"

- **Long-term build-outs**
  "Remember when I should have asked you to build a new production server a month ago? Is that done yet?"

A DBA's Place in the Organization

Organizational skills matter more to a DBA than many other technical jobs, due to the diverse nature of their workload. In addition, the diversity of the workload exposes the DBA to a greater surface area of the organization than is typical for most technical roles. As part of our jobs, we talk to many people:

- **Vendor's technical resources** – mainly to ask why they need "sa" access, but also to request updated pictures of them that are coincidentally the size of a dartboard.

- **Internal development resources** – mainly to ask politely why they decided that a homegrown triple-nested cursor implementation of GROUP BY was a good idea, but also to enquire, for no particular reason at all, about their food allergies.

- **Business stakeholders** – mainly to discuss capacity-planning decisions, but also to find out how to prevent an in-ear Bluetooth headset from affecting one's golf swing.

- **Internal semi-technical resources** (project managers, product managers, business analysts) – mainly to help with decisions about performance, capacity, and future goals for each product that needs database resources, but also to spread misinformation ("What, you didn't know that using the first column in Excel has been outlawed as part of the Patriot Act?").

- **Internal IT resources** – mainly to work with them in configuring and securing the hardware and software platforms on which the DBMS infrastructure depends, but also to trade *Magic: The Gathering* playing cards.

- **Management resources** – to complain about all the above people.

Since we talk to so many people, we are at higher risk of finding ourselves in the crosshairs of the *blame gun*.

The Dark Side of Being a DBA

High risk of exposure to the deadly rays of the blame gun is the primary disadvantage of being a DBA. A blame gun is a device used by the above-referenced people if projects go awry, or you get in the way of their reputational momentum. Even if you're essentially innocent, the blame gun can harm your reputation, career progression, and salary. There is no waiting period for its use and typically the sniper fires from long range.

In my experience, these specific situations, in particular, draw a DBA into the laser sights of the blame gun:

- **A project timeline changes and your tasks suddenly overlap with another project**
  "Well, our project shifted back two weeks and so your part of this project now overlaps with your part of the other project and I miss the part where this is my problem."

- **Unplanned work overwhelms your working time and leaves you unable to execute on any planned projects**
  "He didn't have the development database server ready in time, which is funny, because the word database is in his title."

- **You perform maintenance work, even planned maintenance work**
  "I couldn't care less about Windows updates that you applied last night; I want to know about this security hole I heard about this morning."

- **People "misunderstand" your day-to-day responsibilities**
  "Dave? Oh, he's in charge of making sure we don't use the first column in our public Excel documents."

The more DBAs are exposed to the rays of the blame gun, over time, the more jaded they become, until the unending trail of half-truths and perceived failures turns their beards into Brillo pads of fear and hatred.

OK, I'm being both flippant and melodramatic. The serious, underlying point is that many DBAs are very bad at managing their time, managing expectations, and "advertising" to the organization exactly what it is they do. However, you *can* handle your numerous and diverse projects and you *can* avoid the blame gun, just by applying some simple project management techniques.

The Shield of Project Management

What is project management? Expressed as simply as possible, it is the organization of "things" to get "stuff" done. Normally, we call the things "resources," which is a fancy term for sufficiently employable hominids, which some feel is an advanced term for about 80% of their coworkers.

The non-technical members of your organization expect everyone to know about how to manage a project. Good news: *we are all project managers*. Each time you plan your Saturday you are planning a (probably very lame) project. Every project comprises the following common sense bits of information:

- What are we doing? (project summary)
- Why are we doing this? (project charter)
- Who is doing what? (resource assignment)
- How could it go sideways and fail? (risk plan)
- What is the plan? (project plan baseline)
- How is it going? (project plan)

For every task that takes more than a few hours, you should be prepared to communicate the plan to your manager in the appropriate form. For smaller projects, this may take the form of simple answers to the Who/What/When/Why questions, as illustrated here for an index maintenance task:

- *Why?* Maintaining indexes makes everything faster and brings great honor to our company.

- *When?* We perform the maintenance outside peak hours of usage.

- *Who is doing it?* An automated job, and the Database Team is responsible for making sure it runs.

- *How could it fail?* It could fail to run, or run for too long. It could run and fail and not be noticed.

- *What is the plan?* Every 3rd Tuesday.

- *How is it going?* It's been running cleanly for one week. We made one change to speed it up.

- *What changes to the original plan have occurred?* We changed it so that we have a process to re-evaluate what it does as we add databases and new systems to each machine. The notification system works like this...

As DBAs, we need to learn how to communicate our plans in the correct terms, depending on to whom we're reporting. A manager does not want to hear a winding tale of how there was no 64-bit driver, and the ensuing search for suitable third-party components. They just want to hear about how it affects the plan ("*We burned through 40 hours due to Risk #3, which we couldn't mitigate.*").

For larger projects, we need to create proper documentation. The following sections describe what sorts of documentation are justified in these cases.

Common project management terms cheat sheet

When you communicate your plan, you need to use a commonly understood language.

Project charter

The project charter is a document that explains why you're doing the project. If you have to reread this after every meeting to understand what is going on, then you are officially on a massive corporate project. For the project of getting my family out the door to go to the zoo on a Saturday, our simple example, my project charter might look something like this:

> *We will visit the local zoo and strive to have a safe, fun day in the eyes of our children. We will teach them about animals. We hope not spend more than $500 on food, drink, and gas.*

Work Breakdown Structure (WBS)

A WBS is just a list of all the work the team needs to complete for a project, broken out into appropriate milestones, and with some care taken to list dependencies and parallelize the tasks. Be aware of who is able to complete the tasks for each milestone.

Such a document can assist in further planning and assignment of tasks, and make it easier for us to adjust the plan if people are out sick.

Milestone	Task Name	Can be performed by
Baby bag is packed	Pack formula	Dad or Mom
	Pack bottles	Dad or Mom
	Pack change of clothes	Dad or Mom
Car is ready for transport	Grab umbrella	Dad or Mom or Kid #1
	Put baby bag in car	Dad or Mom or Kid #1
	Pack change of clothes for all non-adults	Dad or Mom or Kid #1
Children are prepared for transport	Kid #1 - dresses self	Kid #1
	Kid #2 - help get dressed	Kid #1
	Kid #3 - dress	Dad or Mom
	Kid #4 - dress	Dad or Mom
	Kid #3 - put in carseat	Dad or Mom
	Kid #4 - put in carseat	Dad or Mom
Everyone is in car	Buckle Kid #2 into their seat	Kid #1
	Put kid #3 in car	Dad or Mom
	Put kid #4 in car	Dad or Mom
Everything is reviewed	Shot of vodka	Dad
	Check that everyone is buckled in	Dad or Mom
	Check that everyone has shoes on	Dad or Mom

Figure 1: The Work Breakdown Structure for the Zoo project.

Critical path / long pole

The "critical path" comprises all the elements that, if you forget any one of them, will put the project's success at risk.

Similar to critical path, the "long pole" refers to the task, or set of tasks which, even after optimization, will take the longest. Ultimately, the long pole defines the minimum amount of time that the project will take; speeding up anything else will not speed up the overall timeline.

For the Zoo project, the long pole is preparing kids #3 and #4 for transport. This milestone, until complete, fully occupies both parents. Everyone else might be ready to go before this happens, but we can't leave until it does.

Resource allocation

This is project management speak for "who is doing what." As the project grows larger, so the terms employed increase in number and complexity. On a two-person project, we assign tasks; on a sixteen-person project, we allocate resources; on a seventy-six-person project, we allocate resources according to the Resource Allocation Matrix Committee Procedure Strategy Giraffe Hat Check-list (OK, I made up the bit about giraffe hats).

The constraint triangle

a.k.a. "The three-sided triangle," a.k.a. "The triangle of project management"

A project has a schedule, a scope, and allocated resources, and a change to one affects the others. Remove a person and it takes longer to complete the same amount of work; if you don't care about quality then you can get done faster; do less (reduce the scope) and you finish early.

It is amazing how often people reference this triangle, often as a defense mechanism against the insanities of requests for large changes in scope without any adjustments to the schedule.

Burndown rate

How quickly you spend the money allocated to a project. An hour into our Zoo project we are all holding large drinks, for which budget was allocated. The large stuffed panda that the 4-year-old is holding was an unforeseen expense.

Checking-in

A term used for the act of a project manager creeping up behind you, during the 30 seconds in which you check your personal email, to see why your task on the critical path is not yet complete. Also called "touching base" and "sync-ing up."

At risk

If a task or project is "at risk," it doesn't mean it grew up in a bad neighborhood: it means it will probably be late.

Specific defensive moves

Armed with some common project management terms, you can now defend yourself from attacks and, over the coming sections, I'll explain how.

Outsource prioritization for items assigned to you

Department A and Department B don't like each other and both have work for you to do. According to the manager of each department, their project is as important to society as the smallpox vaccine, and he or she demands that you work on it until the project is finished and/or you collapse from exhaustion.

Each time you receive a work request, note down a brief description, the name of the stakeholder, the request date, and the priority in terms of expected completion date (at least according to the stakeholder).

Department A's task might look like this:

- **Title**: Create a database server for Department A for the tracking of Department B's birthday cake consumption.

- **Stakeholder**: Department A's assistant manager (a.k.a. *Sudden Def*).

- **Priority**: Should be complete before the next time that you blink or you will be fired in a humiliating way.

- **Date reported**: 3/20/2012 3:02 PM EST.

When Department B's manager swings by, calmly write down the next task:

- **Title**: Create a database trigger on Department A's vendor tracking database that removes every odd invoice record from its database.

- **Stakeholder**: Department B Assistant Manager (a.k.a. *Your Median Nightmare*).

- **Priority**: Should be complete before I get back to my desk or I'll send you an angry email, and then request status updates every 15 minutes until I fill your Inbox quota.

- **Date reported**: 3/20/2012 3:12 PM EST.

What do you work on next? What side do you take? The fact that you have friends in Department A shouldn't really affect which project you work on first thing the next morning.

In fact, you *cannot* make this call. You are here to work on the technical execution, not on sorting tasks based on business priority. Without a clearly established priority, we tend to sort by degree of interest, level of difficulty, or what we can describe best as "DBA order."

None of these is easy to explain to a non-technical person in a heated political situation. You need to stay away from these potential political fights. In all cases, you should outsource the prioritization of your work to your boss, and establish this as an understood process. If you work at a small company, where there is no one who can break these ties in your organization chart, then you simply put the two stakeholders in contact and ask them to arm-wrestle to decide which is the most important. You cannot make an arbitrary call so do not begin work until someone makes a decision.

Never say "No," just communicate that everything has a cost

One tip you pick up from consulting (more useful but equally important as being able to hold an intelligent conversation after three drinks) is the idea that you "Never say No." Does this mean you wind up abused and over-committed, based on the priorities of others? Absolutely, yes...wait, I mean, no! It means that you learn to communicate that every task has an associated cost. This forces the project owner to take more responsibility and think more deeply about hard prioritization tasks.

Let's walk through an example:

Dale: Hey, Dave. I don't think I ever got a chance to thank you for standardizing us on SQL Server after years of a mix of Access, complex systems in Excel, and various versions of custom vendor databases. However, times change and it feels like we need to start moving with the NOSQL flow. I've read several white papers on MongoDB, and talked to a guy with a double nose-ring at Borders, and I'm pretty excited. It's free, fast and elegant. I think it will revolutionize our inventory systems. I need you to sunset SQL Server on these systems, and move to MongoDB immediately across all projects.

Dave: It's a terrible idea on so many levels. Let's fight to the death.

Bad answer; try again.

Dave: OK, cool, that sounds like an exciting move, but let's do some quick pre-planning to decide the best first step.

Moving to MongoDB is a big shift; that's OK but, by my estimate, eight members of staff will require additional training. Let's estimate that each hour a member of the team is not working but instead taking the training hour, as costing us $150/hour. If we assume that two of them will need in-depth training, and the rest need an overview of about a week, then the first two can provide additional internal training for the others. That's four weeks for the pair, plus an additional month tapered out over the next few months, which gives us a total of (*Dave types in Excel like a twitching hamster*) $32,000 for the primary training and $24,000 for the secondary training. Of course, we ought to include a cost estimate for delays to existing scheduled projects during the ramp-up period, let's say $12,000. That gives us a total cost for training and ramp-up, which we will call Milestone 1, of $68,000.

Next, we'd need to enumerate the in-progress projects and the existing systems and decide which ones will be the first to move from SQL Server to MongoDB. We have four projects in progress, one of which is quite large and 80% complete, and 16 existing systems...

Good answer.

Dale: You know what? This has given me a lot of new good information. Let me go back and think about this.

Communicate risk without being obstructive

Every DBA has sat in a meeting, rolled their eyes and thought "Girl, this is a straight-up nasty mess!" Some DBAs open their mouths right after thinking this and say rash things that get them branded as Negative, Not a Team Player, Too Intense, and Distracting. It's all just ammunition for the blame gun. Identify the risks; think a little harder about risk mitigation.

- *Risk*: the thing that is going to make this blow up in your face.

- *Risk mitigation*: the thing that is going to prevent it from being quite so bad.

Feel free to express your concerns, but only if you have a productive solution. Some examples (with the productive part in *italics*):

- This is new technology and I know that everyone is excited about it, as am I. However, we have a lot to learn and I'd hate us to stumble right from the start. It would undermine people's faith in the technology, and possibly prevent us from exploiting it more fully later. *I think we'd be wise to invest some more money on education and prototyping as part of the initial project plan.*

- It seems like nobody knows what is going on with this project, which is understandable, considering how *thinly spread the time of the project leaders is, with all the other projects going on. Would it make sense to shift priorities a bit so that one or two of them can focus more on this project?*

- I agree that moving datacenters is a great idea and that x64 is better than x32 by some unknown mathematical factor, but changing so many systems at once might fail. *I think we should instead identify a system that can transition easily and begin the process with that one. After this, we will have some momentum and learn some valuable lessons to tackle the rest of them. I'm nicknaming this Small Bang and am trademarking it, OK?*

Pay attention to conflicting schedules

One persistent problem makes project planning for a DBA difficult: on an installation or build-out project, the vast majority of the database-related tasks occur at the very beginning and end of a project timeline. At project kick-off, everyone is wide-eyed with enthusiasm and desperately keen to get started, and they need the DBA to set up the required database environment, quickly. They then go off for several months and do unspeakable things to it, and finally come back at "crunch time" begging you to push it to production.

It is during this final stage that the development staff or vendor support people are looking for someone else to take over blame for the project being late, while they wrap up the last 10% of their work (which in some cases is actually 80%).

In order to avoid a blast from the blame gun, it's vital that a DBA avoids scheduling conflicts that involve two projects entering "crunch time" simultaneously. Given that project timelines tend to be about as stable as Jell-O on a treadmill on an airplane, this is easier to say than to do.

However, DBAs must always track potentially conflicting timelines, and throw up a flare as soon as they smell any trouble, as project plans shift.

Make a project plan for recurring, unappreciated tasks

When off-hours maintenance tasks, such as SQL Server upgrades, improving the disaster recovery process, keeping the backups running and so on, run smoothly, they tend to become "invisible" to the DBA's boss.

However, things don't always run smoothly. Consider a simple database procedure that you have to perform weekly, off-hours, and that takes forty-five minutes, in the normal case. At the end of each quarter, that same task might take two hours. In addition, if the development team failed to do the MIQDUT (Most Important Quarterly Data Update Task) on time, you have to perform the steps out of order, in which case it can take up to six hours.

If you hide this complexity from others, including your boss, then you're unlikely to get due credit and appreciation for what might be hours of important and exhausting work. Of course, when things go awry, either due to circumstances beyond your control or because you made a mistake, then suddenly everyone knows about it.

Here are two things you can do to avoid this situation. Firstly, for each task, create a comprehensive check-list of every required step, so that you avoid the sort of simple mistake and subsequent disruption that brings shame to you and your family in a dramatic and highly visible fashion. It is very easy to forget steps as you perform, check, or monitor simple changes, and this is why a simple check-list can be a lifesaver.

I like to ride bicycles and I have a simple check-list of items that I need to remember to take, built from years of mistakes, like forgetting to wear a helmet, or not having cash to bribe a border patrol guard (sometimes I get lost). The list contains cash, ID card, ID on wrist, mobile phone, helmet, 400 calories of food, 16 oz. of water, 2 spare tires, a light, and a knife. I refer to this list, and ensure I have all these items, every time I take a bike ride, even if it is just to ride around the local neighborhood.

Are you doing a manual fix to a log-shipping or replication job? Did you remember to turn the monitoring alarm back on afterwards? A check-list can help you avoid these types of public mistakes, which cause massive delays the next day and expose you to a blame gun firing squad.

Secondly, use each check-list to create a project plan for these off-hours tasks, which makes it clear when these tasks occur and how long they take, so your boss and others fully appreciate the work you do. You can also use this project history to predict future work more accurately.

Figure 2 shows a typical check-list for an "Apply Patches" maintenance task. It exposes the preparation and clean-up tasks that accompany the actual execution, and will give your boss or other stakeholders a proper appreciation of the work involved and how long it takes.

Task Mode	Task Name	Duration
⇨	Notify of beginning of outage window	10 mins
⇨	Run script that puts up maintenance page on website	5 mins
⇨	Reschedule jobs during maintenance window	30 mins
⇨	Perform backup procedures of configuration files and other resources	30 mins
⇨	Apply patches and upgrades	2 hrs
⇨	Restart needed systems in the right order	25 mins
⇨	Reschedule jobs to run in correct order	10 mins
⇨	Monitor regulary scheduled jobs for success	2 hrs
⇨	Answer support phone and explain to business owner that maintenance window is in effect as planned	30 mins
⇨	Monitor logs for any unexpected errors	2 hrs
⇨	Run script that turns off maintenance page on website	10 mins
⇨	Notify of end of outage window	10 mins

Figure 2:   A typical maintenance checklist.

Offensive project management

Up to now, we've discussed ways in which DBAs can use project management techniques to protect themselves from the rays of unwarranted blame. However, project management skills are also an offensive weapon. We can use them to make sure that people make the right decisions, that projects start in the right way, with the required resources, and that we avoid altogether certain types of future maintenance work. Ultimately, good project management skills provide you leverage to advance your career. The following sections describe some specific project management "moves" that can help.

Remove technical debt

All experienced DBAs learn to fear technical debt, *i.e.* any short-term solution to a problem that they know will create, rather than eliminate, future work.

A good example of a technical debt is the patched-up network infrastructure that really doesn't do what you want it to, slows down your backups, and causes occasional failures, which lead you to wake up and fix them about once a month. So how do you convince your boss to spring for that new router and a second NIC on your database server? Many DBAs resort to emotional complaints, such as "Man, that is a pain!" or "I missed watching the American Idol finale last night because the backups failed!"

Unfortunately, your boss doesn't care. However, every time it fails, that flaky network infrastructure is costing your organization money. You need to calculate that amount and communicate it, repeatedly. When you tell your boss, repeatedly, that the network issues are costing the company $13K a year, or $4K every time they cause a failure, then eventually the part of their brain that does mathematics will stage a non-violent sit-in until the hand starts writing checks.

Calculating the cost of an ongoing problem is a complex problem but even a rough estimate can clarify thinking. For a simple down-time event, consider the following costs:

- **Resource time** – how long it takes you and others to deal with the issue. Estimate resource time based on simple aggregates such as $100/hour. Remember that while some people are fixing the problem, others are communicating the problem to clients; include all their time in your estimates.

- **Shifts in schedule** – every time you work to resolve down-time you delay planned work, in a domino effect. Even spending 10–20% of your time on unplanned work can have a big impact on the confidence level you and the organization can place on any future project planning.

- **Business loss** – down-time of internal or external systems means money lost, directly or indirectly, by the business. For external systems, you can estimate the loss based on transactional volumes; for internal systems, estimate based on the time wasted by those that depend on them. For any type of system, keep in mind the reputational cost of a system that your customers or employees can't trust to be available.

- **Cultural costs** – if your organization spends all its time fighting fires then, eventually, only firefighters will be successful and not those that can resolve or prevent the types of problems you are experiencing.

Justify hiring

Are you overworked? How do you prove this? Go to sleep during meetings and send 3 a.m. emails? Dye your hair red and insist people call you "Cranberry Dan the No Sleep Man"? Show your boss your DVR list, with 87 hours of unwatched television?

Again, these responses are too emotional and not likely to have the desired effect, which is to convince your boss to hire someone to help. Put another way, you have to help your boss justify hiring someone to help you, and the correct way to do this is with data.

When you decide you need a hand, you have to build a proper business case to support your cause. Following are the sort of metrics you need to track and report:

- The amount of time you spend on unplanned work.
- The long-term fixes you can't do because you don't have enough time.
- Projects started but now "shelved" due to inadequate resources.
- Projects never started due to lack of resources.
- Projects hamstrung with technical debt and riddled with Band Aids.

- Tasks that are falling through the cracks because nobody is there to catch them (proceed with caution here). Are you planning for future growth, up to date on new security best practices, or fully familiar with new technology that could help your company solve its challenges?

Prove your performance

Most people regard their performance review as a sort of colonoscopy for the mind; unpleasant, necessary, Advil needed immediately afterwards, and more likely to produce confusing or bad news than the reverse. You shouldn't think of it this way, and not only because it is a bad metaphor. You should think of it as a way to prove to your boss how awesome you are, and to show off and reflect on all your amazing feats of the past year.

What can you show them? Well, dear reader, you can show them the project plans for all the projects you completed, your task lists for maintenance work, your analysis of what Band Aids cost the company, and possible solutions, if only resources were available. Since you have also tracked costs carefully, you might even be able to roll up the costs and say things like "I saved the company $200,000 this quarter" with a straight face:

- License cost savings by the consolidation project that moved SQL Server into virtual machines: $87,000.

- Reduction of down-time events by implementing a failover solution for production (reduced average down-time from 2 hours to 10 minutes a month): $105,000.

- Increased productivity by switching the decaf in the break room to Starbucks Extra Addict laced with Red Bull: $8,000.

Ultimately, you need to treat performance reviews as another case where your boss really wants to do something (give you a raise), but needs proof first.

Onwards

It is very easy for highly skilled technical people, with years of experience in a competitive market, to rest on their technical skills to prove their value. However, equally important is the ability to speak the language of the business, track work and costs, and stay out of trouble.

In this chapter, I presented, with a degree of levity, my project management techniques. However, they really can protect you from overwork and under-appreciation, and they can help further your career and build for you a better future.

At some point in your DBA career, you will face the same decision as many other technical roles: should I move into Management or stay Technical? Most organizations will try to support you with either choice. However, only if you have mastered project management will you have any chance of moving into a role where you are making things happen with your team rather than your fingers. Using the techniques discussed in this chapter, tracking the cost, risk, and politics of each task that you do, you will be able to explore either option.

Agile Database Development

Dev Nambi

More and more software development teams use "Agile" methods. Done well, Agile improves software quality and makes development and releases more predictable. Unfortunately, these are not the typical results for "early stage" Agile adopters. Instead, we see:

- an ill-considered rush towards lots of features, with inadequate testing to avoid bugs

- daily, automated deployments, without getting them right

- emergent (read, *chaotic*) system design, and stream-of-consciousness programing leading to "spaghetti code"

- exponentially increasing technical debt and developer frustration.

Teams stop trusting each other. *Human sacrifice! Dogs and cats, living together! Mass hysteria!* Teams adopting Agile take care to improve designs continually, as well as their testing and deployment practices. Agile leaves little room for error; it requires good judgment.

Agile *database* development is particularly hard because databases contain state and must ensure data integrity. They are harder to upgrade or roll back than the front end of a website and so are more amenable to up-front design than continual refinement. Lastly, database developers and DBAs tend to have less experience in Agile practices, leading to additional struggle in the early stages. This chapter will explore the history and principles of Agile development with an emphasis on how we can apply Agile practices successfully to databases.

Agile 101: A History

Agile-style development emerged as a reaction to the practices of what the Agile movement termed traditional Waterfall-style software development. The latter places an emphasis on up-front design, documentation, and completeness, to create a safety net that can produce mission-critical, complex software in a small number of releases.

The "design-first" (so-called "Waterfall") project methodologies originated in the automotive and aeronautics industries, where safety and quality were paramount. The Internet sped everything up and rewarded companies that could rapidly turn an idea into a working product. Development speed became more important than thoroughness and so the main benefit of up-front design vanished. Agile became popular.

Agile development allows teams to spread development and deployment risks over more releases. The shift from plan-driven to feedback-driven work can also reduce business risk, since the team builds fewer unneeded features, potentially reducing technical complexity. Continuous feedback also makes it easier to abandon bad ideas and bad code practices.

Agile development also makes compromises, and adds new risks. The main compromise is trading away time spent up front on design, for more frequent feature delivery. Agile teams spread design time over numerous iterations, but the lack of an initial "unifying" design means that development teams must work hard, adopting best practices and deploying good judgment, to avoid creating incomprehensible system architectures. Maintenance time often suffers too, in the push to iterate and progress continuously. Without careful management, this is what leads to the buildup of the technical debt, *i.e.* the cut corners, inelegant architecture, incomplete tests that, unchecked, gradually take a toll on system performance and developer productivity. This is particularly bad for databases because they often support multiple applications and, unless we take the time to design proper interfaces, database-refactoring can happen only when all coupled applications can change, meaning it happens at the pace of the slowest application team.

The number of deployments increases, requiring investment in streamlined deployment practices. Ultimately, of course, this is a good thing, but the amount and pace of change is a shock for some professionals, and keeping up requires good communications skills. Agile works best with smart, curious, and experienced engineers.

It's all fun and games.

Agile 201: Implications

The early stages of Agile adoption often take a heavy toll on software engineers. Their working lives becomes faster, less certain, and with more change.

There are three reactions: two common and one wise. The first is defensive: *I don't want to do this. It won't work.* The second is the Superhero reaction: *I can do this, I am invincible!* The third reaction is the sensible reaction: *I can do this, but only with help.*

ABC – Automate, Balance, and Communicate

The necessary help starts with the adopting the ABCs: automation, balance, and communication.

Automation

Repetitive tasks haunt the lives of most IT professionals: checking email, filling out reports, responding to bugs and tickets, and so on. However, we can automate or streamline many of these tasks. Most DBAs use SQL Server Agent jobs, scripting languages like PowerShell or Python, SSIS packages, and vendor applications to automate many aspects of their monitoring and maintenance, especially for tasks that happen late at night. Many developers use C#, scripting, and tools such as MSBuild, MSTest and source control command-line applications, to automate their build and test processes.

However, most DBAs *don't* automate documentation, deployments, SQL installs, patching, and so on. Developers don't make the leap from automated builds and testing to continuous integration or tool-aided refactoring work. Even if we can't automate a whole process, we could probably automate *most* of it.

Automating your repetitive tasks

For DBAs, my favorite automation project is to tie together monitoring scripts with the ticketing system. That gets rid of 20% of my day-to-day work right there, if I script it carefully enough. For development work, I like to have a single-command build-and-test script. This prevents me from checking in a broken build or failed unit test at least once per new feature.

Here is my recommendation to help you extend your automation. Start with the automation tools you already know, and get more creative. Then, every four months, pick one additional tool, something that's useful and easy to learn, and add it to your arsenal. Most importantly, spend a little time every week automating away your most common headaches.

A few common tasks take up a lot of time that you can save if you automate them, even partially:

- Automate your monitoring alerts to update your ticketing system (and vice versa).

- Automate your monitoring alerts to trigger your maintenance processes (and vice versa).

- Automate your email inbox to coordinate with your to-do list.

- Automate your build process with your test process and with a developer check-in. Every time a developer checks in a change, build the code and run a set of unit tests against it. This improves code quality almost immediately.

- Build a script that can deploy a single set of changes, either one database or several, to a single environment. Targeting development or test environments is usually safe. Make sure it has a rollback mode.

- Create T-SQL scripts that check for issues such as non-indexed foreign keys, GUIDs in primary keys, tables without interfaces, and permissions without roles. Turn them into database design-validation tests, and make sure they run every time you check in a change.

You will never run out of tasks to automate and streamline. I know three brilliant DBAs who work two hours a day. How? Early on, they spend a month of weekends automating most of their jobs. If something fails three times, the same way, they automate it. They never let on how much of their job they automate. This gives them the time to work with developers, Project Managers and testers to make the databases more stable overall. The key is to make this "automation work" a part of your daily routine.

Balance

Switching to Agile development creates a lot of change, perhaps the most dramatic one being the shift from development work that is planned and deliberate, to intuitive and rapid. This can be perilous. The worst results are:

- **Rampant technical debt** – code bugs and design flaws pile up rapidly and go uncorrected because they compete with user features for developer time.

- **Deployment time and code quality for each release don't improve** despite a dramatic increase in the number of production releases. Every release causes a lot of pain.

- **Business managers**, delighted by the sudden potential for lots more user features, come to expect a feature delivery rate that is often unsustainable.

- **Teams swap current processes and practices for new ones, with reckless abandon**, and without considering their relative merits. Consequently, they encounter problems they previously avoided.

Blessed with logical engineering leaders, we can institute some important **balance** measures. For example, it's a wise practice to set aside 10–20% of development time to pay the "maintenance tax," in other words, reduce technical debt and fix operational bugs.

In addition, allow a fixed, reasonable amount of deployment time per week. Developers can deploy more frequently, in the longer term, if they are allowed time to streamline and clean up each individual deployment.

The key goal is to aim for a steady, sustainable pace. As soon as a Project Manager for an Agile team detects the build-up of technical debt, a large backlog of deployments, or a long list of security patches starting to pile up, then it is time to pay some maintenance tax, and push for a better balance. Ironically, creating a successful Agile team is a marathon, not a sprint.

One great idea that encourages balance is to reward good behavior, and introduce a mild penalty for bad behavior. I worked in a team where developers who broke the build had to bring in donuts for everyone. Conversely, the IT staff rewarded with beer any developers who made the build or deployment process significantly easier. It worked beautifully.

Communicate, constantly

One big change with a switch to Agile is a dramatic decrease in documentation. This can be a benefit; thorough documentation is always out of date and rarely used. Without documentation, *the code, including the tests, is the documentation*. This, coupled with the rapid rate of change of the system design means that **people**, rather than documents, become the primary source of domain knowledge. In order for all of the team to keep up with this pace, and still understand the system and where it is heading, they must communicate *all...of...the...time*.

There are many different ways to communicate. Unless you are telepathic, the fastest way is speaking in person. Face-to-face communication is **high bandwidth**. The second most effective way to communicate is via phone. Spoken language is very efficient; we can convey about 150–200 words per minute, which is 2–4 times faster than we can type. Also, speaking lends itself to back-and-forth communication, which helps people ask questions at just the right time. I'd estimate speaking in person or over the phone is easily 5–10 times more efficient than instant messaging or email, meaning that we should be able to communicate in 10 minutes what would take close to 2 hours of email time.

One of the most common and effective spoken-word communication techniques is the daily scrum or stand-up. Having DBAs and developers at the same daily stand-up works wonders; developers learn about how the system is working, and DBAs learn about imminent code changes.

With this change comes opportunity. For DBAs, constant communication makes it easy to keep developers in the loop about production issues. It also makes it easy to ask for fixes to the most annoying issues of the day, and to get these fixes *quickly*. DBAs also get the opportunity to provide input into design choices that might affect database performance. I have worked in teams where DBAs contributed to all code reviews; the result was *very* stable code.

For developers, constant communication provides feedback about how well our code is doing, both good and bad, and allows us to fix production inefficiencies and bugs. This gradually helps us hone our craft; we learn very quickly what ideas and approaches work, and which ones don't. That means faster, cleaner, *better* code over time.

DDT – Design, Deployments and Tests

Now it's time to use DDT: **Design**, **Deployments**, and **Tests**. Why? *DDT kills bugs*. Most of a database is...code. Databases enable features, and have interfaces. The way we design databases has performance implications. We can deploy patterns in their design, we can refactor them; databases are code. We should treat them in the same way, and apply the same standards of quality to their design, deployment and testing.

Design

Good design saves lives, usually your own. I use the SIIP approach to database design: **Simplicity**, **Integrity**, **Interfaces**, and **Patterns**.

Simplicity

Keep your design as simple as possible. There's a famous acronym for this: KISS (Keep It Simple, Stupid). Features being equal, a simpler design is easier to fix and extend than a complex design. You need to be twice as smart to troubleshoot a system as you do to build one. If you build the most complex system you can, you will not be able to fix it.

The most important objects in a database are its tables. They store the data and enable data integrity. The best way to ensure accurate data is to use a clean and simple data model. For an OLTP database, that means as much normalization as you can handle. Designing to anything lower than third normal form (3NF) usually causes painful headaches. Key-value tables are notoriously painful because they force the application to handle data integrity.

Some database objects are pure code. Stored procedures, views, functions, triggers, and metadata are pure code. They are similar to code objects in other programming languages. They should have the same standards of quality (unit tests, security considerations, versioning, and so on.

Integrity

Data integrity matters in a database. Unlike C# or Java apps, databases *store* data, so data integrity is not optional.

The data integrity features of your database design are of prime importance. Start with data types, primary keys, foreign keys, and check constraints. Beyond that, there are data integrity implications in our choice of nullability, defaults, and the use of triggers. Triggers in particular are a double-edged sword; their hidden nature and support of complexity can lead to unexpected problems.

Interfaces

An interface is the (hopefully) simple contract between your system's guts and any application that calls it. Interfaces enable decoupling: the ability to separate what an application expects from its implementation. I have found that we need interfaces whenever:

- a database is used by multiple applications

- the database and application code change at different speeds.

Inside a database, interfaces are stored procedures, functions, and views. Other types of interfaces are Object Relational Mapping (ORM) and client-side tools. The most important, and most obvious, use of interfaces is to decouple a table's physical schema from the application using it. That way you can change the two independently. Having well-defined interfaces will save you a lot of pain.

Patterns

Use patterns. Similar functionality should look the same. Database developers often use patterns to ensure a set of consistent naming conventions and data type standards. The goal is consistency: stored procedures, tables, column names, security practices, should be similar. Two stored procedures that do almost the same thing, for example, writing one record to a table, should look similar. For example, they should all use the same conventions and standards for parameter names, logging, join patterns, documentation, and so on.

Patterns are effective when they are widely used. Agile is a team sport, so the best way to adopt a set of patterns is through democratic practices like discussion and voting. The same goes for eliminating patterns that the team don't find useful.

Make sure you can enforce patterns automatically. Writing them down in a Word document does nothing at all.

I think I can, I think I can...

These ideas are not new, but they are particularly important in a fast development environment. If your code is changing constantly, your systems and processes will degrade naturally over time, unless you take specific steps to keep them clean and healthy as you progress; it's like entropy.

In an Agile environment, there is rarely the time for drawn-out discussions, so practitioners need to get into the habit of making the right design decision quickly, even intuitively. The best way to acquire this skill is through experience. I find that DBAs and developers with 6–12 months of experience, including *production support*, have the hard-won skill necessary to design intuitively. Weak or counter-intuitive designs lead to anarchy.

Automated validation tests can help guard against some aspects of poor database design. We can create validation tests that fail when a database fails a design check. Start out with the basics, and add additional design checks to clean up your system, over time. For example, we can create validation checks based on querying the system views to look for tables without primary keys, foreign keys without indexes, tables without abstraction views, or objects without permissions, and so on. If someone checks in code that fails one of these tests, they get an email automatically, warning them of their peril. Some tests are widely used already, such as those contained in the highly regarded sp_Blitz tool at (HTTP://WWW.BRENTOZAR.COM/BLITZ/).

If anyone can modify the database design without checks or limitations, then a good database design can turn into an ugly mess within weeks, and you will deeply upset your DBA in the process. Control carefully who has permissions to make database modifications. Ideally, all database changes will take place in Source Control, where they can be tested thoroughly and deployed through the approved process. If necessary, audit direct database modifications using a trigger (see, for example, the *Avoiding Version Drift* section of Alexander Karmanov's article at HTTP://TINYURL.COM/MA7U6A3).

Deployments

Having a set of deployment best practices and tools can make it easy to test and release code, especially if you have multiple environments (development, test, production, and so on).

The following simple equation can help the team estimate what time they need to allocate to manual database deployments:

Total Available DBA Time for Deployments =
*[Manual Time per Deployment] * [Average Risk per Deployment] * [Number of Deployments]*

To increase the number of deployments, the team needs to automate and streamline the deployment process to reduce time and risk, or they need more DBAs! The only alternative, fewer manual deployments, is what happens in many "Waterfall" teams.

Database deployments are different from other application deployments in one critical way: databases contain data. It is relatively easy to upgrade a website because the ASP.NET or PHP pages don't have data in them, so we simply overwrite the entire site. With a database that is impossible, because dropping and re-creating a database drops all of the information, negating its raison d'être.

There are three tenets to database deployments: keep them **robust**, **fast**, and **specific**.

Robust

The first tenet of database deployments: make them **robust**. You should be able to rerun a set of scripts, regardless of whether someone ran them previously, and achieve the same result. As a simple example, instead of having a script that runs:

```
CREATE TABLE dbo.foo…
```

Our scripts should first check for the object's existence.

```
IF OBJECT_ID('dbo.foo') IS NULL
BEGIN
   CREATE TABLE dbo.foo…
   INSERT INTO DeploymentLog (Description) SELECT ('Created table foo')
END
```

Alternatively, we could code this such that, if the table does exist, the script fails immediately.

You should also record the actions of all previous deployments in a deployment log, ideally populated via DDL triggers. Having rerunnable and logged scripts is very useful. If your deployment fails at Step 4, you can restart it from Steps 1, 2, or 3 without worry.

Another pillar of robust deployments: *always* have a rollback mechanism to undo the changes made to your database during a deployment, and return the database schema and objects to their predeployment state.

To roll back a stored procedure change, redeploy the previous version. To roll back a new table, drop it. Instead of dropping a table during an upgrade, rename it out so that, if necessary, the rollback can rename it and put it back into place.

Fast

The second tenet of database deployments: make them **fast**. Agile teams deploy anywhere between once a week, to ten times a day, a pace unthinkable in a Waterfall environment. When dealing with a higher frequency of database deployments, it's important to make sure they don't disrupt users continuously with long (or, ideally, any) service outages.

Code objects

For objects that contain no data, the key goal is to avoid user disruptions during deployment. A common way to change a stored procedure is to drop it, if it exists, then recreate it, as follows:

```
DROP PROCEDURE DoSomething
GO
   CREATE PROCEDURE DoSomething AS …<New Code>
GO
```

The problem here is that if a user session calls the procedure in the period between dropping and creating it, then the user's operation will fail with an "object-not-found" error. This technique also removes any permissions associated with the stored procedure, so we need to reassign them to allow users to access it, once it's re-created.

A better approach is one where we don't drop the object. If the object doesn't exist we **CREATE** it, if it does we **ALTER** it. This technique also keeps the object permissions in place and we can use it for views, functions, triggers, *i.e.* any object that is procedural, or does not contain data.

```
IF OBJECT_ID('dbo.DoSomething') IS NULL
   EXEC ('CREATE PROCEDURE AS BEGIN SELECT ''foo'' END');
GO
ALTER PROCEDURE DoSomething AS ...<Code>
```

The dynamic SQL approach can get messy for anything beyond a very simple stored procedure; the previously referenced article by Alexander Karmanov describes an elegant alternative approach using **SET NOEXEC ON/OFF**:

```
IF OBJECT_ID('dbo.DoSomething') IS NOT NULL
    SET NOEXEC ON
GO
-- skipped, if object already exists
CREATE PROCEDURE DoSomething
AS
    PRINT 'DoSomething: Not implemented yet.'
GO
-- always executed
SET NOEXEC OFF
GO
ALTER PROCEDURE DoSomething AS ...<Code>
```

Indexes

For indexes, the choice is different. It is impossible to change an index definition using `ALTER INDEX`. Instead, we must drop and re-create it. Another option for non-clustered indexes is to create a duplicate index, drop the old one, and rename the new index with the old index's name.

Dropping an index is a quick operation, but creating or altering (rebuilding) an index often requires significant processing time. If your SQL Server edition doesn't support online index operations, or if the specific operation must be offline (such as those on clustered indexes that contain LOB data types), then applications and users will be unable to access the table during the *entire* index operation. That's often unacceptable.

With online index creation, the indexes and underlying tables remain accessible but you can still expect to see an impact on performance during the operation, and users may experience blocking or deadlocking.

I'd recommend creating and modifying indexes when your application is idle. Commonly, teams perform these operations in the middle of the night. The exception is if a table isn't yet in use by applications, in which case there is minimal user impact.

Tables

The most difficult object to deploy is a table. This is especially true if applications query the table directly, without interfaces. In that situation, the table schema is tightly coupled to the applications themselves, and cannot be changed without coordinating the change among application teams. I would recommend implementing an interface first, to decouple the database design from the application design.

There are only a few ways to change a table: we can add or remove a column, or change its definition (modifying a data type, adding a constraint, and so on). Commonly, we might want to change a column name or data type. The former is a metadata-only operation and should have no performance impact on concurrent user operations. Changing a data type, however, can result in SQL Server checking every row, to make sure existing data does not violate the new data type.

Generally, making a column bigger is a metadata-only, quick change. Making a column smaller requires SQL Server to check the entire table for invalid data, resulting in a table scan, which can take considerable time on large tables.

A quick check to see if a change is metadata-only

Turn on STATISTICS IO *before running the* ALTER. *If you see no output, it's a metadata-only change.*

Another common task is to remove an unneeded column. The simplest way to do this is to drop the column (assuming no foreign keys reference that column), but this does not allow for a rollback mechanism.

The key decision is whether to save off the data in the column we wish to drop. To roll back a column drop, first you need to save off all of the data.

```
INSERT    INTO Save_Table
          ( PK ,
            ColumnToDrop
          )
          SELECT  PK ,
                  ColumnToDrop
          FROM    TableToChange
```

Then if we need to undo the change, we simply re-create the column with NULL values and then reload the column with the saved values.

The last common requirement is to add a column to a table and load it with data. If the table is small, we can add it in any way we like, since any blocking from populating the column is likely to be short-lived. For a large table, the way to add a column with minimal user impact is to add it as a NULLable column. If you need to add values into the new column, for existing rows, do so in batches and then set the column to be NOT NULL, if that's required. This minimizes blocking, although it does require several steps.

Similar to indexes, it is best to change tables when your application is idle. However, by following practices such as these you can minimize downtime and disruption. For further reading on how to refactor tables without downtime, I recommend Alex Kuznetsov's article at HTTP://TINYURL.COM/KL8A3DD.

Specific

The third tenet of deployments: keep them **specific**. You should deploy all of the code you have changed, and only the code you have changed. Deployment verification queries are a great help here. For example, if you're deploying a new view, a verification query might look like this:

```
SELECT  CASE WHEN OBJECT_ID('dbo.fooView') IS NOT NULL
             THEN 'View dbo.fooView created'
             ELSE 'View dbo.fooView missing'
        END
```

It should be easy for anyone to identify exactly what is, and what isn't, part of a deployment.

Keep releases *decoupled*, so that you can deploy them independently of other deployments, such as application deployments. For example, deploy a CREATE TABLE script before your application needs to use it. Just in case, make sure your application fails gracefully if the table isn't there. That way, we can deploy either application or database on their own, without any dependencies. That is also an example of forward compatibility.

We should also attach a version number to each database. For example, if we know that a test database is running version 4.1.120, and the production database is running version 4.1.118, we can find the codebase definitions for each version. In addition, we can identify quickly which changes we need to deploy in order to advance the production database to the current version.

Having a good folder-diff tool is a huge benefit. Database code is text, after all. Comparing text files is simple, with the right tool. This is an area in which we can benefit from application developers' solutions, who have had decades to solve the same challenges. Of course, keeping your database code in a source control system is even better, giving access to features such as change history, comments, branching and merging, code review tools and so on.

Tests

Database testing is the third component of DDT. Having a solid set of tests and testing tools increases code quality. Tests ensure that our code works, and that we aren't breaking existing functionality. They give us confidence, and reduce risk.

Focus the majority of your testing efforts on the most critical system components. For databases, I've found that the following factors predict quite accurately how critical a particular piece of database code is:

- it has lots of business logic

- it impacts one of the 20 biggest tables in a database

- it impacts one of the 20 most-commonly-queried tables in a database

- it impacts tables/databases that are used by several different applications

- it changes permissions, or requires odd permissions

- it deletes data from a database via DDL (for example, dropping a column or a table)

- it uses an uncommon piece of the database engine (`xp_cmdshell`, linked servers, service broker, SQL CLR, log shipping).

If we have 100 tests but we only run 20 of them, those 20 are the valuable ones. Tests that aren't run effectively don't exist. Getting developers and testers to use the same set of tests and testing tools is the most important step. Do that, and then incrementally add to your tests.

Test-driven development (TDD) is a very common Agile technique that helps you to make sure you write the tests you need by writing them *before* you write or change code. You know your code works when all of the tests pass. Writing tests first forces you to think about different ways your code can fail.

There are three important categories of tests: **unit**, **integration**, and **performance**.

Unit tests

Put simply, unit tests test a single piece of code in isolation, and make sure it works. For example, having a unit test for a stored procedure makes a lot of sense, especially if the stored procedure has complicated logic. In our team, we have a build-and-test machine that automatically runs unit tests whenever a developer checks in code. It checks our source control system for code changes, rebuilds the entire database chema from the code base and runs a folder full of unit tests against the new database. We catch any test failures instantly, and can notify the developer(s) responsible. This is a *continuous build* system.

Integration tests

While unit tests will check just a particular database object, integration tests will make sure that a change doesn't "break" some dependent database object. In other words, integration tests check code changes to make sure they don't break *other* parts of a system. For example, if we make a change to the database, we should run integration tests to ensure we didn't break any applications or services that use the database. I have found them to be particularly important when working on a database without enough interfaces, or when changing an interface.

The key point with integration tests is to have a good set of cross-application tests running, to make sure that you're simulating system behavior. The emphasis of the test is on integration points; each test creates/modifies data in every application in the system architecture. For an OLTP system, that can mean calling the UI, the business middle-tier, and the database tier.

In our team, we have integration tests for each business feature and we usually try to run them every 1–3 days. When an integration test fails, we email developers on all teams who have made check-ins since the last successful test. Of course, the ideal might be to run them every time we make any change, with every team member getting immediate feedback, before checking in the change.

Performance tests

Performance tests verify that the system meets the identified performance criteria, in terms of query response times under various workloads, and so on. To put it another way, you run a piece of code to see if it is fast enough, and if it scales well under load.

In my experience, development teams don't run database performance tests as often as they should, mainly because running them can require a near-copy of production hardware and they don't have the IT resources or budget to do that.

I have found that the best systems to run performance tests on are restored copies of production databases. It's extremely rare to see test databases with enough data volume and variety comparable to a production environment. A simple PowerShell script can run a set of scripts against a test database and capture the runtime of each query. The best queries to run are copies of the most common ones on the system and the most critical intermittent query, like a monthly billing query.

Our team usually tries to run performance tests at least once per release, especially for changes to large or critical systems. When doing performance testing, define *fast enough* and *scales enough* before you test. Be realistic about your goals.

Conclusion

Agile works very well if you do the right things. It also breaks down quickly if you do the wrong things too often. The key is to know when something is working, and to improve on it. Good judgment, smart people, lots of communication, and a level head are what you really need. With that, you can make Agile work for you, in your own way.

Keep learning, and keep improving. Good luck!

Nine Habits to Secure a Stellar Performance Review

Wil Sisney

I know something about you. I know that you are a motivated database professional, and I know that you're one of the best. How do I know that? Mediocre IT workers don't pick up technical books like this one. They have no interest in attending technical conferences or studying on their own time.

No, you are one of the chosen few, the true engines of any company. You are good at what you do, and more importantly, you want to *get better* at what you do. I don't tell these secrets to just anyone, but thanks to your dedication, I'm going to share with you the nine habits that together form the recipe which will get you the recognition you deserve and secure you a stellar performance review.

I have refined these habits over many years, working with supervisors from both technical and non-technical backgrounds. In fact, when I set out to crystalize this knowledge into a chapter in the book you're holding, I surveyed some of my past supervisors to discover what makes a fantastic employee stand out. I'll also cover how to use your performance review to obtain the best reward for all of your hard work, and how to continue your momentum until next year's equally stellar review.

Habit 1: Work Your Tail Off

Wait, you didn't think this was going to be easy, did you? If you want an amazing performance review, you're going to need to earn it every time you sit down at your desk. Just to be perfectly clear, this chapter isn't about how you can get a fantastic review after turning in mediocre results. This chapter hopes to teach hard-working database professionals how to stand out among the crowd and get the review and the rewards they deserve.

Work doesn't need to overshadow every other aspect of your life, and you don't need to work 80-hour weeks to stay on top. In fact, striking a good work and life balance is a central component of working hard.

The trick is to minimize distractions by developing a diligent work commitment. One method I use to reinforce my commitment is to remind myself at the beginning of every work day exactly why I am there. When I sit down at my desk every morning, I remind myself that by working diligently and avoiding time-wasting activities, I'll be able to accomplish my tasks faster so I can return to my family and life.

The foundation of hard work is a good methodology; choose a system that will help you manage work more efficiently. One excellent system is the **Pomodoro Technique** (HTTP://WWW.POMODOROTECHNIQUE.COM/), based on the idea that you should work in short sprints of 25 minutes at a time, taking 5-minute breaks between each sprint. The technique provides artifacts to help you organize your work, most notably the Activity Inventory Sheet.

Another system I've used in the past is the **Time Management Matrix**. This system divides tasks into one of four quadrants based on the combination of two factors: importance and immediacy. Immediate tasks demand our time even if they aren't important. The most productive work is done in Quadrant 2, where tasks are important but not immediate. Tasks in the fourth quadrant are neither important nor immediate, and so usually represent time-wasters. It's important to eliminate or at least minimize Quadrant 4 tasks in order to focus on the most important jobs.

A third system, which seems to fit the work of database administrators well, is the **Getting Things Done** system (abbreviated to GTD), developed by David Allen and described in his book of the same name. This system focuses on tracking tasks externally (like in an application or a notebook) so that the mind is free from remembering tasks that need to be completed. A "next action" for each task is tracked as well, which means that the next time you visit that task you'll have a plan to work to before you even begin. GTD also encourages a daily and weekly session where tasks are reviewed, statuses are updated, and next actions for new tasks can be assigned. GTD is a solid system, easy to implement, with many resources to help track work, such as smartphone and web applications.

Other useful work management systems

If you work in a development team, you're doubtless familiar with Agile development methodologies such as Scrum, which build in a plan for your daily deliverables and help you stay on track (there are some similarities with GTD). For DBAs, I'd also recommend the Six Sigma process called DMAIC, which Thomas LaRock showed how to apply to database troubleshooting.

In my experience, it doesn't matter which system you use so long as it *works for you* and *you stick to it*. Finding a system that fits your work style will help you manage and prioritize your tasks. Manage your time well and you'll quickly attain rock star status in the eyes of your boss.

Habit 2: Establish the Parameters for Your Success

Despite the results you deliver, it is your boss's perception of those results that will determine your performance review, and thus your rewards. Early in the year, the most important thing you can do is determine what your boss expects of you. The sooner you determine the measures of your success, the sooner you can plot your path.

Your company may establish performance objectives for employees in your position, but these aren't the parameters for your success. Consider these to be only a basic framework for what you need to deliver. More important is what your boss thinks will make you successful, since your boss will be making a decision during your review.

So how do you determine what your boss will base your performance rating on? Ask! This might seem self-explanatory, but have you ever asked your boss what it takes for you to succeed? Simply set up a meeting and ask her how she will judge your success when the year is over. Bear in mind that your boss may be inclined to point you towards the one-size-fits-all performance objectives; if that happens, simply explain that you understand those objectives to be the baseline for your performance, and ask her to expand on what she expects from an *exceptional* employee. Take notes, ask pointed questions, and discuss plans for how you can meet expectations. Once the meeting is complete, compile a summary of your plan for success and send it to your boss. This will give her a chance to refine her expectations. Once that refinement process is complete, you've got a good-faith contract which, if you meet the terms, will deliver the results you expect.

Once these expectations are established, your next job is to create a plan to meet these expectations. Write your plan as you would write effective goals; make sure the plan is *specific* and *measurable*. Establishing your boss's expectations and creating a plan to meet them will position you for success better than most of your peers.

Habit 3: Work with Vision

Your performance objectives work to establish your deliverables, but if you want a stellar performance review you're going to need to go beyond that. How do you figure out what constitutes "above and beyond the call of duty?" Simple: you work with vision.

The vision you are cultivating here is an understanding of how your actions impact the company overall. Start by understanding your place in your organization. Most of us already know this based on our job roles. A database administrator knows that their job is to be the guardian of data. Developers know that they have to deliver efficient and bug-free code. What many people lack is an understanding of how their role contributes to the company's overall success.

Learn what makes your team successful. Once you understand the measures of your team's success, figure out how that success contributes to the company's success. This exercise builds an overall picture of how your daily actions add real value to the company.

The secret to working with vision is to **volunteer to lead when you know the way**. You've sat through that meeting where a problem has been presented and the solution needs to be determined. People may be hesitant to suggest ideas, even though there are several potential solutions. This is your time to shine. If you're able to think up a solution, throw it out there.

Vision is a skill managers always want but rarely see in their employees. Working with vision and putting yourself out there is a key way to stand out, and it provides great material for your highlight reel (that is to say, your performance review).

Habit 4: Train to Gain an Edge

In 2008, IBM conducted a study to determine the return on investment from employee training. The results showed that employees who received 5 hours of training or less delivered only 65% revenue per employee, compared to those employees who received more than 5 hours of training.[1] IBM's study focused on many industries, and I would argue that 5 hours of training is not nearly enough for an IT employee to keep up with changing technology, much less advance their own knowledge.

Should your company pay for training? Absolutely; the fatal flaw of most IT organizations is that they don't budget properly for training. Use every resource your company offers, and don't be afraid to ask for more. Unfortunately, my experience is that you'll have to fight and claw your way to company-paid training. Fortunately, there is a wealth of free and paid resources available for training on SQL Server. I group training into five categories:

1. Blogs.

2. Webcasts.

3. User Group meetings (including webcasts for virtual chapters).

4. Books and white papers.

5. Events (such as the Professional Association for SQL Server's yearly PASS Summit, or a local SQL Saturday event).

You can read more about each of these types of trainings, including recommendations on which are worth your time, at HTTP://WWW.WILSISNEY.COM/FINDTRAINING.

---

1   *The ROI of Employee Training and Development: Why a Hearty Investment in Employee Training and Development Is So Important* – Rachele Williams and Lawson Arnett, APQC. See HTTP://TINYURL.COM/NTYB5KV (requires membership for access).

If finding high-quality training material to study is not the problem, finding time to study it can be more of a challenge. I have a confession to make. When I became a database administrator, I had no idea what I was doing. Thanks to my well-intentioned but non-technical boss at the time, my job title was suddenly Senior Database Administrator and it propelled me into a job for which I had no formal training, and with no one to teach me. I felt like the emperor with "invisible clothes" from the children's fable; sooner or later, someone would spot my ignorance. I hated that feeling, and so I decided to change the situation.

I began studying for *at least* an hour a day, *every* day. When I started the job, I had no clue what I was doing, so I had to study on my own time. At first, it was challenging to find a free hour every day, but after just a few weeks of making this habit a priority, I had no trouble finding time. I'd love to say that after a few weeks I knew everything there was to know about database administration, but we'd both know that was a lie. However, it wasn't long before I was able to hold up my end of a conversation about databases.

I've kept up that pace of *at least* 1 hour of study every day for the last 6 years. Not everyone can study an hour a day, but it's important to make a commitment to your training and establish a regular schedule.

Now when it comes to your performance review, it is critical to **track your training**. There are four things you need to log:

1. The date/time of training.

2. The source and topic of training.

3. The length of training.

4. Brief notes about what you learned.

You can track these four items in many ways; I use a Google Docs spreadsheet so my study log is accessible from any Internet-connected device.

You're going to use this information in two ways. First, you're going to review your notes the day following your training session. According to the *Cornell Note Taking System*, during a learning scenario, such as a lecture, most people will forget 80% of what they've learned unless they take notes *and* review those notes within 24 hours.[2] Spend just a few minutes of each study session reviewing the last session's notes and you'll find that your retention of what you've learned will dramatically improve.

The other way you're going to use your study tracking comes when it is time to write your performance review. We'll discuss that in more detail later. Rest assured that your study commitment will make you more valuable and knowledgeable than most of your peers.

Habit 5: Stand on the Shoulders of Giants

"If I have seen further it is by standing on the shoulders of giants."
– *Sir Isaac Newton, in a letter to Robert Hooke in February 1676*

I've noticed something about the SQL Server community: it is populated with geniuses. Some of the most intelligent and, more importantly, most dedicated people I've met work as database professionals. Strike up a conversation at a technical conference or a user group meeting and chances are that you'll find a lively intellectual with something interesting to say. These are brilliant people and they are doing brilliant work, some of which they've decided to share.

We're going to use and adapt the solutions created by others. Now, I know what some of you are thinking: don't the best database professionals write all of their own solutions from scratch? I used to think that, too. As I monitored resources like Twitter, however, I found just the opposite to be true. The best and brightest among our community were raving about solutions that others had created. They use these solutions. They've learned that by using an off-the-shelf solution they can spend more time working on the projects they are passionate about.

---

2   Source: HTTP://WWW.WWU.EDU/TUTORING/CORNELL%20SYSTEM.SHTML.

There are some rules about using solutions developed by others, rules I have learned through trial and error. First, research the solution to see what kinds of results it has provided for others, and how it addresses your specific need. Go into full research mode. Read blog comments to get a feel for what other people have experienced with this solution and see what alternatives are out there.

The second rule is that you need to read scripts in enough detail that you understand how they work. Make sure you read all code comments. Scan the code for anything that looks suspicious, such as adding new logins with fixed passwords, or dangerous techniques like creating procedures that build and execute dynamic SQL statements. Make informed decisions before releasing potentially dangerous code into your environments. The world of SQL Server is not risk free, so it is up to you to decide what risks are acceptable.

The third rule is that you test the code in your *least important environment* first, and migrate it through environments in order of increasing importance. I'll give you a simple example from my personal experience. I recently went hunting for a trigger-based solution to log user logins on a development server. I found a simple and elegant solution developed by Nicholas Cain, a friend and a recipient of the MCM certification. He's one of those guys you can't help liking, and he's absolutely brilliant. His code used a server-level trigger to track logins, and it provided a daily summary of the data in a rollup table.

His code is flawless; however, I decided to change the name of a security principal for my implementation, but I missed an occurrence of that security principal later in the script. That mistake is forgivable, and is something that would have come out in testing. My mistake, however, was running the script on a busy development server first. Development is less important than production, right? Of course, but I live by the motto that the *development environment is production for my developers.* My slight mistake in code was drastically magnified when suddenly everyone was locked out from the entire server because of my flawed logon trigger. I realized my mistake instantly, but it took me a few minutes to figure out how to fix the problem.

> ### *Dealing with flawed logon triggers*
>
> *To get around a logon trigger that locks everyone out of the server, use the DAC to log in and disable and delete the trigger.*

Once I fixed my mistake, it worked so well that I now use the solution on many of my production servers. The moral of this story is that you need to test solutions in the least impactful environment first. For many of us, that's our local machine's SQL Server Developer Edition instance.

Don't let my cautionary tale dissuade you from using solutions developed by other people. You'll be glad you found something that worked so well for such little effort, and your boss will appreciate that you're using proven solutions that permit you to focus on more important tasks.

Here's a shortlist of my six favorite community solutions on SQL Server, just to help you get started:

- **Ola Hallengren's Backup, Integrity Check and Index Maintenance solution**

  - **What it does:** Makes you look like a genius. Ola has developed some exceptional scripts that do everything SQL Server Maintenance Plans do, but so much better. His backup scripts integrate with third-party backup tools and allow for simple database selection. The index scripts are absolutely amazing. The scripts only do work on objects that require it, and it includes robust logging and excellent statistics maintenance. Suddenly your index management on your data warehouse goes from hours to minutes.

  - **Where to get it:** HTTP://OLA.HALLENGREN.COM/.

- **sp_WhoIsActive from Adam Machanic**

  - **What it does:** Puts important details about currently executing SQL statements at your fingertips. There's so much goodness packed into sp_WhoIsActive that I could have devoted this whole chapter to describing the benefits of this gem.

Consider `sp_WhoIsActive` as the replacement for `sp_who2` or Activity Monitor. When you need to troubleshoot a problem occurring on your SQL Server, `sp_WhoIsActive` is nearly a one-stop shop. Adam has put literally years of work into `sp_WhoIsActive` and has excellent documentation covering the procedure's capabilities.

- **Where to get it:** HTTP://SQLBLOG.COM/BLOGS/ADAM_MACHANIC/.

- **SSMS Tools Pack from Mladen Prajdić**

  - **What it does:** SSMS Tools Pack is an add-in for SQL Server Management Studio that transforms it into a much more robust application. SSMS Tools Pack contains several amazing tools, such as a detailed execution plan analyzer, a handy SQL statement formatter, and a SQL Snippets tool that allows you to store predefined blocks of SQL statements that you type often, which you can then trigger by typing a small shortcut. One of my favorite features comes in the Query Execution History feature, which stores history on each query you run. Since developing on SQL Server is often an iterative process where you build and refine a query one component at a time, this history window is a dream come true. I'm always surprised when I find a new feature in SSMS Tools Pack, and I think you'll find it to be one of the most valuable arrows in your SQL Server quiver.

  - **Where to get it:** HTTP://WWW.SSMSTOOLSPACK.COM/.

- **Sean Elliot's Full Server DDL Auditing Solution**

  - **What it does:** Logs Data Definition Language (DDL) changes across an entire server. Tracking changes to the structure of your databases can be challenging, especially on busy development servers. Sean's solution provides a robust trigger-based logging solution that basically maintains itself. Whenever an object is created, dropped or altered, this solution logs it. Even better, it logs changes in two places – at the database level and at the server level. This feature allows you to reconstruct changes when databases are dropped and restored, and allows you to secure logs in a central location. Sean's solution allows you to know who changed what, and when. I've had situations where two developers have both changed the same stored procedure right after each other and without this auditing solution they'd have had hours of rework

445

to reconstruct what was lost. The brilliant thing about this solution is that it is self-maintaining. When a database is created or restored, the solution automatically creates the objects in that database to enable the logging solution. It is almost a set-and-forget solution. This DDL Auditing Solution isn't source control for databases, but it is darn near close.

- **Where to get it**: HTTP://WWW.SQLSERVERCENTRAL.COM/ARTICLES/DDL/70657/ (Note: this website requires a free registration.)

- **Konesans Custom SSIS Tasks**

  - **What it is:** Custom components for SSIS. Many seasoned SQL Server Integration Services developers don't know that SSIS functionality can be extended using custom data flow tasks. Konesans provides a set of free custom SSIS tasks that can solve common SSIS development challenges. For example, application developers who work with SSIS often wonder how they can use regular expressions – what they call "RegEx" – to validate expressions. SSIS doesn't natively include that functionality; however Konesans has not one, but two components that solve this problem (one is a data cleansing transformation, and the other uses regular expressions like a conditional split transformation). There's a transformation that watches for files to appear in a directory, and there's another that generates row numbers. These tasks can be accomplished using a Script Task component, but that requires that the developer know C# or Visual Basic. These tasks save time and effort, and they work on any server running SSIS (even if the component isn't installed on that server). Test them out and you'll likely find them just as useful as I do.

  - **Where to get it:** HTTP://WWW.KONESANS.COM/PRODUCTS.ASPX.

  - **Pro tip:** If you like these custom components, check out the CodePlex Community Tasks and Components page for additional custom tools. The CodePlex page is located at HTTP://SSISCTC.CODEPLEX.COM/.

- **Management Data Warehouse**

  - **What it does:** The Management Data Warehouse (MDW) collects SQL Server performance information and provides a series of impressive reports to analyze results. I'll admit that the MDW is challenging to install, but once you get past that hurdle you've got a very impressive suite of reports to drill into any performance challenge. The reports start with an overview report, and by clicking on any element within that overview you can drill into very detailed information – all the way down to the execution plan level. The MDW reports are pretty enough that you can show them to management, and they work so well that you can drill into a problem with your boss standing over your shoulder.

  - **Where to get it:** Start with Bill Ramos's article series, where he explains everything you need to know about the MDW and how to install it: HTTP://TINYURL.COM/2EDLDMF.

These solutions are just the tip of the community-contributed iceberg. As a word of advice, don't let your boss or team believe that you developed any of these solutions. Give credit where credit is due, and you'll find that your boss appreciates that you're using proven solutions and saving time.

Habit 6: Control the Headlines

You've heard that old saying that when the database is running well, no one notices. If you're a database professional and doing a good job, it can seem like a thankless task. It doesn't have to be that way, so long as you control the headlines.

This skill is all about getting the highlights of how the databases are running to your boss in a way that isn't annoying. If your boss is like most managers, he will read about twice as many emails per day as his employees. In order to control the headlines, you need to make the information you supply succinct, summarized, and pertinent.

The way we control the headlines depends on our job role. For database and business intelligence developers, our ability to control the headlines starts with project status meetings. If your team doesn't have regular status meetings, take time to write up a weekly status report. The less complex your status report is, the more your boss will appreciate it. Just summarize where your time has been spent, what you'll be doing next, and any barriers that are standing in your way.

Database administrators control the headlines with database status reports. Keep your reports brief – perhaps 1–2 pages. Here are some thoughts on things that you might want to include in your status reports:

- **Total instances and total databases being managed:** The larger your shop, the more often this number changes. Tracking this week over week is a good way for your boss to judge the team's capacity.

- **Successful backups:** This figure is the percentage of database backups that were successful on first attempt. If there is a common theme between the database backups that failed, be sure to note that in the Emerging Problems section (explained below).

- **Number and percentage of successful recovery tests:** Backups aren't successful until it's proven that you can recover from them. Since few of us have the resources to restore all of our backups, many DBA teams pick a percentage of backups to perform recovery tests on.

- **Unplanned outages:** Were there any unexpected periods of downtime? Did a server crash unexpectedly? Keep track of these things in this section of your report. If you're going to include this section, it is *absolutely critical* that you also include 1) the root cause, and 2) what you did to solve the problem. This is where you show your boss that your job is challenging, but you have the solutions to the complex problems your databases face.

- **Emerging problems:** Is disk space running out on a critical production server? Is the tape backup system running too slowly to keep up? As the database administrator, you often see problems emerging before they cause serious challenges. This is where you tell your boss what is coming up, and where you provide suggested solutions.

- **Sections highlighting your specialties:** We are all good at working on SQL Server in certain ways. If your passion is performance tuning, add a section that summarizes your tuning efforts. Tell your boss how many procedures you tuned, and highlight the statistics that matter (such as how much time your tuning efforts shaved off of execution times). If it is your job to deploy new databases and instances, track here how many were deployed and how long it took. Did you handle the release this weekend? Tell your boss how much time it took, what was deployed, and suggest ways to make the release even smoother next time.

Those are just a few options. This is your report, so customize it to cover the things that are most important to your shop. As a word of caution, don't try showing everything as always operating smoothly. Your boss needs to know what problems exist and that you're on top of them. If you demonstrate that metrics are improving over time, you're controlling the headlines like a champ.

It's just as important to control the headlines when things go badly as when everything is going well. If you run into a crisis, control the headlines by focusing on what you've done, or are doing, to fix the problem. Never try to hide a problem; your boss needs to know what you're up against. Communicating statuses and solutions underway during a crisis makes the best of a bad situation. Don't forget to follow up with a detailed analysis of the root cause of the problem and suggestions on how to prevent it in the future.

Habit 7: Write a Self-Appraisal that Sparks Memory of Success

OK, all of your hard work this year is about to pay off. Now it's time to write your self-appraisal, and you are going to write the best damn self-appraisal you can.

Before deciding what to write, think about what your boss wants to read. Think about what your boss does during the year-end review process. In most companies, your boss sits for hours reading self-appraisals and decides how to divide rewards fairly. Your boss wants to read self-appraisals that are short, concise and based on fact. Your boss doesn't want to read a ten-page rant that talks about how much you deserve the best rating. This feels like emotional warfare and will only point out your flaws to your boss. By simply writing your review to fit what your boss wants, you're already going to be standing out from the crowd. Keep it concise, focused and based on fact.

Deciding what to include in your self-review should be simple because you've been preparing all year to write this review through the habits you've been practicing. The purpose of your self-review is to remind your boss of your successes. You've tracked your accomplishments throughout the year via your status reports. Review them and select the top achievements from each, summarizing achievements where possible. Prioritize the list of achievements, giving weight to those with numeric facts to demonstrate results, and select the top 10–12 achievements. If you can tie the achievements in with cost savings or profit for the company, do so. Some of us don't have that ability, but so long as you keep your achievements based on numbers, your boss will have the material to evaluate your performance properly.

Now that you've got a shortlist of the best work you did this year, it is time to set some goals for next year. You'll add these to the performance review. Approach this in the same way you'd tackle the inevitable "What are your weaknesses?" question in an interview. Choose three areas to improve and, at this point, keep your choices broad. For example, someone who wants to learn more about SQL Server can choose to improve their technical skills.

For each area of improvement that you've identified, write two goals. Make them specific and measurable. Include these goals in your review, and then work towards them the next year. Don't be afraid to write goals to which your employer will need to contribute as well.

Last, take a peek at your training logs. Sum up the hours you've spent training; you'll add this to your review later. Showing how many hours you've trained will set you apart from your peers. You've probably learned a great deal over the year. If you can, pick common themes from your training and summarize them into a bulleted list.

Each employer typically has a self-review template to use, so it will be up to you to determine how best to fit your achievements in. On the off-chance that you don't work for a company that requires self-appraisals as part of the review process, you're still going to write a self-review. Your boss needs to read this. Even though self-review templates vary, you should be able to incorporate the list below into that review.

Your review should include the following:

- A two- to three-sentence introductory paragraph that discusses your role and contributions to the company.

- A bulleted list of your top 10–12 achievements, with numbers-based measurements.

- A one-sentence statement explaining your work management system and how well it has helped you meet your goals. Don't be afraid to name the system you selected.

- A statement explaining your passion for studying SQL Server and the total hours you've spent studying. If you feel it is appropriate, include a one-sentence statement discussing the focus of your training.

- Next, write a forward-looking statement about your plans to build upon your successes this year by working to improve three areas next year.

- List each area of improvement with your two goals for each area. If you wish, you can include a statement about the value each of these goals will bring to the company. It is also a good idea to include a statement asking for your company's help to meet these goals.

- A final paragraph summarizing your successes this year and your eagerness to continue these successes to help the company succeed in the coming year.

I use this pattern every year when writing my review, and I've proven it repeatedly with many managers of different styles. When describing your achievements, you'll have a tendency to be verbose. Fight it; your boss wants as little reading as possible, so keep everything you write relevant, brief and factual.

Most people loathe writing self-appraisals and put them off until the last minute. One last tip is to get your review submitted well before the deadline to give your boss plenty of time to read it.

If you follow these seven steps, you'll have done everything you can to secure a stellar review. Next, we'll talk about what to do with it.

Habit 8: Use Your Review to Negotiate Rewards

Now that you've done everything in your power to get the stellar review you deserve, it's time to put it to use. You're about to play the very challenging game of negotiating your reward for that hard work. And don't forget that you are negotiating here. All too often I see co-workers or friends who take a meager raise without considering what they could get.

The first rule of negotiating your merit increase (the salary increase most companies reward competent workers with) is to **know what you are worth**. Usually, salaries aren't discussed openly, even among good friends, so how do you find out if your salary measures up to others? Salaries also vary widely by region, so how can you know how your location affects your salary?

I have two suggestions. First, if you work at a larger company with a Human Resources department, they've probably calculated a market value for your position. Don't be afraid to ask them what it is. In my experience, "market values" tend to be estimated at only 85–90% of actual median salaries, but your mileage will vary depending on your company's corporate philosophies.

Second, make use of your friend, the Internet, to tell you what you're really worth. My favorite website for salary comparisons is www.Glassdoor.com. The idea behind Glassdoor is simple: post your salary anonymously, associated with your company and job type, and you get access to salary information others have posted.

Other sites, such as WWW.PAYSCALE.COM get very detailed about total rewards, including things like health benefits and paid vacation, to determine a total value for the job. Use as many resources as you can to put together a picture of a salary, and don't forget to adjust the figure based on your experience and your region.

Average pay raises for competent employees hover around 3% of current salary, with this value fluctuating based on the economy. Top performers, surprisingly, typically only net 5% raises. The percentage you're shooting for will depend on how far off your base salary is from your market value. Except in situations where your salary is far under market value, it is rare to see even exceptional employees getting a raise over 8%.

There are a few things to keep in mind when talking money with your boss. The time for salary negotiations comes after you receive your performance review. Let your boss present the proposed merit increase to you. This does two things: first, it lets you know how far apart you are in your expectations; second, it gives your boss a chance to discuss factors that might be affecting the proposed increase. Your boss almost certainly has been given a limited budget for merit raises, so your raise needs to be balanced against the other members of your team.

Another critical thing to keep in mind when negotiating your raise is that you need to keep your personal life out of the conversation. You can't guilt your boss into a raise because your kid needs braces. Guess what? Her kid needs braces, too. Even if you can guilt her into a raise based on your personal situation, don't. This amounts to emotional warfare and it will come back to bite you in the end. Instead, focus on the results you get. Your review is proof now that the company agrees that your contributions were a major factor in your department's success. Focus your negotiations on the value you've brought to the company. Results are what matters, and they form the entire platform to build your case on.

If you're satisfied with the proposed raise, leave well enough alone. You've proven your worth to your boss, so if you get a solid raise offer, she's probably done her best for you. If your performance review was great and the proposed amount doesn't fit your expectations, begin negotiating.

On rare occasions, no matter how fiercely you negotiate, your boss is simply unable to provide you with the raise you want. Factors such as the economy and company's stock price can make it impossible for your boss to give you the raise you deserve. Fortunately, there are still options for you to get non-traditional rewards as alternatives. Ask your boss to send you to that training event or technical conference you've always wanted to attend. Negotiate a better shift, or ask for that office you've had your eye on. Your boss wants to reward you for your hard work, and creative solutions can work well for both of you.

Habit 9: Don't Rest on Past Success

Congratulations on your stellar review! You've put yourself on the fast track to success. But here's the thing – your past success doesn't influence future performance. The bar is raised every year, and you're going to have to put just as much or more effort into securing your next stellar performance review.

The good news is that you have the tools you need to repeat this cycle. Reassess your standing after your review, and then begin the process again. Be sure to focus on re-establishing the parameters for your success, using those measures to set new goals to fit the evolving nature of your job role.

You have the tools you need to succeed, and by following these nine habits, you'll stand out clearly as an exceptional employee that the company will strive to retain.

Index

CPSIA information can be obtained at www.ICGtesting.com
Printed in the USA
BVOW06s1121201013

334208BV00005B/61/P